The Degradation of the International Legal Orde

The Rehabilitation of Law and the Possibility of Politics

Providing the basis for critical engagement with the pessimism of the contemporary age, *The Degradation of the International Legal Order?* argues passionately for a rehabilitation of the honour of historic events and processes, and of their role in generating legal concepts. Drawing primarily from the Marxian tradition, but also engaging with a range of contemporary work in critical theory and critical legal and human rights scholarship, this book analyses historical and recent international events and processes in order to challenge their orthodox interpretation. What is thus proposed is a new evaluation of international legal principles and human rights norms, the revolutionary content of which, it is argued, turns them from mere rhetoric into powerful weapons of struggle.

Accessibly written, but theoretically sophisticated, this original and timely book is intended for critical teachers and students of international law, human rights, and international relations, as well as legal and political activists.

Bill Bowring is Professor of Law at Birkbeck, University of London, and a practising barrister. His research interests include international law, human rights and Soviet and Russian law. He is also a legal and political activist and has taken many cases to the European Court of Human Rights.

The Degradation of the International Legal Order?

The Rehabilitation of Law and the Possibility of Politics

Bill Bowring

Routledge·Cavendish
Taylor & Francis Group
a GlassHouse book

First published 2008 by Routledge-Cavendish
2 Park Square, Milton Park, Abingdon, Oxon OX14 4RN

Simultaneously published in the USA and Canada
by Routledge-Cavendish
270 Madison Ave, New York, NY 10016

*Routledge-Cavendish is an imprint of the Taylor & Francis Group,
an informa business*

A GlassHouse book

Typeset in Times by
RefineCatch Limited, Bungay, Suffolk
Printed and bound in Great Britain by
TJ International Ltd, Padstow, Cornwall

British Library Cataloguing in Publication Data
A catalogue record for this book is available from the British Library

Library of Congress Cataloging-in-Publication Data
Bowring, Bill.
  The degradation of the international legal order: the
rehabilitation of law and the possibility of politics / Bill Bowring
        p. cm.
  Simultaneously published in the USA and Canada.
  Includes bibliographical references
1. International law – Philosophy. 2. Human rights – Political
aspects. 3. Iraq War, 2003–   4. Habermas, Jürgen. I. Title.
  KZ3400.B69 2008
  341 – dc22
                                    2007036667

ISBN10: 1–904385–99–0 (hbk)
ISBN10: 1–904385–36–2 (pbk)
ISBN10: 0–203–93012–6 (ebk)

ISBN13: 978–1–904385–99–8 (hbk)
ISBN13: 978–1–904385–36–3 (pbk)
ISBN13: 978–0–203–93012–1 (ebk)

Contents

Table of cases

Introduction

This book seeks to provide a diagnosis of and a tentative prognosis for the present impasse of international law and international relations both before and after the invasion and occupation of Iraq. International law found itself in a divided world prior to 1989,[1] but those divisions have been transfigured in less than two decades. The book traces the paradoxes of the simultaneous revival of liberal-Kantian conceptions of international law, the unexpected collapse of the USSR, and the apparent apotheosis and simultaneous mortal crisis of human rights. I argue for the radical defence of the real achievements of the UN system in the period of decolonisation – and for a substantive account of human rights.

My response to the blatantly unlawful behaviour[2] of the US and UK in the invasion and occupation of Iraq (2003 to the present),[3] which cannot have come as a surprise after the experience of the first Iraq war, Kosovo and Afghanistan (see Chapter 2 of this book), is to defend the solid principles of international law developed since the Second World War, which I explore in detail in Chapter 1. I argue that these principles resist illegality not because of their exalted legal status, but because they have a determinate content – that is, a symbolic, material content – born out of struggle, out of real human achievement.

This book therefore seeks to make the case for a radical, dialectical re-reading of international law and human rights.

I am writing in the context of the apparent triumph of capital – of the capitalist system – in almost every territory of the planet since the collapse – through its own rottenness and corruption – of the USSR in 1991. This has often been described as some novel form of 'globalisation' a term which is

---

1 Cassese (2005).
2 See BBC 16 September 2004, 'The United Nations Secretary-General Kofi Annan has told the BBC the US-led invasion of Iraq was an illegal act that contravened the UN charter', at http://news.bbc.co.uk/1/hi/world/middle_east/3661134.stm
3 See a full account in Sands, Philippe (2006).

often made to bear far too much explanatory weight.[4] As good a recent attempt as any at a definition for my critical purposes can be found in Adam Gearey's *Globalization and Law*. His 'working definition' is as follows: 'The term describes a complexity, a manifold of social, political, economic and cultural forces interacting on a global scale.'[5] But surely that definition could be applied to every period of human history; and most certainly to the nineteenth century. Gearey therefore goes on to specify that the term describes the '... transition from the colonial empires of "old" Europe to an international order defined at the end of the Second World War'. For Gearey, this order is characterised by a '... qualified hegemony of America and of European and Asian trade blocs'. Although 'formal decolonisation' has taken place, there is still a division, he says, between developed and developing countries. He also refers to the foundation of 'powerful supranational agencies' dealing with the operation of the world economy and human rights.

In a footnote, he argues: 'It is important to resist a simple description of ideological/regional blocs or a trite division between rich and poor countries while maintaining that world economy is structured by underlying inequalities of power and wealth.'[6]

While acknowledging the richness and radical approach of Gearey's book taken as a whole, I contend that the phrase 'underlying inequalities' misses the systemic nature of what is happening now to the whole of the planet.[7] Commenting in passing on Hardt and Negri's *Empire*[8] and on the work of Deleuze and Guattari,[9] Gearey appears to adopt the notion that the social is 'no more than an expression of power'. This '... builds on Marx's insights but does not see all social relationships in terms of class interest. As a theory of global power, it describes the operation of a complex system dedicated to its own reproduction.'[10] In passing, I rather doubt that Marx ever saw all social relationships in terms of class interest.

My argument is, on the contrary, that the proper name for this 'complex system' is 'capitalism', of which imperialism is an inescapable feature. I am not proposing, however, to write yet another text seeking to explain why capital's victory must inevitably lead to the abandoning of every radical or systemic response to the threats, environmental and humanitarian, posed by

---

4 See, of hundreds of titles, Baylis and Smith (2004); Wolf (2005); Aart Scholte (2005).
5 Gearey (2005) p. 2.   6 Gearey (2005) p. 23.
7 For an excellent critique of 'globalisation theory' see Rosenberg (2002) – he analyses deep intellectual confusions that stand in the way of a clear understanding of the modern world, and shows how these confusions ultimately condemn globalisation theorists to a peculiar and quixotic stance: the more clearly they attempt to articulate their arguments, the more equivocal and evasive those arguments become, yielding at best the intellectual equivalent of an architectural folly; and for a remarkably incisive theoretical approach, Wallerstein (2004).
8 Hardt and Negri (2000).   9 Deleuze and Guattari (2004).
10 Gearey (2005) p. 13.

capital's relentless pursuit of growth and profit. That is, I do not join the growing contingent of those postmodern theorists for whom 'power' leaves no space for collective resistance.

I am of course obliged to say at this point what I mean by 'capital' and, indeed 'capitalism' – the system driven by capital's unceasing urge to valorise itself, in which every social relationship, every intellectual creation, and every human appropriation of the material world is reducible to money. I note that neither term appears in the index to Gearey's book, and his chapter on the IMF, GATT and WTO does not mention the possible existence of a system. So I may be out on a limb, and must anyway justify myself.

I have been much influenced in this regard by the work of Christopher Arthur, and the school of Marxist scholarship of which he is the latest representative – the scholars of the 'value form approach to *Capital*', exemplified by the Soviet scholar of the 1920s, Isaak Rubin.[11] For this school, to which I subscribe, capital seeks remorselessly to transform, to transmute, all real human relations, especially those protected by notions of human rights, into the abstract monetary 'value' which is its only aim. This set of understandings is, in my view, the only key to understanding developments in international law and international relations.

This approach has a thorough-going philosophical framework, grounded in Hegel, Marx, and Adorno. In Arthur's words, Rubin '. . . stresses that all the material and technical economic processes are accomplished within definite historically specific *social forms*. Things, such as commodities, are assigned a social role as *mediators* of production relations.'[12] This is a very different approach from that of Pashukanis, whose work is considered in Chapter 1 of this book.

In a recent book, Arthur wrote a chapter on 'The Spectre of Capital'.[13] For Arthur, '. . . value is an unnatural form that clings, vampire-like, to labour, and feeds off it'.[14] In order to explain the content he gives to this metaphor, Arthur draws from Roy Bhaskar's notion of *real* negation or absence, as opposed to 'ontological monovalence, the purely positive account of reality'.[15] That is, if absenting (for example, the deprivation of human rights) is a real process, what has become absent through such a process leaves not simply 'nothing', but a 'determinate nothing' 'structured by the specific process that brought it about'.[16] Bhaskar's position is best described as 'emergent powers materialism',[17] for Arthur's purposes 'the emergent properties of the determinate absence of use value', that is, the alienation from human beings of the enjoyment of the products of their labour, in the bizarre world of capital. As Arthur puts it, 'there is a void at the heart of capitalism . . .

11 Rubin (1928).   12 Arthur (2004) p. 11.   13 Arthur (2004) p. 153.
14 Arthur (2004) p. 157.   15 Bhaskar (1993) Chapter 2.   16 Arthur (2004) p. 160.
17 Bhaskar (1993) p. 397.

the circulation of commodities and money as seemingly material objects supports a world of pure form'.[18]

At this point he enters the imaginary world of Marx – with his references to 'ghostly objectivity', 'sensuous supersensuousness', 'mysteriousness' and so on – and of Jacques Derrida's homage to the specters of Marx.[19] In a bravura passage, Arthur describes the lethal emptiness at the heart of capital:

> If we treat value as the spiritual essence of the capitalist economy, its range of incarnations all centre on a single origin, namely money, the transubstantiated Eucharist of value; 'the spectre' is this hollow armour, at once mute metal and possessor of the magical power to make extremes embrace. The spirit is made metal and stalks among us. The spectre interpellates all commodities as its avatars, an uncanny identity of discernibles, a spectral phenomenology. This negative presence, posited thus, fills itself out through emptying them of all natural being, and forming for itself a spectral body, a body of spectres. In capitalism all is *always* 'another thing' than what it is.[20]

Arthur also devotes a chapter[21] to the collapse of the USSR. Arthur argues that '. . . in the Soviet Union capital's metabolism was disrupted without an alternative being established; lacking organic coherence, the system could not survive once the exceptional conditions of revolutionary mobilisation, of terror, and of war, passed. The USSR has to be seen as the negation of socialism within socialism . . .'[22]

The pivotal role played by the collapse of the USSR is also a reason why much of the empirical focus of the book is on the former Soviet Union and especially Russia. This is, as it happens, the field of my own scholarly endeavours. But it is also, and that is perhaps why I have been drawn to focus on this region of the world, the most exacting experimental laboratory for the efficacy of international law and of human rights.

Arthur shares Adorno's anguish as to the extraordinary damage caused by capital. Adorno remarked that '. . . the whole is false.'[23] But he does not share Adorno's pessimism. He concludes:

> We take our stand with what escapes the totality, yet supports it, social labour, the exploited source of capital's accumulated power, no matter that this is denied. We saw, with Marx, that (form determined as wage labour) living labour realises itself only by its de-realising itself,

---

18 Arthur (2004) p. 167.   19 Derrida (1994).   20 Arthur (2004) p. 167.
21 Arthur (2004) Chapter Ten, 'A Clock Without a Spring: Epitaph for the USSR'.
22 Arthur (2004) p. 222.   23 Adorno (1978) p. 50.

producing 'the being of its non-being', capital. Only through the negation of this its negation can labour liberate itself, humanity, and Nature, from the succubus of capital.[24]

I could not put this better myself. Indeed, if this book has the only result of encouraging its readers to study Arthur's work, I would be well content.

Another radical account of capitalism is to be found in Badiou's text on *Saint Paul*, in the first chapter, 'Paul: Our Contemporary'.[25] Badiou insists that the contemporary world is not nearly as complex as those who wish to ensure its perpetuation would claim. Marx's inspired prediction has been fulfilled: the world finally *configured*, but as a world-market. He highlights the following paradox: 'in the hour of generalised circulation and the phantasm of instantaneous cultural communication, laws and regulations forbidding the circulation of persons are being multiplied everywhere.'[26] He adds:

> Deleuze put it perfectly: capitalist deterritorialisation requires a constant reterritorialisation. Capital demands a permanent creation of subjective and territorial identities in order for its principle of movement to homogenise its space of action; identities, moreover that never demand anything but the right to be exposed in the same way as others to the uniform prerogatives of the market.[27]

It is on this basis that Badiou launches a stinging attack on contemporary human rights orthodoxy; I explore this in a later chapter.

Part of the purpose of this book is to explore the role that human rights can or ought to play in the resistance of social labour, in its attempt to 'negate the negation'. Again, Gearey provides a good point of departure. He asserts that human rights can be approached as 'manifolds of power relationships' in the relations between sovereignty and power.[28] He refers to Karel Vasak's notion of three generations of rights,[29] and notes that the third generation of 'solidarity rights' (or peoples' rights) are legal claims that function politically, so that it is 'hardly surprising that their articulation relates in part to the struggles against colonialism'. This is perhaps what he means by the 'agonistic character' of rights.

However, it is my case, elaborated in this book, that each of the three generations of human rights had its origins in revolutionary struggles, and that each therefore has a substantive, not simply a rhetorical character. For this reason among many others I would take issue with Gearey when he asserts that 'we can now posit a fourth generation of rights: rights that justify

---

24 Arthur (2004) p. 244.   25 Badiou (2003a) pp. 4–15.   26 Badiou (2003a) p. 10.
27 Badiou (2003a) p. 11.   28 Gearey (2005) p. 13.   29 Vasak (1977).

military intervention in the name of humanity'.[30] Intervention or interference, however they are characterised, and in the name of whichever honour-
able motives, have never been – and most certainly are not now – part of
the struggle of individuals or collectivities. I have written previously about
the French intervention in Rwanda, which was supposed to exemplify a new
'right and duty'.[31] Recent disclosures support my contention that the motiv-
ation for that exercise, as with all others of its kind, was purely cynical.

This book also argues for the possibility of politics. I agree with Slavoj
Žižek that '. . . politics cannot be reduced to the level of strategic-pragmatic
interventions. In a radical political act, the opposition between a "crazy"
destructive gesture and a strategic political decision breaks down.'[32] This
clarification is important because, for me, human rights are precisely those
scandalous ruptures with pre-existing modes of social existence which have
arisen in the context of great historical events, the French Revolution, the
Russian Revolution and the de-colonisation struggles of the 1960s. Human
rights are invested with content and regain their significance through social
struggles. They are a significant part of the possibility of politics. Žižek adds:
'The point is not simply that, once we are thoroughly engaged in a political
project, we are ready to put everything at stake for it, inclusive of our lives, but,
more precisely, that *only such an "impossible" gesture of pure expenditure can
change the very coordinates of what is strategically possible within a historical
constellation.*' He adds: '. . . an act is an "excessive", transstrategic, intervention that redefines the rules and contours of the existing order.'[33]

Chapter 1 plays several important roles in situating the argument of the
book. For me, the most important achievement of the United Nations has
been – against itself – the firm establishment of the right of peoples to self-
determination, first as a principle, then as a right in international law. It is
now recognised by the International Court of Justice as *jus cogens*, binding
on all states. This achievement owed much to the former USSR and its allies,
and had its roots in the theoretical and practical engagements of V. I. Lenin;
but in a thoroughly paradoxical manner. In order to trace the transformation
of Soviet international law into the epitome of positivism, I analyse the work
of Yevgeny Pashukanis; and this continues my debate – a debate which has
already borne real fruit – with China Miéville and his outstanding attempt to
work out a Marxist theory of international law. My disagreement with him is
not only, as he recognises, on our very different accounts of human rights,
and, indeed, of the rule of law; but also as to the significance of the Soviet
understanding of international law during Pashukanis' time and later, as
against Soviet support for national liberation movements. In Chapter 2 I
analyse the apparent degradation of international law through the policy of

30 Gearey (2005) p. 14.   31 Bowring (1995).   32 Žižek (2004a) p. 510.
33 Žižek (2004a) p. 511.

the United States and United Kingdom in the wars from 1990, the end of the Cold War, in Iraq, Serbia, and Afghanistan, through the optic of the analyses of leading scholars of international law, as well as the robust attacks on human rights made by the international relations scholar David Chandler. This engagement enables me to set out my main theses.

In Chapter 3, I review some of the scholarly literature on the Iraq war of 2003 to the present, not simply its illegality, on which there is broad consensus, but also the reasons given by the UK and USA for invading Iraq without the sanction of the UN Security Council. I also explain why Tony Blair and his colleagues should be investigated for war crimes. This leads me, in Chapter 4, directly to the challenge not only to international law, but to the 'self-contained regimes' (Martti Koskenniemi) of humanitarian and human rights law. Does the former take precedence over the latter in conditions of armed conflict; and are human rights mechanisms capable of dealing with the challenges thrown up by the use of force? I explore the experience of Russia in Chechnya – I have been directly involved in bringing cases to the Strasbourg Court – and to the prospects of complaining of violations by the UK.

Chapter 5 engages critically with the work of one of the most trenchant critics of international law, Susan Marks. Her path-breaking work takes me to a critique of a philosopher for whom I have respect and affection, Jürgen Habermas. I argue that his post-Marxist attempt at theoretical and practical reconciliation is itself a pernicious ideology, in the sense of obscuring the conflict at the heart of the international order.

At this point I clarify my own position on international law and human rights, taking the necessary next step from the arguments of Chapter 1. Chapter 6 contains my own attempt to work out a 'substantivist', Aristotelian – by which I mean Marxist – account of human rights, based very much on the evidence I present as to the origins in theory and practice of the key right of the UN system, and of the 'third generation' of human rights. I do this through my own regular – pedagogic – encounter with the leading contemporary Aristotelian, Alasdair MacIntyre. I start of course with his *After Virtue*,[34] which contains a passage now cited as an example of 'human rights nihilism'. In fact, two years before its publication, MacIntyre delivered a lecture in which he declared:

> Just because natural rights are philosophical fictions, political appeals to natural rights are always systematically misleading . . . A certain lack of principle will appear in their use as it has from the beginning . . . in that theatre of the absurd, the United Nations, human rights are the idiom alike of the good, the bad and the ugly.[35]

---

34 MacIntyre (1985).   35 MacIntyre (1983) p. 19.

Having presented my own position, I engage with some of the other contemporary critics of human rights.

Chapter 7 takes issue with two leading contemporary scholars who have issued especially trenchant challenges to the discourse and the practice of human rights, Slavoj Žižek and Alain Badiou. However, my critique does not lead me to reject their arguments out of hand. On the contrary, their radical proposals are designed to re-establish the possibility of politics. It is precisely in the renewal of politics that human rights, on my reading, also re-acquire their scandalous symbolic resonance and materiality. Chapter 8, on the other hand, interrogates two rather more friendly – at first glance – critics of human rights, Costas Douzinas and Colin Perrin. However, my reading of their work, highly interesting and important as it is, has a sharper edge. In my opinion, neither of these scholars leads human rights into anything other than a dead end. The latest theoretical 'turn' by Douzinas is especially surprising.

This leads me in Chapter 9 to deepen my critique of methodological individualism in the theory of human rights, and in particular the rights of minorities. I declare myself in this chapter as in others as a student not only of Marxism but also of Roy Bhaskar's early critical realism. The object of my critique is the widespread reluctance of human rights scholars to recognise the existence of groups or of group rights.

Chapter 10 turns to another dimension of the struggle over the content of human rights, one which is especially relevant in the UK. My field of enquiry here is that of social and economic rights, and the extraordinary allergy to them to be found in the Common Law world. At the same time, I argue that my substantive, historical account restores this often neglected 'second generation' of rights to their proper place in partnership with the civil and political rights enshrined in the French Declaration of 1789. Minority rights are another actual and highly politicised dimension of human rights and international law. It is here that an engagement with political science becomes a necessity.

Chapter 11 turns to yet another example of the way in which human rights theory and practice problematise themselves at every step. In this case, my object of critique is the question of 'legal transplantation', which logically follows from the frequently heard condemnation of human rights discourse as irredeemably Western.

This brings me to my conclusion.

Chapter 1

Self-determination – the revolutionary kernel of international law

Introduction

In this chapter I set the scene by examining the historical origins of what is for me the most significant gain of post World War II international law, the right of peoples to self-determination.[1] It is my case that this was welded to international law in the context of the Russian Revolution, in theoretical and practical struggles both before and after October 1917. This leads me to an analysis of the contradictions of Soviet international law, and, necessarily, to the question whether a Marxist theory of international law is possible. This section takes the form of a respectful engagement with the work of China Miéville, whose *Between Equal Rights* is the most important recent contribution to the field. Finally, I contrast the Soviet theory of international law, positivist to the core, with Soviet practice. The USSR gave crucial support for the anti-colonial movement, while ruthlessly suppressing deviation within the Soviet camp.

Soviet international law neglected

The Soviet theory and practice of international law, if it is the subject of any consideration today at all, is usually dismissed as a purely historical example of an extreme species of positivism, and of no contemporary interest. Most often it is ignored. For example, in his article 'What Should International Lawyers Learn from Karl Marx?',[2] Martti Koskenniemi does not mention Soviet international law at all. Even an avowed Marxist scholar of international law does little more. In his article,[3] 'An Outline of a Marxist Course

---

1 Mine is by no means the only radical interpretation – see also Anghie (2007), arguing that the colonial confrontation was central to the formation of international law and, in particular, its founding concept, sovereignty; and Knop (2002), who, from a Feminist perspective, seeks to move from articulating the right to interpreting it – for her, the practice of interpretation involves and illuminates a problem of diversity raised by the exclusion of many of the groups that self-determination most affects.

2 Koskenniemi (2004).

3 In the same special issue of the *Leiden Journal of International Law*.

on Public International Law'[4] B. S. Chimni contrasts the definition of 'treaties' in what he terms 'Mainstream International Law Scholarship':

> ... with the definitions offered by the Soviet scholars Korovin and Pashukanis: 'Every international agreement is the *expression of an established social order*, with a *certain balance of collective interests*';[5] 'A treaty obligation is nothing other than *a special form of the concretization of economic and political relationships*'.[6] These definitions, through drawing in extra-textual reality, offer greater insight into the meaning of a treaty than the formal definition offered by MILS. They refer us to both the fact of an established (capitalist) social order and to its concretization as economic and political rules embodying a certain balance of collective (class) interests.[7]

However, these authors are not introduced save as 'Soviet scholars', no context at all is given, nor the fact that they were bitter enemies. Soviet international law even in this Marxist account barely exists; in the standard genre of the history of international law it is mentioned only to be dismissed.

I wish to take a very different position. I seek to argue in the following paragraphs that the contradictions of Soviet international law have generated some of the most important propositions and principles of contemporary international law, and are of continuing relevance.

This chapter starts with a typical description in the standard genre, by a distinguished contemporary international legal scholar. I then trace the development of Soviet international law through a double refraction: what it said about itself, in some bitterly fought theoretical struggles; and what was said about it by the attentive scholars of the United States. For this purpose I trace the trajectory of Yevgeny Pashukanis, the best known Marxist theorist of law in the West, in part as refracted in the writings of US scholars of international law. I show that despite following developments in Soviet international law with close interest, these observers entirely misunderstood what they sought to analyse. It should be said that the leading Soviet theorists did so too. This tradition of misunderstanding has continued until the present day. I contend that this is true also of the most sophisticated and committed of contemporary Marxist scholars of international law, China Miéville. I engage respectfully with his impressive work.

More importantly however, there was in my contention a clear-cut contradiction between the positivism of the legal textbooks, and the actual practice of the Bolshevik and then Soviet doctrine of the 'Right of Peoples to Self-Determination'. Thus, the USSR gave enormous material and moral support to the National Liberation Movements, and led the successful drive to see the

---

4 Chimni (2004).   5 Korovin (1928).
6 Pashukanis (1980) p. 181 (emphasis added).   7 Chimni (2004) p. 12.

principle and then right to self-determination placed at the centre of public international law in the twentieth and twenty-first centuries.

The standard account of Soviet international law

Western scholars are familiar with what is generally termed the 'Marxist-Leninist theory' in international law, and with its standard characterisation.[8] Iain Scobbie in a recent comparison of Soviet and 'New Haven' theories refers to 'the Soviet theory of international law propounded by G. I. Tunkin'.[9] For Scobbie, Soviet theory amounted to a 'constitutive' (rather than a 'facilitative') theory.[10] It relied on 'the objective rules of societal development and the historical inevitability of socialism'.[11] That is, it was thoroughly mechanical in spirit and exposition.

There can be no surprise that Scobbie refers only to Tunkin. William Butler's translation of Tunkin's textbook made available to a Western audience the only substantial Soviet text in English on international law.[12] Tunkin, born in 1906, died aged 87 in 1993, while completing the last edition of his *Theory of International Law*, and having just submitted an article – on customary international law – to the *European Journal of International Law*. Here he wrote of the attempt '. . . to create a new world order based on the rule of law'.[13]

Scobbie comments that Soviet theory was structurally highly traditional, and firmly rooted in Marxist-Leninist theory to the extent that 'at times, it seems simply to amount to taking the dogma for a walk'.[14] This was certainly true of Tunkin's textbook. It was also very conservative, recognising only rules and State consent to rules: as Damrosch and Müllerson explained it, Soviet theory treated 'the existing corpus of international law as a system of sufficiently determinate principles and norms which all states are obliged to observe in their mutual relations . . .'.[15] As a direct consequence, Soviet theory rejected 'the general principles of law recognised by the civilised nations'.[16]

The existence of two opposed social systems meant that the only norms of 'customary' or 'general' international law could be those which were neither socialist nor capitalist. Tunkin asserted that: 'only those international legal norms which embrace the agreement of all states are norms of contemporary general international law.'[17] Thus, Soviet theory recognised only treaties and custom – narrowly defined as above – as sources of international law.

---

8 Scobbie (2006) p. 84.   9 Scobbie (2006) p. 92.   10 Scobbie (2006) p. 92.
11 Scobbie (2006) p. 96.   12 Tunkin (1974).   13 Tunkin (1993) p. 534.
14 Scobbie (2006) p. 97.   15 Damrosch and Müllerson (1995) p. 9.
16 Article 38(1)(c) of the Statute of the International Court of Justice.
17 Tunkin (1974) pp. 250–251.

The US scholar Alwyn Freeman (1910–1983),[18] writing much earlier, also noted that Soviet international law embraced:

> ... the most extreme form of positivism ... The Soviet brand of positivism is much more restricted, much narrower, and is, in sum, a rejection of a great portion of international legal principles ... Soviet positivism has been distinguished by the exclusion of customary practice as a source of international obligations. It views international law as embracing only those principles to which states have expressly consented through an international agreement or have otherwise manifested their acquiescence.[19]

Indeed, writing in 1948, at the time of his frenetic activity in the United Nations as leader of the Soviet delegation, the notorious Andrey Vyshinsky[20] wrote that: '... the Soviet theory of international law regards the treaty, resting on the principles of sovereign equality of peoples and the respect for mutual interests and rights as the basic source of international law. This secures for international law and its institutions full moral as well as juridical force since at their base will lie the obligations agreed to and voluntarily assumed by nations.'[21]

There is, however, a point at which this conservatism shows another, opposite side. Freeman did not fail to notice it, in his discussion of sovereignty. He explained that the Soviets '... retain the classical, strict conception of states alone as the subjects of international law, with a rigid insistence on sovereignty in its most extreme form, a form which must deny the paramount nature of international law over national law. They do, however, recognise an exception in favour of peoples fighting for "national liberation".'[22] It is very odd, however, that Freeman did not notice the basis for such a claim: the right of peoples to self-determination. This 'principle' had become a 'right' as the

---

18 Freeman was an editor of the American Journal of International Law from 1955 to 1972, worked on international claims cases while in the US State Department, and served in the Army Judge Advocate General's Office in World War II, on the staff of the Senate Committee on Foreign Relations, and as an official of the IAEA.

19 Freeman, A. (1968) p. 713.

20 Andrey Vyshinsky was born in Odessa, Russia, on 28 November 1883. As a young man he joined the Social Democratic Party. In the 1903 split, he sided with the Mensheviks. Vyshinsky became a lawyer and after the October Revolution he joined the Bolsheviks. He taught law at Moscow State University until becoming a state prosecutor. Between 1934 and 1938 Vyshinsky was the leading prosecutor in the 'show trials' of Stalin's opponents. In 1940 he was given the responsibility of managing the (illegal) occupation of Latvia. He also helped establish communist rule in Romania before becoming Soviet foreign minister in March 1949. He survived the purge that followed the death of Joseph Stalin in 1953 and continued as the Soviet representative in the United Nations. Vyshinsky died in New York on 22 November 1954.

21 Vyshinsky (1948) cited in Triska (1958) p. 713.   22 Freeman, A. (1968) p. 716.

common first article of the two International Covenants of 1966 – the 'International Bill of Rights'.

Scobbie quite rightly notes the notorious so-called 'Brezhnev doctrine', that relations between socialist states are not based on 'peaceful co-existence', but on 'proletarian internationalism'. This hypocritical policy justified the invasions of Hungary in 1956, Czechoslovakia in 1968, and Afghanistan in 1980.[23] But, curiously, he says nothing about the application of the 'right of peoples to self-determination' to Soviet support for the national liberation struggles of three decades from World War II.

In the next section of this chapter, therefore, I analyse the origins of the Soviet doctrine of the right of nations to self-determination. It should be noted that in Russian as in many other languages, 'nation' and 'people' are practically synonymous.

The Bolsheviks and self-determination

Bolshevism versus Austro-Marxism

The Bolshevik and then Soviet doctrine of the right of nations to self-determination had its origin in the uncompromising pre World War I struggle between Lenin, Stalin and Trotsky (and orthodox Marxists with Karl Kautsky at their head) on the one side, and the Austro-Marxist theorists such as Karl Renner and Otto Bauer on the other.[24]

Austro-Marxist ideas of non-territorial personal autonomy, developed as a possible antidote to the dissolution of the multi-national Austro-Hungarian Empire, found a ready audience among the Jews of the Russian Empire. The Jews had no 'historic' or 'consolidated' territory. The Jewish 'Bund' (*Algemeyner Yidisher Arbeter Bundin Lite, Poyln un Rusland*) was founded in Vilna (now Vilnius, capital of Lithuania) in 1897, as a Jewish political party espousing social democratic ideology as well as cultural Yiddishism and Jewish national autonomism.[25] The First Congress of the Russian Social Democratic Labour Party in 1898 decided that the Bund 'is affiliated to the Party as an autonomous organisation independent only in regard to questions specifically concerning the Jewish proletariat'.[26] It was from the start influenced by the ideas of Renner and Bauer, although Renner's model did not allow for diasporas or scattered minorities.[27] As Yves Plasseraud points out:

23 Scobbie (2006) p. 99.   24 Bowring (2005a).

25 In the Bund Archive at the Russian State Archive of Social and Political History (GRASPI), Moscow.

26 *The CPSU in Resolutions and Decisions of Its Congresses, Conferences and Plenary Meetings of the Central Committee* (Moscow: Progress, 1954) Part 1, 14.

27 Plasseraud (2000).

> The leaders of the Bund and the Jewish Socialist Workers Party therefore took on the task of adapting Renner's ideas to the situation of the Yiddish-speaking Jews of Central and Eastern Europe . . . The Bundist leaders proposed that Russia, like the Austro-Hungarian Empire, should become a federation of autonomous peoples.[28]

Vladimir Ilich Ulyanov (Lenin), the leader of the Bolsheviks following the split in the RSDLP in 1903, was a bitter opponent of the Bund and of the Austro-Marxist prescription. In October 1903 he published an article entitled 'The Position of the Bund in the Party'.[29] He was especially critical of the Bund's idea of a Jewish nation. He argued that: 'Unfortunately, however, this Zionist idea is absolutely false and essentially reactionary. "The Jews have ceased to be a nation, for a nation without a territory is unthinkable", says one of the most prominent of Marxist theoreticians, Karl Kautsky.' Lenin was wholly in agreement with Kautsky on this point.

Lenin thus adopted Kautsky's orthodox 'scientific' definition of the concept 'nationality', with two principal criteria: language and territory.[30] Both Lenin and Kautsky were in favour of Jewish assimilation.

At the January 1912 Conference of the RSDLP(B), the Jewish Bund declared that it had been influenced by Austro-Marxist theories of personal or non-territorial national cultural autonomy. Consequently, at the August conference of the RSDLP(B), it adopted a resolution 'On National Cultural Autonomy', including it in the programme of the Bund.[31]

Lenin's reply was uncompromising. In 1913, in his 'Draft Platform of the 4th Congress of the Social Democrats of the Latvian Area', he denounced the 'bourgeois falsity' of the slogan of 'cultural national autonomy'. He asserted that in Russia only the Jewish Bund members – 'together with all the Jewish bourgeois parties' – had so far defended this concept.[32] Later that year he devoted an article to 'Cultural-National Autonomy'.[33] He once more denounced this plan as 'an impossibility':

> A clear grasp of the essence of the 'cultural-national autonomy' pro-
> gramme is sufficient to enable one to reply without hesitation – it is
> absolutely impermissible. As long as different nations live in a single state
> they are bound to one another by millions and thousands of millions of
> economic, legal and social bonds. How can education be extricated from
> these bonds? Can it be 'taken out of the jurisdiction of the state', to
> quote the Bund formula?

Lenin particularly mocked the references to Austria:

28 Plasseraud (2000) p. 4.   29 Lenin (1968a).   30 Kautsky (1903).
31 Filippov (1998) p. 66.   32 Lenin (1968b).   33 Lenin (1968b) p. 503 n. 30.

... why should the most backward of the multinational countries be taken as the *model*? Why not take the most advanced? This is very much in the style of the bad Russian liberals, the Cadets, who for models of a constitution turn mainly to the backward countries such as Prussia and Austria, and not to advanced countries such as France, Switzerland and America!

Stalin's 'scientific' contribution

Also in early 1913, J. V. Stalin published, under Lenin's instruction, his one substantial work of theory, *Marxism and the National Question*.[34] This devoted a whole chapter to 'Cultural-National Autonomy', and was primarily designed as a reply to the Bund. Stalin attempted his own definition of a nation:

> A nation is a historically constituted, stable community of people, formed on the basis of a common language, territory, economic life and psychological make-up manifested in a common culture.

It is noteworthy that Stalin's definition of the nation is not so far from contemporary orthodoxy. Anthony D. Smith defines *ethnie* as:

> ... a named unit of population with common ancestry myths and shared historical memories, elements of shared culture, a link with a historic territory, and some measure of solidarity, at least among the elites.[35]

Note the importance of the link to territory. Again, he defines the modern nation, in ideal-typical terms, as '... a named human population sharing a historic territory, common myths and historical memories, a mass, public culture, a common economy and common rights and duties for all members'. John Hutchinson, too, contends that: '... Nations are distinguished in addition by a commitment to citizenship rights, and the possession of a high literate culture, a consolidated territory and a unified economy.'[36]

They are all agreed on the importance of territory.

Stalin's next move was a critique of Renner and Bauer, insisting on the importance of territory: 'Bauer's point of view, which identifies a nation with its national character, divorces the nation from its soil, and converts it into an invisible, self-contained force.' Stalin answer was as follows: '... there is no doubt a) that cultural-national autonomy presupposes the integrity of the multi-national state, whereas self-determination goes outside the framework

---

34 Stalin (1913).   35 Smith, A. D. (2001) p. 19. See also Smith (2002).
36 Hutchinson (2001) p. 75.

of this integrity, and b) that self-determination endows a nation with complete rights, whereas national autonomy endows it only with cultural rights.' And he further warned: 'Springer's and Bauer's cultural-national autonomy is a subtle form of nationalism.'

The Bolshevik origins of the right to self-determination

Applying his definition and critique to the national question in Russia, Stalin started from the assertion that 'the *right of self-determination is an essential element* in the solution of the national question.' For 'crystallised units' such as Poland, Lithuania, the Ukraine, the Caucasus, etc he believed that *national* autonomy could not solve the problem, and the only correct solution was *regional* autonomy, for a definite population inhabiting a definite territory. The national minorities in each of these territories need not fear the result: 'Give the country complete democracy and all grounds for fear will vanish.' This would include equal rights of nations in all forms – liberty of conscience, liberty of movement, languages, schools, etc.

In December 1913 Lenin himself began to write on the question of the 'right of nations to self-determination'. In a short polemic[37] on the question of independence for Ukraine, he insisted on '. . . *freedom* to secede, for the *right* to secede', while conceding that '. . . the *right* to self-determination is one thing, of course, and the *expediency* of self-determination, the secession of a given nation under given circumstances, is another.' Later in December 1913[38] he again declared: 'A democrat could not remain a democrat (let alone a proletarian democrat) without systematically advocating, precisely among the Great-Russian masses and in the Russian language, the "self-determination" of nations in the political and not in the "cultural" sense.' The latter, he said, meant only freedom of languages.

In April–June 1914 Lenin published his own substantial work on the question, a polemic against Rosa Luxemburg, who opposed the break-up of the Tsarist Empire, 'The Right of Nations to Self-Determination'.[39] In the first chapter, he insisted that '. . . it would be wrong to interpret the right to self-determination as meaning anything but the right to existence as a separate state.'[40] Furthermore, '. . . the national state is the rule and the "norm" of capitalism: the multi-national state represents backwardness . . . from the standpoint of national relations, the best conditions for the development of capitalism are undoubtedly provided by the national state.'[41]

His understanding of the historical significance of the demand is highly significant for this chapter:

---

37 Lenin (1913).   38 Lenin (1913a).   39 Lenin (1914).
40 Lenin (1914) http://www.marxists.org/archive/lenin/works/1914/self-det/ch01.htm, p. 2.
41 Lenin (1914) http://www.marxists.org/archive/lenin/works/1914/self-det/ch01.htm, p. 5.

The epoch of bourgeois-democratic revolutions in Western, continental Europe embraces a fairly definite period, approximately between 1789 and 1871. This was precisely the period of national movements and the creation of national states. When this period drew to a close, Western Europe had been transformed into a settled system of bourgeois states, which, as a general rule, were nationally uniform states. Therefore, to seek the right to self-determination in the programmes of West-European socialists at this time of day is to betray one's ignorance of the ABC of Marxism.

In Eastern Europe and Asia the period of bourgeois-democratic revolutions did not begin until 1905. The revolutions in Russia, Persia, Turkey and China, the Balkan wars – such is the chain of world events of *our* period in our 'Orient'. And only a blind man could fail to see in this chain of events the awakening of a *whole series* of bourgeois-democratic national movements which strive to create nationally independent and nationally uniform states. It is precisely and solely because Russia and the neighbouring countries are passing through this period that we must have a clause in our programme on the right of nations to self-determination.[42]

Thus, Lenin's conception of self-determination in 1914 was wholly and necessarily relevant not only to the Tsarist Empire but also to the European colonial empires. He spelt this out further in 1915, in a polemic with his fellow revolutionary Karl Radek:

We demand freedom of self-determination, i.e., independence, i.e., freedom of secession for the oppressed nations, not because we have dreamt of splitting up the country economically, or of the ideal of small states, but, on the contrary, because we want large states and the closer unity and even fusion of nations, only on a truly democratic, truly internationalist basis, which is inconceivable without the freedom to secede. Just as Marx, in 1869, demanded the separation of Ireland, not for a split between Ireland and Britain, but for a subsequent free union between them, not so as to secure 'justice for Ireland', but in the interests of the revolutionary struggle of the British proletariat, we in the same way consider the refusal of Russian socialists to demand freedom of self-determination for nations, in the sense we have indicated above, to be a direct betrayal of democracy, internationalism and socialism.[43]

Finally, in 1916, in a long article entitled 'The Discussion on Self-Determination Summed Up',[44] Lenin wrote, with regard to the colonies:

---

42 Lenin (1914) http://www.marxists.org/archive/lenin/works/1914/self-det/ch03.htm.
43 Lenin (1915).   44 Lenin (1916).

Our theses say that the demand for the immediate liberation of the colonies is as 'impracticable' (that is, it cannot be effected without a number of revolutions and is not stable without socialism) under capitalism as the self-determination of nations, the election of civil servants by the people, the democratic republic, and so on – and, furthermore, that the demand for the liberation of the colonies is nothing more than 'the recognition of the right of nations to self-determination'.

It is, therefore, perfectly clear that Lenin's conception of self-determination had nothing in common with that propounded by US President Woodrow Wilson after World War I. It should be recalled that standard texts on international law usually refer only to Wilson as progenitor of the concept. For Wilson, self-determination applied – and applied only – to the former Ottoman, Austro-Hungarian and Russian empires. The British, Belgian, French, Dutch, Spanish and Portuguese empires were in no way to be threatened. And American interests in Puerto Rico and the Philippines were also sacrosanct. Lenin's approach, on the other hand, was consistent, and revolutionary.

Self-determination put into practice

I wish to maintain that, for Lenin at least, self-determination was not a mere slogan, but a principle he put into practice with immediate effect within the former Russian Empire following the Bolshevik Revolution. According to Igor Blishchenko (1930–2000), one of the best Soviet scholars of international law,[45] in a text published, ironically, in 1968, the year that the USSR crushed the 'Czech Spring', Lenin's Decree on Peace of 26 October 1917, for the first time extended the principle of the right to self-determination to all peoples, thereby discarding the imperialist distinction between 'civilised' and 'uncivilised' nations.[46]

In fact, the Decree declared that:

> By annexation or seizure of foreign territory the government, in accordance with the legal concepts of democracy in general and of the working class in particular, understands any incorporation of a small and weak nationality by a large and powerful state without a clear, definite and voluntary expression of agreement and desire by the weak nationality, regardless of the time when such forcible incorporation took place,

45 I worked with Blishchenko for a number of years, in particular on the draft of the Rome Statute of the International Criminal Court; for a touching obituary by the International Committee of the Red Cross, see http://www.icrc.org/Web/eng/siteeng0.nsf/html/57JREV.
46 Blishchenko (1968) p. 69.

regardless also of how developed or how backward is the nation forcibly attached or forcibly detained within the frontiers of the [larger] state, and, finally, regardless of whether or not this large nation is located in Europe or in distant lands beyond the seas.

If any nation whatsoever is detained by force within the boundaries of a certain state, and if [that nation], contrary to its expressed desire whether such desire is made manifest in the press, national assemblies, party relations, or in protests and uprisings against national oppression, is not given the right to determine the form of its state life by free voting and completely free from the presence of the troops of the annexing or stronger state and without the least desire, then the dominance of that nation by the stronger state is annexation, i.e., seizure by force and violence.[47]

In his article, Blishchenko moved next to answer a series of Western scholars who argued that the Decree was entirely hypocritical, first having no application to peoples within the USSR, and second, having been applied only to Finland in the former Tsarist Empire. He pointed to the substantial autonomy, if short of secession, enjoyed by Union and Autonomous Republics in the USSR in accordance with Article 17 of its Constitution. More importantly, he underlined the extent to which the principle was indeed put into practice by Lenin in the early years of the USSR. What he failed to point out, not surprisingly in 1968, is the fact that one of Lenin's most bitter struggles with Stalin concerned independence for Georgia.[48]

In a much later text,[49] Blishchenko showed that the early Soviet government was entirely consistent in implementing self-determination. On 4 (17) December 1917 the Soviet government recognised the right to self-determination of Ukraine. In response to the request of the Finnish government, the Soviet of Peoples' Commissars on 18 (31) December 1917 resolved to go to the Central Executive Committee with a proposal to recognise Finland's independence. In fact, it was the Whites, seeking to restore the Empire, who opposed Finnish independence. By a Decree of 29 December 1917 (11 January 1918) the right of the people of 'Turkish Armenia' to self-determination was recognised. In answer to a request from the government of Soviet Estland, on 7 December 1918 Lenin signed a Decree on recognition of the independence of Estonia, Latvia and Lithuania.

On 5 February 1919 the Presidium of the All-Union Central Executive of Soviet Russia insisted, in a principled manner, that in implementing the principle of self-determination, the issue was resolved by the self-determining nation itself, by the people itself. The dictatorship of the proletariat was

47 http://www.firstworldwar.com/source/decreeonpeace.htm.   48 See Lewin (2005).
49 Blishchenko (1998) p. 71; see also, on national liberation movements: Baratashvili (1967).

not a condition for self-determination, which applied equally to bourgeois independence movements. Thus, the Soviet government recognised the republics of Bukhara and Khorezm, which were not socialist.

This was the profoundly significant historical context in which Yevgeny Pashukanis became the acknowledged theoretician and leader of a Marxist account of law and of international law.

The real significance of Yevgeny Pashukanis

Pashukanis' history

Pashukanis was born in what is now Lithuania in 1891, and was liquidated in 1937, condemned as a member of a 'band of wreckers' and 'Trotsky-Bukharin fascist agents'.[50] He was a pupil of the Latvian-born legal theorist Piotr I. Stuchka, his senior by 25 years (Stuchka lived from 1865 to 1932, when, unusually for those times, he died of natural causes).[51] Chris Arthur has described Pashukanis' 'important contribution to the materialist critique of legal forms' as 'to this day the most significant Marxist work on the subject'.[52] I do not disagree. At the same time I hope to demonstrate that the paradoxical effects of Soviet practice (as opposed to the positivist theory they propagated) played a key role in developing and putting in place one of the most important principles of international law, the right of peoples to self-determination.

Pashukanis was, from 1925 to 1936, the leading theorist of law in the USSR, recognised as such by none other than Stuchka himself, who wrote that the *General Theory of Law and Marxism* was 'to the highest degree a valuable contribution to our Marxist theoretical literature on law and directly supplements my work, which provides only an incomplete and greatly inadequate general doctrine of law'.[53] This was a period of 'passionate legal debate', well analysed by Michael Head.[54]

Pashukanis was the Director of the Institute of Law of the Soviet Academy of Sciences, and effectively the country's director of legal research and legal education. He made significant changes to legal education, including the virtual elimination of civil law subjects from the educational curriculum, and replacing them with an emphasis on economics and economic administration.[55] John Hazard (1909–1995),[56] who studied under him, recalled

---

50 Arthur (1983) p. 10.   51 Stuchka (1988) pp. x–xi.   52 Arthur (1983) p. 9.
53 Stuchka (1988) p. xvii.
54 Head (2001). See also the extracts from Pashukanis and Stuchka in Zile (1992).
55 Garlan (1954) p. 303.
56 Hazard was a founder of the field of Soviet legal studies in America who taught at Columbia for 48 years. Upon his graduation from Harvard Law School, he was sent by the Institute of Current World Affairs as the first American to study Soviet law at the Moscow Juridical

another side of his character: in the Institute the situation where he '. . . projected a theory said to be infallible, and where those who strayed from Pashukanis' line were castigated like Korovin or denied faculty appointments, promotions and salary raises was novel to me'.[57] That is probably disingenuous of Hazard, a native of American academe; but seems to be accurate.

Edwin Garlan, writing in 1954 for an American audience during the Cold War, identified two conclusions reached by Pashukanis on the basis of his analysis of basic legal categories. First:

> Only bourgeois-capitalist society creates all the conditions essential to the attainment of complete definiteness by the juridic element in social relationships.[58]

And second:

> The dying out of the categories . . . of bourgeois law by no means signifies that they are replaced by new categories of proletarian law – precisely as the dying out of the category of value, capital, gain and so forth will not (with the transition to expanded socialism) mean that new proletarian categories of worth, capital rent and so forth appear. The dying out of the categories of bourgeois law will in these conditions signify the dying out of law in general: that is to say, the gradual disappearance of the juridic element in human relations.[59]

As Garlan notes, it follows from these propositions that the transition period of the dictatorship of the proletariat had to take the form of bourgeois law. Thus, the task of transition law was to eliminate itself, by way of a rapid movement to policy – technical – administration as opposed to civil and criminal law.[60]

Pashukanis revived: China Miéville

China Miéville, with his reworking of the 'commodity-form theory of international law',[61] has provided the most serious and sophisticated attempt in

---

Institute. Only a handful of scholars were concerned with Russian diplomacy and business then, and scholarship on Russia was limited principally to historical studies. He approached the field of Soviet law as a pioneer and received the certificate of the Juridical Institute in 1937. He was the author of widely used textbooks and studies of Soviet law and public administration, and served the US government during World War II, helping to negotiate the Lend-Lease agreement with the Soviet Union.

57 Hazard (1979).   58 Pashukanis (1924) p. 110.   59 Pashukanis (1924) p. 122.
60 Garlan (1954) p. 303.   61 Miéville (2004).

recent years at a Marxist account of international law.[62] The final sentence of his powerful book truly sums up his conclusion: 'The chaotic and bloody world around us *is the rule of law.*'[63] International law and human rights are at best distractions, on his account, and at worst potent weapons in the hands of the enemy. As he points out in his Introduction to *Between Equal Rights*, Miéville draws extensively from Pashukanis, who was one of the most serious Marxist legal theorists of the USSR or anywhere. Miéville traces and explains his arguments in Chapter Three, and seeks, through 'immanent reformulation', to answer some criticisms of Pashukanis.[64]

China Miéville identifies in Critical Legal Studies and other so-called 'New Stream' theories of international law an 'implicit theory of the social world, an idealist constructivism',[65] in which international law is sometimes depicted as a 'constraining myth' inherited from the past, or where structures of everyday life such as international law are deemed to be 'the accretion of ideas'. For Miéville, this privileges '. . . abstract concepts over the specific historic context in which certain ideas take hold, and how'. Miéville upholds a resolutely 'classical' version of Marxism.[66] As it happens, I agree with this. However, as explained by Miéville, Pashukanis argues that *the logic of the commodity form is the logic of the legal form.* In commodity exchange, he continues, 'each commodity must be the private property of its owner, freely given in return for the other . . . Therefore, each agent in the exchange must be i) an owner of private property, and ii) formally equal to the other agent(s). Without these conditions, what occurred would not be commodity exchange. The legal form is the *necessary form* taken by the relation between these formally equal owners of exchange values.'[67] For Miéville, law is called forth as a 'specific form of social regulation . . . *That form is law,* which is characterised by its abstract quality, its being based on the equality of its subjects and its pervasive character in capitalism.'[68] Miéville refers with approval to Pashukanis' '. . . assertion that private law, rather than public law, is the "fundamental, primary level of law". The rest of the legal superstructure can be seen as essentially derived from this.'[69]

In fact, Pashukanis' assertion goes rather further, and is as follows:

> Yet while civil law, which is concerned with the fundamental, primary level of law, makes use of the concept of subjective rights with complete assurance, application of this concept in public-law theory creates misunderstandings and contradictions at every step. For this reason, the system of civil law is distinguished by its simplicity, clarity and perfection, while theories of constitutional law teem with far-fetched constructs

---

62 Miéville (2005). 63 Miéville (2005) p. 319. 64 Miéville (2005) pp. 6–7.
65 Miéville (2004). 66 Miéville (2005). 67 Miéville (2005) p. 78.
68 Miéville (2005) p. 79. 69 Miéville (2004), and (2005) p. 86.

which are so one-sided as to become grotesque. The form of law with its aspect of subjective right is born in a society of isolated bearers of private egotistic interests . . .[70]

It is clear that Pashukanis knew Marx's *On the Jewish Question*,[71] and it must be said that the passage just cited is highly reminiscent of what Marx had to say about the 'rights of man':

None of the so-called rights of man, therefore, go beyond egoistic man, beyond man as a member of civil society, that is, an individual withdrawn into himself, into the confines of his private interests and private caprice, and separated from the community.[72]

Later in the same passage, Marx expressed ironic puzzlement that in the French Declaration of 1789 '. . . finally, it is not man as *citoyen*, but man as *bourgeois* who is considered to be the *essential* and *true* man.'

Pashukanis' limitations

I am also a great admirer of Pashukanis' early work. However, I doubt very much whether his work on the commodity theory of law can really serve as the basis for a new theory of international law. Miéville himself at several points recognises Pashukanis' limitations and contradictions. Here are some important objections.

First, Pashukanis' theory strongly suggests that there was no law as he defines it before the development of the commodity form, which only appeared with the development of capitalism. That must be either wrong or circular, a definition that depends upon itself. Miéville does not neglect this problem, and effectively criticises Pashukanis for 'eliding' the distinction between the *logical* movement from simple to capitalist commodity exchange, and the *historical* movement from exchange of commodities under pre-capitalist societies to that in capitalism itself.[73] Miéville is forced to assert: 'A history of the development of the legal form *can* be developed using Pashukanis' theory.'[74] Chris Arthur notes this problem from a different point of view in his *Introduction*:

A difficulty that arises from a Marxist point of view is that the bourgeois regime is one of *generalised* commodity production; that is, it treats labour-power as a commodity and pumps out surplus labour from the

---

70 Pashukanis (1983) p. 103.   71 Pashukanis (1983) p. 132, note 43.
72 K. Marx (1975a) p. 164.   73 Miéville (2005) pp. 96–97.
74 Miéville (2005) p. 97.

wage-workers. Yet Pashukanis makes reference to commodity exchange without taking account of the various forms of production that might involve production for a market . . .[75]

In other words, Pashukanis has failed to take into account the whole of human pre-capitalist history.

Second, Mieville, it seems to me, takes insufficient notice of Bob Fine's critical remarks, which go to the heart of this particular reappropriation of Pashukanis. First, as Fine points out, 'Whereas Marx derived law from relations of commodity production, Pashukanis derived it from commodity exchange.'[76] This, according to Fine, leads Pashukanis to a conclusion that was plainly wrong:

> Instead of seeing both the content and the forms of law as determined by and changing with the development of productive relations, Pashukanis isolated law from its content and reduced quite different forms of law, expressing qualitatively different social relations, to a single, static and illusory 'legal form'.[77]

And any 'legal form' must be bourgeois. As Fine explains, this led Pashukanis in 1924 to argue that the Soviet Union of the New Economic Policy (NEP) was not yet ready for the abolition of law, and that, since law is in any event bourgeois, there can be no such thing as proletarian law. More to the point, Pashukanis was obliged by the logic of his own position to see the transition from capitalism to socialism simply as the replacement of commodity exchange by planned production, that is, the replacement of bourgeois (legal) forms by socialist (technical forms).[78] Thus, as Fine points out, in 1929 he accepted Stalin's view that communism was being achieved through the first Five-Year Plan.[79] Miéville has read Fine,[80] but seems entirely to have missed the point of his criticism.

Third, Miéville's reprinting and discussion of Pashukanis' short essay on international law[81] from 1925, fails to take account not only of the fact of Pashukanis' intellectual trajectory until his death at the hands of Stalin in 1937, but, more importantly, the way in which that trajectory was already determined by Pashukanis' early accommodation to Soviet technicism. Indeed, the essay formed part of the three volume *Encyclopedia of State and Law* which was launched and edited by Stuchka. Pashukanis' contribution was entirely consistent with Stuchka's overall line and policy. But the reasons for this went deeper than a mere desire for conformity, which in any

---

75 Arthur (1983) p. 29.   76 Fine (2002) p. 157.   77 Fine (2002) p. 159.
78 Fine (2002) p. 167.   79 Fine (2002) p. 168.
80 Miéville (2005) p. 101, notes 122, 123.
81 Miéville (2005) pp. 321–335; Pashukanis (1925).

event was not in Pashukanis' character. As Fine explains, 'Not only did Pashukanis invert the relationship between law and bureaucracy envisaged by Marx, he lost all sight of the democratic nature of Marx's critique of the state, according to which its withering away was to be the result of its ever more radical democratisation.'[82]

Pashukanis' official trajectory

Pashukanis was a staunch loyalist in relation to the regime – by conviction rather than any sort of pressure. Thus, by 1932, Pashukanis, by then editor in chief of the official law journal *Soviet State*, was able to write a 'hallelujah' in response to Stalin's letter 'Some questions on the history of Bolshevism'.[83] Pashukanis' major work on international law, *Essays in International Law*, appeared in 1935.[84] Within two years he was dead, following *Pravda*'s announcement on 20 January 1937 that he had been found to be an enemy of the people – just two months after he had been named by the regime to supervise the revision of the whole system of Soviet codes of law. Michael Head's analysis leads to a critical assessment of Pashukanis' legacy:

> He offered profound insights into the economic roots of the legal form, even if displaying several basic confusions in Marxist economics. However, he was weaker on the ideological and repressive role of law and the state apparatus. And key aspects of his theory served the interests of the emerging Stalinist bureaucracy, with whom he aligned himself against the Left Opposition.[85]

Indeed, scholars such as Christine Sypnowich, who presents Pashukanis as an orthodox Marxist, coupling 'Marx and Pashukanis',[86] and Ronnie Warrington,[87] for whom, following the US scholar Robert Sharlet, Pashukanis was an orthodox 'Old Bolshevik',[88] miss the extent to which Pashukanis' theories led him inexorably to support for Stalin's policies.

As I show below, Pashukanis also entirely missed the revolutionary context for his analysis of international law. Moreover, his denunciation in 1937 and, posthumously, for the remainder of the Stalin period was based on the assertion that he failed to point out that 'international law must be defined as class law in terms so simple and expressive that no one could possibly be deceived'.[89]

---

82 Fine (2002) p. 169.   83 Pashukanis (1932).   84 Pashukanis (1935).
85 Head (2004) p. 272.   86 Sypnowich (1990) p. 8.   87 Warrington (1981) p. 181.
88 This, as Michael Head shows, is quite wrong – Pashukanis, like Vyshinsky, was a Menshevik and only joined the Bolsheviks in 1918 – see Head (2004) p. 274.
89 Hazard (1938) p. 246.

According to the US scholar Hazard, the Soviet reader was supposed by Soviet orthodoxy to be able to find 'simple proof of the theoretician's argument that foreign policy is shaped to fit the demands of the struggle between the classes, and that international law as the tool of that policy is no more than a reflection of class conflicts calling for some attempts at solution'.[90]

As against Korovin, for whom a change of form must follow a change of substance, so that the Soviet Union had brought with it a new form of international law, the 'international law of the transition period', Pashukanis had argued for a continuation of old forms, including diplomatic immunity, the exchange of representatives, and the customary law of treaties, not least since these gave the Soviet Union considerable protection.

Pashukanis roundly condemned Korovin's doctrine:

> ... scholars such as Korovin who argued that the Soviet Government should recognise only treaties [as a source of] international law and should reject custom are absolutely wrong. An attempt to impose upon the Soviet Government a doctrine it has nowhere expressed is dictated by the patent desire to deprive the Soviet Government of those rights which require no treaty formulation and derive from the fact that normal diplomatic relations exist.[91]

Pashukanis also came in for particular criticism because he called the principle *rebus sic stantibus* 'healthy'.[92]

Most copies of the *Essays* were destroyed after he was denounced in 1937, but in this culminating work he declared that any attempt to define the 'nature of international law' was scholastic.[93] In his view, such attempts were the result of the continuing influence of bourgeois legal methodology, which, he said, rested on the association of law with substance developing in accordance with its own internal principles. For him, in 1935, international law was a means of formulating and strengthening in custom and treaties various political and economic relationships between states, and the USSR could use international law to further Soviet interests in the struggle with capitalist states. He saw no reason to believe that in using these principles of international law for its own purposes the USSR was compromising its principles, in a world in which most states were capitalist. For Pashukanis there was no point in seeking to determine whether international law was 'bourgeois' or 'socialist'; such a discussion would be 'scholastic'.[94]

This approach to international law is as far as it could be from a 'commodity-form' theory. It is utterly positivist in its approach, in precisely

90 Hazard (1938) p. 246.   91 Pashukanis (1935), cited in Triska (1958) pp. 704–705.
92 Hazard (1938) p. 250.   93 Pashukanis (1935) p. 16, cited in Hazard (1957) p. 387.
94 Hazard (1957) p. 387.

the manner described by the 'standard genre' to which I referred above. For Pashukanis, international law is composed simply of the treaties concluded by states, and such customary law as every state could agree on.

It should be no surprise that Pashukanis' apparent theoretical stance changed as it did between 1925 and 1935. The context had completely changed. In his 1925 essay, Pashukanis was writing when the world appeared to be divided into two camps, capitalism and workers' power, and when much of the planet was subject to colonialism. He wrote, quite correctly: 'The historical examples adduced in any textbook of international law loudly proclaim that *modern international law is the legal form of the struggle of the capitalist states among themselves for domination over the rest of the world.*'[95] In the 1935 textbook he said that international law as practised between capitalist states was one of the forms with the aid of which imperialist states carry on the struggle between themselves for territory and super-profits.[96] He also declared that the earliest international law appeared with the earliest class society, that is, with the development of the slave-holding state which grew out of the tribal civilisation of primitive man as division of labour and acceptance of the concept of private property stratified society into classes.[97]

Vyshinsky, Pashukanis' nemesis – and Stuchka's theoretical successor – was diametrically opposed to this:

> Only one who is consciously falsifying history and reality can perceive in capitalist society the supreme and culminating point of legal development . . . Only in socialist society does law acquire a firm ground for its development . . . As regards the scientific working out of any specific problems, the basic and decisive thought must be the aspiration to guarantee the development and strengthening of Soviet law to the highest degree.[98]

Indeed, Pashukanis' 1935 textbook is absolutely standard in the ordering and style of its presentation. The exception is Chapter III, '*Istoricheskii ocherk mezhdunarodnoi politiki i mezhdunarodnovo prava* (Historical sketch of international policy and international law)',[99] which presents, with some references to Comrade Stalin, and 'the thesis of the victory of socialism in a single country', a strictly factual account of the history of international law and policy from ancient times to 'International relations in the period of the breakdown of capitalist stabilisation and the struggle of the USSR for peace', with the most attention given to the October Revolution of 1917 and the post World War I period.

Pashukanis' 1925–1927 conception that 'The real historical content of

95 Pashukanis (1925).   96 Summarised at Hazard (1938) pp. 245–246.
97 Pashukanis (1935) cited in Hazard (1938) p. 251.
98 Cited in Garlan (1954) p. 304.   99 Pashukanis (1935).

international law, therefore, is the struggle between capitalist states'[100] rapidly gave way to 'socialism in one country' and 'peaceful co-existence'. As Hazard pointed out in 1938: '. . . throughout the whole of any future discussion, the (Soviet) writer must re-emphasise the struggle for peace which is being waged by the USSR, and show how this struggle rests upon the sanctity of treaties and the observance of international obligations.'[101] The political context for this new orientation was the fact that the USSR was admitted to membership of the League of Nations on 18 September 1934, and, up to its aggression against Finland in December 1939, it was the leading protagonist of the League and of 'collective security'.[102]

Within a year the Molotov–Ribbentrop pact and Hitler's attack on the Soviet Union would bring an end to such political and scholarly imperatives.

In the circumstances, Pashukanis could not possibly have predicted the thoroughly contradictory developments which followed World War II, in particular the creation and transformation of the United Nations, the development of the great multilateral, in some cases universal, international treaties, and the consolidation of political principles such as self-determination into fundamental principles – legal rights – of international law. Indeed, it was his own theoretical position which prevented him from doing so. E. A. Korovin, writing as early as 1923, placed particular emphasis on 'Sovereignty as national self-determination', 'The legal form of self-determination', 'Bourgeois self-determination and the method of "Balkanisation" '.[103] Korovin was much more a Bolshevik – a Leninist – than Pashukanis ever was.

Why did Pashukanis miss the significance of self-determination?

At this point there is an absence in Pashukanis' work which is key to the argument of this chapter. He made only one reference to the 'right of nations to self-determination', despite the fact that this was the centre of Lenin's approach to international policy in the immediate post-1917 period. A factual account of 'imperialist usurpation' is analysed only in relation to Lenin's work on 'imperialism as the highest stage of capitalism'. On Pashukanis' 1935 account, the 'basic fact of world history' after the October Revolution is the 'struggle of two systems': capitalism, and socialism as constructed in the USSR. The most important feature of the 'Decree on Peace' of 8 November 1917 is the rejection of secret treaties. At this point Pashukanis introduced the following: 'The declaration of the rights of the peoples of Russia proclaimed the right of each people to self-determination right up to secession and forming an independent state.'[104] Pashukanis said nothing about any significance this might have for the imperialist and colonial systems.

100 Miéville (2005) p. 325.   101 Hazard (1938) p. 252.   102 Prince (1942) p. 429.
103 Korovin (1923).   104 Pashukanis (1935) p. 38.

Pashukanis noted the creation of several new states on the ruins of the Austro-Hungarian and Ottoman empires, and the existence in most of them of significant national minorities – but he did not breathe a word on self-determination. The same is true of his account of the recognition by the USSR and conclusion of treaties with Estonia (2 February 1920), Lithuania (12 July 1920), Latvia (11 August 1920), and Finland (14 October 1920).[105] The whole analysis is centred on the USSR and its interests. Thus, Pashukanis related, '. . . the sympathy of the oppressed peoples of the colonies for the Soviet Union aroused the anger of the imperialists.'[106] The Soviet Union, on the other hand, was 'guided by support for the workers within the countries and in the whole world'.[107]

Pashukanis was quite clear that the many bilateral treaties concluded by the USSR from 1932, when Hitler came to power, onwards, were not directed against any third state, but were based on the policy of supporting peaceful relations with all states 'and guaranteeing our socialist construction against the threats of intervention'.[108] Thus, the culmination of Soviet diplomatic efforts by 1935 was the invitation by 34 states on 15 September 1934 for the USSR to join the League of Nations, and its accession on 18 September 1934, with only three states voting against and seven abstentions.[109] According to Pashukanis, the 'brilliant success' of Soviet foreign policy was based on the internal policy of strengthening the dictatorship of the proletariat and construction of a classless socialist society. The 'thesis of the possibility of the victory of socialism in one country' had determinate significance for resolving the problems of foreign policy. A list of principles contains, after breaking with the policy of the Tsarist and Provisional governments, exit from the wars, proposing peace to all warring countries, publishing and denouncing all secret treaties, cancelling debts, '. . . winning the trust and sympathy of the proletariat and oppressed peoples of the whole world, the proclamation of the principle of self-determination of nations and brotherly solidarity of the proletariat and the colonial peoples of the whole world . . .'.[110]

Pashukanis was incapable of recognising the significance of self-determination for international law. In my view, this was not simply the result of the limitations imposed by the period in which he was living, or the necessity to adapt to Stalin's ideology, but was the direct consequence of his own theoretical position, worked out in the early 1920s. Miéville does of course notice these developments, in particular the fact that the UN Charter proclaimed the 'equal rights and self-determination of peoples'.[111] However, although he acknowledges that the struggles for decolonisation after World War II represented a radical change in international law in relation to

105 Pashukanis (1935) p. 44.   106 Pashukanis (1935) p. 49.
107 Pashukanis (1935) p. 50.   108 Pashukanis (1935) p. 55.
109 Pashukanis (1935) p. 62.   110 Pashukanis (1935) p. 63.
111 Miéville (2005) p. 264.

colonisation, he argues that in its *content* it is a mere continuation of the universalising trend in the *form*. By this he means that the logic of international law is and was 'universalising', or, in other words, imperialist. Following Eric Hobsbawm's 1994 *Age of Extremes*, Miéville notes the fact that waves of decolonisation struggles broke out first in Asia, then North Africa and the Middle East, then Sub-Saharan Africa. This was the point at which the United Nations General Assembly, twice the size that it was at the foundation of the UN, adopted the watershed *Declaration on the Granting of Independence to Colonial Countries and Peoples.*[112]

Miéville fails to note the following salient points. First, as I have already outlined, 'self-determination of nations' was the principled position thoroughly worked out by V. I. Lenin before World War I, and put into practice by him in the context of the former Russian empire after World War I. Second, the principle was anathema to the Western imperialist powers, which were content for the former Russian, Austro-Hungarian and Ottoman empires to break up into new nations. Self-determination limited to these cases was quite acceptable to the major imperialist powers. Third, the UN Charter contains a statement of principles including self-determination, but does not proclaim a right. This was a victory of the Western allies over the USSR and its partners. Fourth, it is significant that only in the context of victories of the national liberation movements did the principle of self-determination become a right in international law.

In fact, both Pashukanis and Miéville seem to overlook the significance of the principle, then right, to self-determination. Pashukanis' emphasis on the commodity form, and insistence that law only comes into its own in the context of capitalism, blinded him to the importance for international law of the political events in the midst of which he lived and worked. This may well have been a consequence of the perspective given to him by his own time and place. But it was much more the inevitable consequence of his own theoretical position.

The USSR and self-determination after World War II

Decolonisation

Blishchenko, writing in 1968, celebrated the break-up of the colonial system of imperialism, and the broad national liberation movements in Asia, Africa and Latin America after World War II, which had posited the right of peoples to self-determination with new force. He asserted, with reason, that

---

112 UN Resolution 1514 (XV) 947th plenary meeting, 14 December 1960, text at http://www.gibnet.com/texts/un1514.htm (accessed 19 March 2006).

the USSR had done everything to ensure that the right became one of the fundamental principles of contemporary international law. This was due in part to the work of the Soviet Delegation at the San Francisco Conference[113] which drafted the Charter of the UN, as a result of which Article 2(1) of the Charter refers to 'respect for the principle of equal rights and self-determination of peoples . . .'.[114]

As Morsink points out,[115] in 1914 Lenin calculated that more than one half of the world's population lived in colonies, which covered three-quarters of the world's territory, a calculation that was still roughly correct at the end of the 1940s. The UN's Universal Declaration on Human Rights was drafted just as the European empires began to break up. Two leading participants, Malik from Lebanon and Romulo from the Philippines, were from countries which became independent in 1946, together with Syria. India, Burma and Pakistan gained their independence in 1947, together with Ceylon in 1948. India and Pakistan were both active players in the drafting process.

Andrei Zhdanov, Stalin's favourite, delivered the key speech at the founding meeting of the Cominform (Communist Information Bureau), and announced that the world was divided into two camps, 'the imperialist and anti-democratic camp' led by the United States, and the 'democratic and anti-imperialist camp' led by the USSR. He asserted that there was a 'crisis of the colonial system' and that 'the peoples of the colonies no longer wish to live in the old way. The ruling classes of the metropolitan countries can no longer govern the colonies on the old lines.'[116] Cassese relates that the Dumbarton Oaks Proposals, the basis for the UN Charter, did not contain any reference to self-determination, but this was reconsidered at the end of April 1945, at the UN Conference on International Organisation in San Francisco – at the insistence of the USSR.[117] Thus, a draft was presented referring to '. . . respect for the principle of equal rights and self-determination of peoples'.

As Tunkin noted in 1970, at the Second Session of the UN General Assembly the Soviet delegation proposed an article for the Universal Declaration on Human Rights as follows: 'Each people and each nation has the right to national self-determination. A state which has responsibility for the administration of self-determining territories, including colonies, must ensure the realisation of that right, guided by the principles and goals of the United Nations in relation to the peoples of such territories.' However, under pressure from the colonial powers this proposal was rejected, with the result that the principle of self-determination does not appear in the UDHR.[118]

---

113 United Nations Conference on International Organisation, 1945, v. III, 622; and see Tunkin
     (1970) p. 67.
114 Blishchenko (1968) p. 75.   115 Morsink (1999) p. 96.
116 Cited in Morsink (1999) p. 97.   117 Cassese (1995) p. 38.
118 Tunkin (1970) p. 69.

Dmitrii Grushkin notes[119] that one key factor at the end of World War II was the strengthened role of the USSR and the appearance of a whole bloc of states oriented towards it. Further, a bi-polar system took shape in international relations in which the contradictory interests of the two sides could be clearly traced. Third, the role of the mass character of politics significantly grew during World War II: 110 million people from 72 states took part. It was a war of peoples, not of governments. Fourth, in place of the League of Nations a global international organisation appeared with real resources and much more effective instruments. The UN sought to create on the basis of new principles (human rights, self-determination, sovereign equality of states) a powerful and effective international legal system. In the documents adopted by the UN, the idea of self-determination received new support, but also aroused bitter disputes. However, the USSR, with the support of the socialist countries and the newly independent states of Asia, campaigned for the establishment of a practically unlimited right to self-determination of colonial and dependent countries and peoples.

At the Tenth Session of the UNGA in 1955 the opponents of including the right to self-determination into the Covenants argued that the UN Charter only refers to a 'principle' and not a 'right' of peoples to self-determination, and that in various instruments the principle is interpreted in different ways. To the extent that the right to self-determination is a collective right, they declared, then it was inconsistent to include it in a document setting out the rights of individuals. Supporters, however, responded that despite the fact that the right to self-determination is collective, it affects each person, and that to remove it would be the precondition for limiting human rights. Furthermore, a state accepting the UN Charter and recognising it must respect the 'principle of self-determination' and the 'right' flowing from it. The latter point of view triumphed, and the new 'right' found its way into the common Article 1 of both the International Covenants on Civil and Political Rights, and Social, Economic and Cultural Rights, respectively.[120]

The right to self-determination in international law

Heather Wilson reminds us[121] that the admission of 17 newly independent states at the opening of the Fifteenth Session of the General Assembly had a decisive effect on the UN. On 23 September 1960, the Soviet Union, grasping the opportunity presented by this dramatic development, requested the addition of a 'declaration on the granting of independence to colonial countries and peoples' to the agenda.[122] This was a truly climactic moment in the development of contemporary international law.

---

119 Grushkin (1997) p. 10.   120 Grushkin (1997) p. 12.
121 Wilson (1988) pp. 67–68.   122 UN Doc A/4501, 23 September 1960.

It was the USSR which submitted to the Fifteenth Session of the UN General Assembly the draft of the historic Resolution 1514 (XV) of 14 December 1960, the 'Declaration on the granting of independence to colonial countries and peoples'. This historic resolution aroused a whole wave of reactions and protests, but, none the less, was adopted. This document noted the connection between the right of peoples to self-determination and individual freedoms. Following on the heels of Resolution 1514 (XV) came a whole series of documents of a similar type: Resolution 1803 (XVII) of 14 December 1962 on 'Inalienable sovereignty in relation to natural resources'; Resolution 2105 (XX) of 20 December 1965 'On the realisation of the Declaration on the granting of independence to colonial countries and peoples' – the General Assembly recognised the legitimacy of the struggle of colonial peoples against colonial domination in the exercise of their right to self-determination and independence, and it invited all states to provide material and moral support to national liberation movements in colonial territories.

In the 1966 Covenants on human rights, which to begin with were developed as a single document, it was decided that the provision on self-determination be included on the basis that:

a) it '. . . is the source or essential foundation for other human rights, since there cannot be authentic realisation of individual rights without realisation of the right to self-determination';
b) in drafting the Covenants the realisation and protection of the principles and goals of the UN Charter must be taken into account, including the principles of equal rights and self-determination of peoples;
c) a series of provisions of the Universal Declaration of Human Rights are directly connected to the right to self-determination;
d) if the right was not included in the Covenants, they would be incomplete and ineffective.[123]

Writing in 1970, Tunkin also pointed out that if in 1919 as many as 64 per cent of the population of the planet lived in colonies and semi-colonies, then at the start of 1969 only 1 per cent of humanity remained in colonies. It was on this basis that both the International Covenants have a common Article 1, on the right in international law of peoples to self-determination. This was a remarkable achievement by the USSR and its allies in the decolonised world.[124]

The National Liberation Movements

The success of the USSR and its allies in the 1960s had momentous consequences for the legal and political process of decolonisation. Later resolutions

---

123 Grushkin (1997) p. 12, citing Kristesky (1981).   124 Tunkin (1970) p. 70.

of the UNGA ensured that the so-called 'national liberation movements'[125] were recognised as the 'sole legitimate representatives' of the relevant peoples. In other words, ex-territorial social and political organisations were in fact made equal to sovereign subjects of international law. Examples were the Palestine Liberation Organisation (PLO), the South West African Peoples Organisation (SWAPO), the ANC (African National Congress) and the PAC (Pan African Congress). In 1973 the UN declared that it recognised SWAPO as the 'sole authentic representative of the people of Namibia'. And in 1974 the PLO was recognised by the majority of member states of the UN as the lawful representative of the Palestinians, with corresponding status at the UN.

There are writers such as Christopher Quaye, who ignore the Soviet role in promoting the legal right to self-determination or supporting the national liberation movements.[126] However, Galia Golan, although seemingly unaware of the international law dimension, wrote in the context of national liberation movements that: 'The term preferred by the Soviets [to "independence"] as an overall, all-inclusive type of objective was self-determination.'[127] Her book demonstrates the huge resources devoted by the USSR to support of all kinds for a very wide range of national liberation movements in the Third World. Tables she prepared list 43 movements in 26 countries, with 13 instruments of 'Soviet behaviour'.[128] Roger Kanet noted that 'Soviet trade with the developing nations increased more than eleven times from 1955 to 1970'. In 1970 it increased an additional 15.7 per cent.[129] Furthermore, Bhabani Sen Gupta pointed out that 'in cultivating friendly, viable forces, the Soviet Union has persistently tried to satisfy some of the *felt* needs of the power elites of Third World societies. In South Asia, they have come forward to provide aid for industrialisation programs in India, for which the Indians could not secure resources either domestically or from Western nations . . .'[130]

I would contend, contrary to these authors, that it was not as a result of Soviet propaganda, but through the logic of the new international law, developed through the efforts of the USSR and its allies, that a people with the right to self-determination faced with aggressive attempts to deny that right enjoyed the right of self-defence under Article 51 of the Charter, and was in all respects to be considered a subject of international law. Thus, Portugal was at that time waging war against the peoples of Angola and Mozambique; those peoples were therefore victims of aggression and enjoyed the right of self-defence, and third party states had the right and duty to come to their assistance.[131] G. I. Tunkin, a year earlier, in a more formal article, defending the dubious concept of 'proletarian internationalism', also linked

125 See Golan (1988).   126 Quaye (1991).   127 Golan (1988) p. 136.
128 Golan (1988) pp. 262–267.   129 Kanet (1974) p. 1.   130 Gupta (1974) p. 123.
131 Blishchenko (1968) pp. 76–77.

the 'struggle for international peace and security' with the 'struggle for the freedom and independence of peoples', with reference especially to Resolution 1514 (XV).[132]

Vietnam and the Czech Spring: Further contradictions in self-determination

The year 1968 was not only the year of the Soviet invasion of Czechoslovakia, but also a crucial moment in the US war in Vietnam. The invasion of Czechoslavkia took place against the background of the emergence of a new 'socialist international law', with a new approach to traditional concepts of sovereignty. G. I. Tunkin published a revised second edition of his textbook on *International Law*.[133] According to him, it appeared to commentators in the United States that the new Soviet position could be dated back to Pashukanis' conclusion in the 1920s that the Soviet Union could and did utilise generally accepted norms of domestic and international law both in the administration of state affairs and in conducting relations with foreign states. Through this practice, it gave the bourgeois norms a new Socialist content.[134]

Dealing with the Czechoslovak events, Tunkin argued that these were a logical extension of the concept already well developed and applied in Hungary in 1956. This was the legal prevention of inroads by capitalist influences into a socialist state.[135] The international law framework is provided through an analysis of the concept of sovereignty. Tunkin noted that both general and socialist international law respected the concept of 'sovereignty', but concluded that respect is not the same thing in the two systems.[136] Socialist states would continue to insist on respect for the principle as developed in general international law when speaking of the relationships between themselves and capitalist states so as to prevent capitalist states from intervening in the internal affairs of socialist states, but the concept of sovereignty had evolved within the conceptual framework of 'proletarian internationalism' as regards the mutual relationships of socialist states. His translator, William Butler, commented: 'The Soviet invasion of Czechoslovakia plainly was a difficult moment for his approach to international law, and his treatment of a "socialist international law" impressed, rightly or wrongly, as something less than enthusiastic.'[137]

Tunkin's arguments should be contrasted with what, in the same year, the US scholar Alwyn Freeman was able to write:

---

132 Tunkin (1967a) pp. 144–146.   133 Tunkin (1970), and Tunkin (1974).
134 Hazard (1971) p. 143.   135 Tunkin (1970a) p. 493, cited in Hazard (1971) p. 145.
136 Tunkin (1970) p. 495.   137 Butler (2002) p. 394.

In the years following World War II increasing interest has been evidenced in the extent to which Soviet theory and practice may have influenced the development of the law of nations. This is to be expected in view of the prominence and power which the USSR has come to enjoy in the world community.[138]

Freeman denounced what he saw as a 'political dogma dressed in treacherous legal trappings', namely the official Soviet doctrine of 'peaceful coexistence'. He referred, as do so many American scholars of the period, as well as President Kennedy in his post-inauguration speeches, to an alleged address by Khrushchev to a Soviet Communist Party audience on 6 January 1961.[139] In one account:

> Soviet Premier Nikita Khrushchev delivered a speech behind closed doors in which he asserted that 'a mighty upsurge of anti-imperialist, national-liberation revolutions' was sweeping through the 'third world.' He went on to say that 'Communists fully and unreservedly support such just wars . . . of national liberation.'[140]

The impact of Khrushchev's words was felt in the US itself and in its subsequent policy:

> The speech, published in the Soviet press just two days before the newly elected President John F. Kennedy took his oath of office, had a profound effect on the new administration which regarded it as a portent of wars to come. Kennedy and his advisers concluded that the Cold War was entering a new phase which would take place in the 'third world,' and would be characterized by guerrilla wars. Accordingly, they sought to improve the nation's ability to conduct counter insurgency warfare by dramatically expanding the Army's Special Forces or, 'green berets.' Before Kennedy's assassination in Dallas in 1963, he had dispatched over 16,000 of them to South Viet Nam in order to engage in just such a conflict. The war for the 'third world,' and a new phase of the Cold War had gotten under way in earnest.[141]

This address may well be apocryphal; it has proved impossible for me to track down a definite reference. But there is every reason to believe that its effect was as described. It had its effect on the scholars too. For Freeman, while

---

138 Freeman (1968) pp. 710–711.
139 Quoted in the American Bar Association (1964) *Peaceful Coexistence: A Communist Blueprint for Victory*, 14.
140 http://hnn.us/roundup/comments/19470.html   141 Speed (2005).

accommodations of mutually acceptable principles were possible in 1968, no progress in international law was possible until 'the Soviet Union is prepared to abjure its messianic and compulsive espousal of the doctrine of world revolution'.[142] Freeman was of course writing at the height of the Vietnam War: he expresses outrage that the public opinion barrage orchestrated by the USSR '... actually inhibited the United States from using tear gas where such use was in the interest of humane treatment of the civilian population'.[143]

The leading Soviet scholars were, in the end, obliged to abandon both positivism and the revolutionary content of self-determination. Writing in 1991, just before the dissolution of the USSR, and using the new language of 'perestroika', 'common human values' and 'common European home', Blishchenko also argued for 're-thinking the periodisation of the contemporary history of international law, and for reading its formation not in the October Revolution of 1917 but the French bourgeois revolution, for the first time promoting such generally recognised norms and principles of international law as the right of peoples to self-determination ...'.[144]

However, the principle, then right, of self-determination played in my view a much more significant role, both in its practical effects in the international order, and as the 'obscene other' of Soviet positivism in international law.

This paradoxical, dialectical aspect of Soviet international law is entirely missed by Miéville. In this, it has to be said, he takes his place in a well-established tradition of the critique of 'socialist law'. It seems to me that a radical reworking of Pashukanis' contribution is required in order to account satisfactorily for the role of law in a world in which capitalism has – as it must, and as Marx predicted – spread to every corner. Turbulence has grown proportionately with interdependence. The Iraq adventure is a compelling example not of the omnipotence of US power, but of its radical limitations, and the indomitable human spirit.

What Miéville quite rightly draws from Pashukanis is what he terms 'materialism', that is, the crucial importance of economic and political investigation and analysis for analysing developments in law, without forgetting law's real existence and relative autonomy as a constant but endlessly metamorphosing aspect of human existence – like religion, with which, as a human construct, it has so much in common.

The right of peoples to self-determination in international law achieved the status of a right in the context of decolonisation and – thoroughly paradoxical and hypocritical – Soviet support both for the principle and for national liberation movements. It was law, indeed a pillar of the international rule of law.

---

142 Freeman (1968) p. 722.   143 Freeman (1968) p. 720.
144 Blishchenko (1991) pp. 135–136.

Conclusion – and another account

At this point I would like to propose an alternative reading to China Miéville's relentlessly pessimistic account of the post World War II movements for decolonisation, and 'peoples' rights', especially the right to self-determination and the right to development – the *New International Economic Order* which he mentions in passing.

Here a thoroughly dialectical case can be made. There is no question that the movements for colonial freedom and decolonisation were, as shown above, bitterly opposed by all the imperialist powers. In each case – France in Vietnam and Algeria, Britain in Kenya and Malaysia, the US, to this day, in Puerto Rico, Portugal in Mozambique and Angola, the South African and Israeli experiences – the response of imperialism was ferocious and bloody. It is not enough to note that some of these became petty imperialisms in their own right, or in many ways simply served the interests of the former colonial power.

For me, it is vitally important to note that the demand for self-determination became a vitally important part of the external legitimation and ideological self-empowerment of these movements. In a paradoxical – and dialectical – fashion, the USSR, notwithstanding the profound deracination of its approach to international law, as exemplified by Vyshinsky[145] and Tunkin,[146] found itself obliged to give very considerable material support to self-determination struggles, despite the fact that this was not only extremely costly but often contrary to its own geopolitical self-interest. I mean dialectical in the following way: the content of the proposed norm often came into sharp conflict with its juridical form, and in the process the content was imbued with a new significance, in due course transforming the form as well.

In every case the process was not ideal – it was not the work of professors – but thoroughly material. This is what Patricia Williams in *The Alchemy of Race and Rights* refers to as the subversion and appropriation of bourgeois legal norms – a process of alchemy.[147] Thus, the United Nations itself was transformed, not in effectiveness or ultimate independence, but in the unique possibility it gives for the less powerful states – and international civil society – to gather and speak.

145 Vyshinsky (1979).   146 Tunkin (1974).   147 Williams (1991).

Chapter 2

The degradation of international law?

Introduction

This chapter explores the recent pre-history to the present crisis of international law; and sketches a means of escape from the impasse.

Some years ago, Tony Carty wrote of 'The Decay of International Law'.[1] In a prescient passage, he argued:

> Official argument is, inevitably, confined to one-sided assertions of legal principle which it is thought are likely to appeal, along with many other 'non-legal' factors, either to a domestic audience or to particular allied powers. Attempts to 'persuade' the adversary are exceptional. Legal doctrine tries to carry the discourse further to precisely this stage. It has nothing to lose but its reputation for integrity.[2]

In 2002, following the US and UK response to the events of September 11, David Chandler instead proclaimed the 'degradation' of international law. Now, following the invasion and occupation of Iraq from 2003 to the present, is hard to argue with his conclusion that 'International law is no longer accepted as a legitimate curb on the use of force by Western powers, while coercive intervention by Western powers against other states is increasingly legitimised through the framework of "international justice" . . . The gap between "justice" and what is "legal" has led to the degradation of international law rather than to its development.'[3] This point is echoed by Noelle Quenivet, in her survey of literature from the European continent, asking whether international law has really changed since September 11.[4] Her conclusion is bleak. The principal consequence seems to have been '. . . the greatly enhanced respectability of the use of military force in response to terrorism . . . the extent to which some version of "just war" doctrine has been relied upon to justify such an approach provides little comfort. As Delcourt has

1 Carty (1986).   2 Carty (1986) p. 115.   3 Chandler (2002) p. 158.
4 Quenivet (2005).

noted,[5] this development seems primarily to signal "the degeneration of international law and devitalisation of the system of collective security", mainly caused by the emergence of a "hegemon".'[6]

This chapter is an attempt at reflection on what has befallen the law, and at resolution of the question whether law and power can once again be brought into a relationship in which there is a perspective for justice. I say 'once again', since it is contended here that the development of international law during the 'Cold War' was, for reasons which are entirely democratic, progressive and humane. This position is what I describe in this book as 'revolutionary conservatism'.

My starting point in this chapter, following my reference to capital in my introduction, is a ghoulish metaphor, a macabre prelude to what follows. Although this chapter comprises a tragedy in three acts – Iraq (starting in 1991), Serbia (starting in 1999) and Afghanistan (starting in 2001 and by no means resolved at the time of writing) – my starting point is 1986, when an act of vengeance and a chilling prophecy could encourage the delusion that history is simply a vicious circle. It is also noteworthy that none of the three disasters I describe has achieved closure. Each continues to wreak vengeance, in part at least through the law of unintended consequences, a law which applies with remorseless lack of irony to the United States especially. This is all the more the case in Iraq since March 2003.

A further element of counterpoint is added by an ironical accompaniment: the words of the most sunny optimist, the normative liberal par excellence, the true believer in the legitimacy of norms and rules in international law, Thomas Franck.[7]

This chapter focuses primarily on scholarly writings concerning the three events noted above. I bear in mind Hilary Charlesworth's forthright critique of the development of international legal scholarship through the examination of 'crises',[8] and plead guilty. Nevertheless, Charlesworth herself suggests that: 'One way forward is to refocus international law on issues of structural justice that underpin everyday life. What might an international law of everyday life look like?'[9] One purpose of the present analysis will be to seek to show how both international human rights, and international law, of which human rights comprise a sub-set, may be vindicated when understood not as a discourse in which a 'degraded vision of the social world' serves to 'sustain the self-belief of the governing class',[10] but as a product of and catalyst of real struggles. This is the substantive account of human rights for which I argue later in this book.

---

5 Delcourt (2002) pp. 214–215.   6 Quenivet (2005) p. 577.
7 Franck and Patel (1991), Franck (1999), Franck (2001).   8 Charlesworth (2002).
9 Charlesworth (2002) p. 391.
10 Chandler (2002) p. 235, citing K. Malik *The Meaning of Race: Race, History and Culture in Western Society* (London, Macmillan, 1996) p. 105.

Not least, this chapter seeks to corroborate Michael Byers' position, reflecting in 2002 on the previous decade of forceful measures against Iraq: 'Although law is necessarily the result and reflection of politics, law nevertheless retains a specificity and resistance to short-term change that enables it to constrain sudden changes in relative power, and sudden changes in policy motivated by consequentially shifting perceptions of opportunity and self-interest.'[11] This is especially the case if law is the result and reflection not only of power, but of struggle and resistance: that is perhaps how law itself can offer resistance.

Vampires

If international law has been degraded, it has also been violated; but violated to all appearances with its own full, enthusiastic participation. The three exemplary uses of armed force against Iraq, Serbia and finally Afghanistan appear as three acts in a tragedy of intimate deception, a macabre vampire–bride relationship between law and power. The three stages can be described as follows. First, *consummation*, when law and power, freed by the end of the Cold War, seemed set for the longed-for happy alliance; second, *seduction*, when power sought from law invasion of its means of creation, international custom; third, *rejection*, when power, having taken and ravished the law, turned its back and walked away.

Antonio Cassese, in his first reaction to the US response to September 11, identified another vampirish activity, the reproduction of vampires through the poisoned bite. 'In sum, the response to the appalling tragedy of 11 September may lead to acceptable legal change in the international community only if reasonable measures are taken, as much as possible on a collective basis, which do not collide with the generally accepted principles of that community. Otherwise, the road would be open to the setting in of that *anarchy* in the international community so eagerly pursued by terrorists.'[12] That is, stated less politely, terrorism has bred terrorism; its victim, its own sworn enemy, is only too willing, it turns out, to repeat the cycle of death and destruction.

Some black-letter international law – revolutionary conservatism

On one matter this chapter adopts a resolutely positivist, black-letter approach – revolutionary conservatism. I have in mind the plain words of the UN Charter, taken together with the hard-won state practice and *opinio juris*

---

11 Byers (2002) p. 35.   12 Cassese (2001) p. 1001.

concerning the use of force, the 'inherent' right to self-defence, and especially the slippery doctrine of 'anticipatory' self-defence.[13]

Since 1945 it has been an unambiguous principle of international law that the United Nations has, with one strictly limited exception, a monopoly of the use of force in international relations. This is the effect of Article 2(4) of the UN Charter, which prohibits 'the threat or use of force against the territorial integrity or political independence of any State, or in any other manner inconsistent with the Purposes of the United Nations'.

All UN members are strictly bound by this Article – the UN Charter is a binding treaty. Indeed, the UN was established to prevent a repetition of the horrors of World War II.

Only the United Nations Security Council, acting under Chapter VII of the Charter, is entitled to 'take action by air, sea, or land forces as may be necessary to maintain or restore international peace and security' (Article 42). The Security Council may, as in the case of the Gulf War, delegate the execution of such action to states or groups of states. But it must do so expressly, and must remain in charge.

The only exception to this principle is contained in Article 51 of the UN Charter: the right of self-defence if an armed attack occurs against a Member of the United Nations. Customary international law, which long pre-dates the UN,[14] makes it clear that self-defence only warrants measures which are proportional to the armed attack and necessary to respond to it. This principle, and the status of the doctrine of self-defence as customary law independent of the UN Charter, was confirmed by the International Court of Justice in *Nicaragua v US* in 1986.[15]

Furthermore, Article 51 also states that self-defence may only be used *until* the Security Council has taken measures necessary to maintain international peace and security.

While it is accepted and indeed urged that the Security Council, its composition and its role are in need of democratic reform, and its dispositions with regard to the existence of a threat to or breach of international peace and security ought to be subject to review by the International Court of Justice,

---

13 In the first edition of his *International Law* (Oxford, Oxford University Press, 2001) Antonio Cassese reviews practice and *opinio juris*, and concludes, 'In the case of anticipatory self-defence, it is more judicious to consider such actions as *legally prohibited*, while admittedly knowing that there may be cases where breaches of the prohibition may be justified on moral and political grounds and the community will eventually condone them or mete out lenient condemnation' (pp. 310–311). This is at p. 362 in his second edition (2005).

14 See the *Caroline* case, 1837: 29 British and Foreign State Papers 1137–38, and 30 British and Foreign State Papers 195–6.

15 *Nicaragua Case* (1986) ICJ Reports 14. See also the UK response to the 1982 Falklands/Malvinas invasion as a necessary and proportionate act of self-defence – Byers (2002a) p. 406.

the Security Council itself is in need of protection. In Professor Quigley's phrase, it is in danger of becoming a 'helpless hostage'.[16] He points, with substantial incriminating evidence, to the following:

> Four categories of situations have arisen that reflect the Security Council's inability to fulfil its functions properly as a result of United States dominance. First, in 'threat to the peace' situations, the United States has asserted dubious facts before the Security Council, and the Council has acted as if those facts were true, without investigation. Second, the United States has at several times acted purportedly on the basis of powers granted by the Security Council, but in fact outside any powers actually granted. Third, the United States has convinced the Security Council on several occasions to authorise it to take military action unilaterally rather than under Council control. Fourth, the United States has, by use of its veto power, blocked the Security Council from dealing with the United Nations' longest standing territorial dispute, that over Israel–Palestine.[17]

Professor Quigley's words were prophetic; the Israel–Palestine conflict is the inescapable foundation, playing the roles of cause and effect, in propaganda and in reality, to the events of September 11, and the war in Afghanistan.

Yet I would argue, with hindsight, that the UN system, itself the result of compromise between the First and Second Worlds, the capitalist and communist systems, acquired its most important concepts and juridical content through the process of decolonisation. It is no accident that the principles of state sovereignty and non-interference, brought to life by the hard-won legal right of peoples to self-determination, became the main source of legitimacy for the United Nations as a focus for the aspirations of new states and aspiring peoples.

The start of a vicious circle – the bombing of Libya

The late 1980s were a turning point in the fate not only of the (former) USSR, but of international law as a potential source of protection from strong states. In 1986 the United States lost the case brought against it in the International Court of Justice by Nicaragua.[18] And on 15 April 1986 the United States attacked five targets in Libyan territory, having sought and obtained the agreement of Margaret Thatcher for the use of the UK as a staging post for its bombers. Not only for the purpose of this chapter, the events of 15 April 1986 serve as an awful warning for what took place on 11 September 2001. As was recognised at the time, the civilian deaths in Tripoli and Benghazi, if scaled up

---

16 Quigley (2002).   17 Quigley (2002) p. 130.
18 *Nicaragua Case* (1986) ICJ Reports 14.

from the tiny population of Libya to the huge population of the United States of America, would have represented a strike on New York and Washington causing at least tens of thousands of innocent victims. Neither international law nor justice can countenance an eye for an eye, violence for violence. But the action of the United States in April 1986 was at the very least an awful harbinger, and perhaps one of the causes, of the events of 11 September.[19]

However, the purpose of this section is to recall the prophetic words of Professor Paust, writing shortly afterwards.[20] It should be noted at once that Paust was not writing to condemn the United States. Far from it. His conclusion was in essence a premonition of Kosovo and Afghanistan. 'Indeed, if the state dominated system did not recognise that the use of force is permissible when reasonably necessary to defend fundamental human rights, such a denial would inexorably demonstrate its own illegitimacy.' At first sight, of course, this is a non-sequitur, but we will let that pass. More interesting is the path of Paust's reasoning, and the demonstration he offers of the iron consistency of US policy, with regard to international law.

Paust starts with the now forgotten 'Schultz doctrine', enunciated on 15 January 1986, before the bombing of Libya. George Schultz, then US Secretary of State, stated in a speech at the National Defense University: 'It is absurd to argue that international law prohibits us from capturing terrorists in international waters or airspace, from attacking them on the soil of other nations even for the purpose of rescuing hostages, or from using force against states that support, train and harbor terrorists or guerillas.' He added: 'A nation attacked by terrorists is permitted to use force to prevent or pre-empt future attacks, to seize terrorists, or to rescue its citizens, when no other means is available.'[21]

Paust contrasts this assertion with the near-unanimous (the US abstained) condemnation by the UN Security Council of Israel's use of force in 1985 against the PLO in Tunisian territory. The Security Council condemned this action as a 'flagrant violation of the Charter of the United Nations, international law and norms of conduct',[22] and the 'sincere condolences over the loss of life of its citizens' extended to the Government of Tunisia by Ambassador Vernon Walters, when explaining US abstention.[23]

For Paust, 'One is left necessarily then with the following set of questions: is it permissible under international law to attack terrorists on the soil of

---

19 It is worth noting that the UN Security Council condemned the attack as a violation of the UN Charter. The vote was 9–5–1, with the US, UK, France, Australia and Denmark voting no, and Venezuela abstaining.

20 Paust (1986).

21 The speech is reprinted at 25 *International Legal Materials* 204 (January 1986).

22 UN Doc S/RES/573 (4 October 1985), vote 14–0–1, also 24 *International Legal Materials* 1740–41 (November 1986).

23 US Mission to the UN Press Release No. 106(85), 4 October 1985.

another nation without the consent of such a nation-state? Indeed, is it permissible to attack states that support, train, or harbor terrorists?'[24]

Having reviewed the UN Charter, the 1970 Declaration on Principles of International Law, and the many authoritative condemnations by a wide range of scholars – two full pages of footnotes – of both pre-emptive and retaliatory reprisal actions, Paust concludes: 'For this reason, implementation of the "Schultz doctrine" by the use of preemptive or retaliatory use of force would place the United States in violation of international law and must be opposed.'[25]

Paust clearly did not wish to adopt a position which would give the United States no response to terrorism. He therefore considered that 'situations may arise when the use of force is reasonably necessary to assure an overall serving of the purposes of the Charter', when the United Nations machinery is not functional.[26] However, he added that 'circumstances would have to be compelling and the actual use of force would have to be reasonably necessary and proportionate and not otherwise involve an impermissible targeting of individuals or objects.'[27]

I argue that the law of self-defence is very much more tightly circumscribed. Indeed, a central focus of this analysis will be the legal justifications – if any – offered by the US and UK with respect to their actions against Iraq, Serbia and Afghanistan respectively. What was offered with respect to Libya? Paust points out[28] that shortly after the bombing raid the US made 'confused' – an understatement – references to several wildly differing claims of justification of the attack. First, it was said that force had been used as a reprisal action or retaliation for a prior (10 days previously) terrorist act in Berlin – the death of an American serviceman in an explosion at a nightclub.[29] Second, force had been 'mainly a signal to Colonel Qadaffi to cease terrorist acts'.[30] Third, the US intended to intimidate the elite Libyan guard relied on by Qadaffi.[31] Fourth, it believed it was carrying out pre-emptive self-defence.[32]

---

24 Paust (1986) p. 714.   25 Paust (1986) p. 719.   26 Paust (1986) p. 721.

27 Paust (1986) p. 722, also citing Paust (1983) pp. 307, 310.   28 Paust (1986) pp. 729–730.

29 See 'US Calls Libya Raid a Success' *New York Times* 16 April 1986.

30 See 'US Aides Deny Attack Is Start of an Escalation' *New York Times* 16 April 1986; and Ambassador Vernon Walters, statement to the UN Security Council on 15 April 1986, 'to deter future terrorist acts', reprinted in (1986) 80 *American Journal of International Law* p. 633.

31 See 'Chose Targets to Fuel Coup Against Kadafi, Schultz Says' *New York Times* 16 April 1986.

32 Ronald Reagan 'We Have Done What We Had to Do' *Washington Post* 15 April 1986; also Legal Adviser Abraham Sofaer testified before a House subcommittee that the US 'military action in self-defense . . . in order to preempt and deter' Libya and 'to conduct a military strike . . . in its own territory falls within the specific terms of' the War Powers Resolution: (1986) 80 *American Journal of International Law* 636. Sofaer defended the constitutionality of the actions taken against Libya on two grounds: (1) Presidential power to use force in self-defence; and (2) implicit approval by Congress through appropriations.

Fifth, the action was self-defence against ongoing attacks on United States nationals and embassies abroad.[33] Paust demolished each of these comprehensively. He concluded – and put it mildly – that the US action was 'highly suspect' under international law.[34]

This confusion – or rather negligent disdain – as to justification in international law looks remarkably like the arguments concerning Afghanistan and, later, Iraq.

The Gulf War – consummation

Now we come to the apparent consummation – or so it seemed to the enthusiasts of the time – of international law, in 1991. Remember that only three years passed between the Libya raid and the fall of the Berlin Wall in October 1989. The USSR itself was about to collapse in ignominy, its ideological foundations having rotted away. Moreover, preparation for the new events at the theoretical level was timely indeed. Thomas Franck's *The Power of Legitimacy Among Nations* appeared in 1990.[35] Not, of course, as a consequence of this book's publication, on 2 August 1990 Iraq invaded Kuwait, and – after a remarkably lengthy pause – on 29 November 1990 the UN Security Council adopted Resolution 678.[36] This Resolution appeared to mark the end of the stifling of the Security Council, so much a feature of the Cold War. The system appeared to be about to come into its own.

In part, the delay was caused by the need to win the near-unanimous vote (China was not present) that the United States wanted. In order to win Soviet support for the vote, the United States, according to news reports, agreed to help keep the three Baltic republics out of the November 1990 Paris summit conference,[37] and pledged to persuade Kuwait and Saudi Arabia to provide the USSR with the hard currency it desperately needed – they did so,[38] though only shortly before its demise.

It will be recalled that Resolution 678 '[a]uthorises Member States co-operating with the Government of Kuwait . . . to use all necessary means to uphold [the earlier resolutions] and to restore international peace and security in the area'. For the first time since Security Council Resolution 84 of

---

33 'US Defends Raids Before UN Body' *New York Times* 16 April 1986; and statements of Ambassadors Okun and Walters before the UN Security Council on 14–15 April 1986.

34 Paust (1986) p. 732.   35 Franck (1990).

36 See (1990) 29 *International Legal Materials* 1565.

37 Apple 'Summit in Europe: East and West Sign Pact to Shed Arms in Europe' *New York Times* 20 November 1990.

38 T. Friedman 'Mideast Tensions: How US won Support to Use Mideast Forces. The Iraq Resolution: a US–Soviet Collaboration – A Special Report' *New York Times* 2 December 1990.

7 July 1950,[39] recommending unified military action against North Korea, military action was taken with the approval of the Security Council.

Thomas Franck and Faiza Patel were unambiguous in their response to these events.[40] 'The UN System seems politically to be developing the capacity to substitute police enforcement for vigilante violence . . . Now, surely, is the time to embrace, to encourage, the new policing system before settling forever for sovereign wars of self-proclaimed self-defence.'[41]

However, there were a number of cogent criticisms at the time.[42] Eugene V. Rostow commented: 'Except for the word "authorises", the resolution is clearly one designed to encourage and support a campaign of collective self-defence, and therefore not a Security Council enforcement action.'[43] Burns H. Weston went further, questioning the legitimacy of the resolution and the action which followed.[44] For him, this had four aspects. First, the indeterminacy of the legal authority of Resolution 678; second, in the great-power pressure diplomacy that marked its adoption; third, in its wholly unrestricted character; and finally 'in the Council's hasty retreat from non-violent sanctioning alternatives permissible under it'.[45]

The Security Council held no meetings on the Gulf crisis between 29 November 1990 when Resolution 678 was adopted, and 14 February 1991, when it met in secret session to discuss the political aspects of the end of the war. On 3 April 1991 the Security Council adopted Resolution 687,[46] Iraq accepted it on 6 April, and the Security Council declared it to be in effect on 11 April.

In one respect, the Security Council did in fact set itself a new precedent; this was indeed to be a new era for the authorised use of force. Christine Gray points out that since Operation Desert Storm the Security Council has authorised member states to take action in Somalia (1992), Yugoslavia (from 1992), Haiti (1994), Rwanda (1994), the Great Lakes (1996), Albania (1997), the Central African Republic (1997), Sierra Leone (1997) – as well as Kosovo in Resolution 1244 and East Timor under Resolution 1264: 'it has not concerned itself with identifying a legal basis for such authorisations beyond a general reference to Chapter VII of the UN Charter.' All were internal conflicts, with the debatable exception of the former Yugoslavia.[47]

But Resolution 687 did not bring about any closure in respect of the war against Iraq. Earlier in 2002 the *European Journal of International Law* devoted a whole issue to 'The Impact on International Law of a Decade of Measures against Iraq'.[48]

39　SC Res 84, 5 UN SCOR (Res & Dec) at 5.　　　40　Franck and Patel (1991).
41　Franck and Patel (1991) p. 74.
42　See also Glennon (1991); Caron (1991); Damrosch (1991); Meron (1991).
43　Rostow (1991) pp. 508–509.　　　44　Weston (1991).　　　45　Weston (1991) p. 518.
46　Security Council Resolution 687, 30 ILM 846 (1991).　　　47　Gray (2002) pp. 3–4.
48　*European Journal of International Law* Vol. 13, No.1, February 2002.

Operation Desert Storm was soon followed by Operation Provide Comfort by the USA, UK and France in protection of the Kurds of Northern Iraq in April 1991.[49] Part of the justification for this was that the action was taken 'in support of Resolution 688', ignoring the fact that this resolution was not adopted under Chapter VII, and did not authorise the use of force. In January 1993 the USA and UK carried out attacks on Iraqi missile sites in the no-fly zones. The Secretary General of the UN argued that this action was mandated by the Security Council according to Resolution 678, because of Iraq's violation of the ceasefire resolution.[50] Gray points out that the Secretary General never reverted to this argument, and it has been criticised for arrogating to individual states powers which belong to the Security Council.[51]

Very similar justifications were used to justify Operation Desert Fox in December 1998, in response to Iraq's withdrawal of co-operation with UN weapons inspectors. This operation, which lasted four days and four nights, saw the use of more missiles than used in the whole of the 1991 crisis. The UK and US referred to Security Council Resolutions 1154 and 1205 as providing the legal basis for the use of force. But, as Gray points out, these resolutions had been passed under Chapter VIII, but made no express provision for the use of force.

As Mary Ellen O'Connell points out, the first of the post Cold War sanctions regimes was that imposed on Iraq.[52] On 6 April 1990, a few days after Iraq's invasion of Kuwait, the Security Council adopted Resolution 661, which imposed a comprehensive ban on trade and financial transactions with Iraq. Resolution 666 expanded the economic sanctions, but with exceptions for humanitarian considerations. In Resolution 670 of 1991, air links were prohibited. In 1995, the Security Council, 'concerned by the serious nutritional and health situation of the Iraqi population' passed Resolution 986, 'food for oil'. Nevertheless, the sanctions remain in force. Karima Bennoune, former Legal Adviser at Amnesty International, expresses the view of many critics of economic sanctions against Iraq: '. . . these sanctions appear to have been relatively useless in undermining the power of the Iraqi regime and on the other hand have had an apocalyptic effect on the population of Iraq.'[53]

Indeed, the contradiction between Robin Cook's objectives set out on 12 May 1997[54] that British foreign policy should contain 'an ethical dimension', and this among other policies led to the abandonment of the so-called 'ethical foreign policy', and its replacement in early September 2000 by the objective of making 'Britain strong in the world'.[55] Paul Williams notes 'the sustained criticism which has emerged from a variety of groups opposed to British support for sanctions against Iraq despite repeated attempts by ministers to

49 Malanczuk (1991); Franck (1995) pp. 235–236.   50 Weller (1993) p. 741.
51 Gray (2002) p. 12.   52 O'Connell (2002) p. 67.   53 Bennoune (2002) p. 252.
54 Cook (1997).   55 Williams (2002).

defend the government's record'.[56] But Williams said nothing about the war against Serbia.

The war against Serbia – seduction

On 24 March 1999, after the breakdown of the Rambouillet negotiations over the fate of Kosovo and the Kosovars, Operation Allied Force was launched. This was the start of a 78-day bombing campaign.[57] As Biddle points out, NATO won: not surprising, when it is considered that the combined population of NATO's 19 countries exceeded Serbia's 11 million by a factor of 65; NATO's defence budget was 25 times larger than Serbia's entire economy; and its armed forces outnumbered Serbia's by 35 to 1.[58]

In many ways, the war against Serbia provided the bridge between the wars against Iraq and Afghanistan. 'Even as NATO bombs fell on Belgrade, US and British aircraft were continuing their sustained (if nearly invisible) war on Iraq, one that expended more than 2,000 bombs and missiles in 1999 alone – not nearly the number used in Kosovo but still a sizeable show of force. And the 2000–1 campaign in Afghanistan was both a clear descendant of and a reaction to the military model unveiled in Kosovo.'[59] In his review for *Foreign Affairs*, Biddle makes no mention at all of international law, or of the United Nations.

The argument that the bombing was necessitated by the need to avert humanitarian disaster – a new law of humanitarian intervention – had such moral appeal that critics of the action were few, at least in Northern Europe. There were exceptions. Michael Byers and Simon Chesterman responded polemically on 19 April 1999: 'Nato's unilateral intervention in the Balkans has frightened Russia, isolated China, and done little to help the million or so Kosovars in whose name Serbia is being bombed. Its principal achievements may be to ensure the death of the "new world order" famously heralded by George Bush after the liberation of Kuwait in 1991, and to destroy an institution that has helped to prevent international wars for over half a century.'[60]

Thomas Franck pointed out one of the crucial differences between the Gulf War and the Kosovo War – the distinction between '. . . mitigation and justification. Neither the US Department of State nor NATO seriously attempted to justify the war in international legal terms.'[61] He was forced to this conclusion by Bruno Simma's unanswerable critique[62] of the war's legality. Franck responded:

. . . while UN authorisation of collective military action did break new

---

56 Williams (2002) p. 59, citing Herring (2002).   57 See Murphy (2000).
58 Biddle (2002) p. 138.   59 Biddle (2002) p. 139.   60 Byers and Chesterman (1999).
61 Franck (1999) p. 859.   62 Simma (1999).

ground, there was little new about armed response to outright aggression. Resolution 1244, on the other hand, endorses the deployment of collective (regional) armed force to counteract, not aggression, but gross violation of humanitarian law and human rights . . . There is, however, another notable distinction between Resolutions 687 and 1244. The former established an international regime for Iraq wrought by the triumph of the Security Council-authorised forces. The latter imposed a regime on Yugoslavia after a campaign by NATO that the United Nations had not authorised. Although the Council had previously invoked Chapter VII and 'stresse[d]' the need for a 'negotiated political solution', it had stopped short of authorising NATO to bring about the results it later embraced in Resolution 1244 . . . This has made it hard to disagree with the disquieting conclusion of Professor Bruno Simma . . . that NATO's military action was in breach of international law.[63]

The main issue, however, was whether the actions of NATO, especially the United States, had the effect of bringing about, in record time, a new creative development in customary international law through state practice and *opinio juris*. That is, did the imperative – as presented by NATO – of averting a humanitarian disaster in Kosovo, namely the genocide or at any rate ethnic cleansing of Kosovars by the Serbs, trump the provisions of the UN Charter prohibiting the use of force? This was the issue highlighted in Rwanda in 1994, when it appeared that Bernard Kouchner's doctrine of *droit et devoir d'ingérence*, was the main justification for the French intervention, *Operation Turquoise*, approved ex post facto by the Security Council.[64]

The debate was conducted primarily in the pages of the *EJIL*. Bruno Simma was answered by Antonio Cassese, whose principled position on the question of anticipatory self-defence has been noted above. Cassese submitted two anguished essays.[65] In answer to the question whether international law was moving towards a new customary law of 'forcible countermeasures' in response to humanitarian disaster or gross and massive violation of human rights, Cassese argued that if such a new law was indeed developing, then practice and *opinio juris* could at the most justify measures taken only in extreme circumstances, where the intervenors had a reasonable subjective opinion that only prompt intervention could avert disaster, and only then until the Security Council could take control.

Most remarkably, the Independent Commission on Kosovo,[66] comprising such progressive luminaries as Hanan Ashrawi, Richard Falk, the Russian diplomat Oleg Gordievsky, and chaired by Richard Goldstone, came to the conclusion that the intervention was 'illegal but legitimate'.[67] For Jack

---

63 Franck (1999) p. 858.   64 Bowring (1995).   65 Cassese (1999a); Cassese (1999b).
66 Independent Commission on Kosovo (2000).   67 Independent Commission (2000) p. 4.

Donnelly, this displays 'tension' – but is 'entirely appropriate'.[68] David Rieff is much less kind in his assessment: he describes the Report as 'the wishful thinking of eminent persons'[69] – in other words, of 'the great and the good of the international social-democratic establishment'.[70] He makes the valid, for me, point that 'States in the poor world oppose the intervention in Kosovo because they continue to believe that sovereignty remains the best protection against foreign hegemony.'[71] More controversially, he argues: '. . . such interventions, no matter how disinterested, or wrapped up in the mandate of the UN or new international law, are colonising enterprises.'[72] He is especially opposed to the 'human rights understanding of the world', because it is 'curiously indifferent to history'.[73] Thomas Weiss, on the contrary, applauds the Commission's report, and contends that 'Humanity, or the sanctity of life, is the only genuine first-order principle for intervention. The protection of the right to life, broadly interpreted, belongs in the category of obligations whose respect is in the interest of all states. All others – including the sacred trio of neutrality, impartiality and consent, as well as legalistic interpretations about the desirability of UN approval – are second-order principles.'[74]

Legal scholars have not failed to notice the political imperatives which law was made to serve. Christine Gray points out that Kosovo is another instance (following Rwanda, Albania and Haiti) of the desire for legitimacy which influenced the USA, the UK and other NATO states in claiming a Security Council basis for their use of force in Kosovo.[75] She adds: 'It is no longer simply a case of interpreting euphemisms such as "all necessary means" to allow the use of force when it is clear from the preceding debate that force is envisaged: the USA, UK and others have gone far beyond this to distort the words of resolutions and to ignore the preceding debates in order to claim to be acting on behalf of the international community.'[76] Christine Chinkin used an article in the *AJIL* itself to aim the most succinct and deadly criticism of the Kosovo War:

> Finally the Kosovo intervention shows that the West continues to script international law, even while it ignores the constitutional safeguards of the international legal order . . . All these incidents serve to undermine the Charter on an ad hoc selective basis without providing clear articulation of the underlying principles, or even assurance of future acceptance by those who currently espouse them. The case of Kosovo may have highlighted the continuing chasm between human rights rhetoric and reality. It does not resolve the way this can be bridged.[77]

---

68 Donnelly (2002) p. 101. 69 Rieff (2002). 70 Rieff (2002) p. 111.
71 Rieff (2002) p. 116. 72 Rieff (2002) p. 117. 73 Rieff (2002) p. 118.
74 Weiss (2002). 75 Gray (2002) p. 8. 76 Gray (2002) p. 9.
77 Chinkin (1999) p. 846.

One purpose of this book is to argue for a substantivist account of human rights, rooted in history, on the basis of which the rhetoric can be wrested from the USA and UK and turned, as the most powerful of weapons, back upon them. International law itself can be presented in a quite different light.

Thus, the doyen of American international lawyers, Louis Henkin, was quite firm as to the international law: '. . . the law is, and ought to be, that unilateral intervention by military force by a state or group of states is unlawful unless authorised by the Security Council.'[78] The human rights scholar Jack Donnelly, while conceding that this was the view of most commentators, added: '. . . the moral arguments for humanitarian intervention should not be ignored.'[79] His argument is that 'When faced with a conflict between legal and moral norms, political considerations, rather than a corrupting influence, ought to weigh heavily in decisions to act and in judgements of such actions.'[80]

Nevertheless, in the end Thomas Franck permitted himself an optimistic conclusion, in line with his theories of legitimacy and fairness in international law: 'A final lesson of Kosovo is that, in the end, the United Nations – albeit disdained and circumvented – again became an essential facilitator in ending the conflict. It is not the only forum for the exercise of creative, sustained multilateral diplomacy, but it remains a resilient and irreplaceable one.'[81]

However, as with the war against Iraq, the war against Kosovo has had continuing and perhaps unintended consequences.

First, the legitimacy of both the International Criminal Tribunal for the Former Yugoslavia and the European Court of Human Rights has been called into question. The Prosecutor of the ICTY refused to contemplate a prosecution of responsible persons in NATO states for alleged violations of humanitarian law during the bombing of Serbia.[82]

This contrasts with the approach in relation to Article 18(1) of the ICTY Statute taken by the Prosecutor when asserting her right to investigate allegations of crimes committed by Serb forces in Kosovo.[83] The threshold test expressed therein by the Prosecutor was that of '*credible evidence tending to show that crimes within the jurisdiction of the Tribunal may have been committed in Kosovo*' (emphasis added). That test was advanced to explain in what situation the Prosecutor would consider, for jurisdiction purposes, that she had a legal entitlement to investigate. (As a corollary, any investigation failing to meet that test could be said to be arbitrary and capricious, and to fall

---

78 Henkin (1999).   79 Donnelly (2002) p. 101.   80 Donnelly (2002) p. 103.

81 Franck (1999) p. 860.

82 Final Report to the Prosecutor by the Committee Established to Review the NATO Bombing Campaign Against the Federal Republic of Yugoslavia (2000) 21:4–7 *Human Rights Law Journal* pp. 257–272.

83 *Request by the Prosecutor, Pursuant to Rule 7 bis (B) that the President Notify the Security Council That the Federal Republic of Yugoslavia Has Failed to Comply With Its Obligations Under Article 29*, dated 1 February 1999.

outside the Prosecutor's mandate.) Thus formulated, the test represents a negative cut-off point for investigations.

As to the use of cluster bombs by NATO, the Review Committee decided as follows:

> 27. Cluster bombs were used by NATO forces during the bombing campaign. There is no specific treaty provision which prohibits or restricts the use of cluster bombs although, of course, cluster bombs must be used in compliance with the general principles applicable to the use of all weapons. Human Rights Watch has condemned the use of cluster bombs alleging that the high 'dud' or failure rate of the submunitions (bomblets) contained inside cluster bombs converts these submunitions into antipersonnel landmines which, it asserts, are now prohibited under customary international law. Whether antipersonnel landmines are prohibited under current customary law is debatable, although there is a strong trend in that direction. There is, however, no general legal consensus that cluster bombs are, in legal terms, equivalent to antipersonnel landmines . . .

The Prosecutor accepted the Review Committee's conclusion that:

> On the basis of the information reviewed, however, the committee is of the opinion that neither an in-depth investigation related to the bombing campaign as a whole nor investigations related to specific incidents are justified. In all cases, either the law is not sufficiently clear or investigations are unlikely to result in the acquisition of sufficient evidence to substantiate charges against high level accused or against lower accused for particularly heinous offences.

This decision by the Prosecutor has been widely criticised. For example, Ronzitti argued that this was 'equivalent to a *non liquet*'.[84] Difficulties in interpretation are not a good reason for not starting an investigation. There are fields of humanitarian law, as with any body of law, which are not *sufficiently* clear. However, the task of law interpretation and 'clarification' is entrusted to the Tribunal, which thus cannot conclude by saying that it cannot adjudicate the case, since the law is 'not clear'. The *non liquet* is not part of the jurisprudence of the Hague Tribunal nor of any other tribunal.'[85]

And Professor Benvenuti submitted:

> . . . notwithstanding the recommendation of the Review Committee, an

---

84 The Latin phrase '*non liquet*' literally means 'it is not clear', that is the facts (and/or law) are insufficient to provide the basis for a decision. It is the technical term given to a verdict given by a jury when a matter is to be deferred to another day of trial.
85 Ronzitti (2000).

in-depth investigation should be started because the above-mentioned grounds, as summarized by the Review Committee, are insufficient to exclude that grave breaches of IHL within the competence of the Tribunal may have occurred. If, in the opinion of the Review Committee, 'the law is not sufficiently clear', this ought to be the very reason for starting an in-depth investigation, thus allowing the ICTY to clarify the law . . . If, in the opinion of the Review Committee, 'investigations are unlikely to result in the acquisition of sufficient evidence of charges' (though such an opinion does not exclude the possibility that grave breaches of IHL may in fact have occurred), this would be a good reason for the Prosecutor to start an investigation making use of the very strong powers she (and the Tribunal) have resorted to in other cases (such powers were not at the disposal of or used by the Review Committee).[86]

In its response to the ICTY's decision not to investigate NATO actions, Amnesty International (AI) noted the admission by the Review Committee that in answering the allegations of war crimes made against it, NATO had 'failed to address the specific incidents' with which it was charged. Five of these are among the incidents identified by AI in its 7 June 2000 report.[87] The Committee's report documenting why a criminal investigation should not be conducted into NATO also revealed that it had 'not spoken to those involved in directing or carrying out the bombing campaign'. Nonetheless, it came to the conclusion set out above. Amnesty International pointed out that the Review Committee's report did not explain what difficulties it anticipated in gathering evidence against NATO or its officials.

And on 12 December 2001 the Grand Chamber of the ECtHR found the applications of a number of Serbian civilian victims (represented by US and UK lawyers including Prof Françoise Hampson of Essex University) of the NATO bombing of the Belgrade TV station on 23 April 1999 to be inadmissible.[88] These apparently one-sided results, no doubt highly satisfactory for the NATO states, provided ammunition for Slobodan Milosevic in his own trial at The Hague.

Second, the legal status of Kosovo, whether as a continuing part of Serbia, as an autonomy of some description, or as a fully independent entity, remains unresolved. The character of the UN administration, first under Bernard Kouchner (see above) as special Representative of the Secretary General of the UN, has been a source of considerable concern. The UN military presence, KFOR, and the civil administration, UNMIK, operate with effective

---

86 Benvenuti (2001) pp. 504–505.   87 See http://www.amnesty.org/ailib/intcam/kosovo/.
88 Application no. 52207/99 by Vlastimir and Borka Banković, Živana Stojanović, Mirjana Stoimenovski, Dragana Joksimović and Dragan Suković against Belgium, the Czech Republic, Denmark, France, Germany, Greece, Hungary, Iceland, Italy, Luxembourg, the Netherlands, Norway, Poland, Portugal, Spain, Turkey and the United Kingdom.

immunity from legal challenge in ordinary courts. Only the Ombudsperson Institution in Kosovo, led by the former member of the European Commission of Human Rights Marek Antoni Nowicki was able to challenge a number of disturbing phenomena.

Thus, in April 2001 he was obliged to challenge the incompatibility with recognised international standards of the scope of the grant of immunity to KFOR and UNMIK in their institutional capacities.[89] In June 2001 he found that '. . . deprivations of liberty imposed under "Executive Orders" or any other form of executive instruction, decree or decision issued by the Special Representative . . . do not conform with recognised international standards'.[90] He found that any such deprivation of liberty and the absence of judicial control over deprivations of liberty imposed under Executive Orders violated Article 5 of the European Convention on Human Rights.

The elections of 17 November 2001 and the election of Nexhat Daci as President of the Kosovo Assembly, under the Constitutional Framework for Provisional Self-Government gave rise to hopes that the rule of law might in future be obeyed. But when the question of the entry of the Federal Republic of Yugoslavia, the FRY, arose in March 2001, the Ombudsperson wrote that the current status of Kosovo as an international protectorate outside the jurisdiction of FRY 'is to place Kosovo completely outside the purview of any international human rights monitoring and/or judicial mechanisms, where it will remain for the conceivable future'.[91]

Thus, as with the war against Iraq, the war against Serbia has led to a continuing denial, by the United Nations itself, of fundamental human rights. In this way, not only is the legitimacy of the Security Council challenged, but the reputation and integrity of the United Nations itself is undermined by its own actions.

The war against Afghanistan – rejection

One of the more extraordinary responses to the aftermath of September 11 was the article by Jamie Shea, NATO Director of Information, and voice of NATO during the war against Serbia, 'NATO – Upholding Ethics in

---

89 Special Report no.1 of 26 April 2001 'On the compatibility with recognised international standards of UNMIK Regulation No. 2000/47 on the Status, Privileges and Immunities of KFOR and UNMIK and Their Personnel in Kosovo (18 August 2000) and on the Implementation of the above Regulation' at http://www.ombudspersonkosovo.org/doc/spec%20reps/spec%20rep1_summary.htm.

90 Special Report no.3 of 29 June 2001, 'On the Conformity of Deprivations of Liberty under "Executive Orders" with Recognised International Standards'. http://www.ombudspersonkosovo.org/doc/spec%20reps/spec%20rep3_summary.htm.

91 Letter from Marek Antoni Nowicki to Bruno Haller, Secretary General of the Parliamentary Assembly of the Council of Europe, 11 March 2002; on http://www.ombudspersonkosovo.org/reports_other.htm.

International Security Policy'.[92] Ethics, for Shea, is the content of Article 5 of the Washington Treaty, invoked by the 'Alliance' on 12 September. 'The acceptance of such shared destiny is at the heart of ethics in international security policy, for it makes opting out or neutrality in the face of the new, transnational terrorist threats much more difficult to justify.'[93] He makes no mention of international law, or any relation between ethics, law or rights.

There is, however, every reason why we should ask why the US and UK did not seek the explicit authority of the Security Council, which alone should be able to decide questions of pressure, sanctions, or the use of force. This failure was repeated in every detail in relation to Iraq in 2003.

It is noteworthy that the two Security Council Resolutions, 1368 (2001) of 12 September 2001, and 1373 (2001) of 28 September 2001, while reaffirming the right of self-defence contained in the Charter, do *not* authorise any use of force, the bombing or any other – unless one accepts the arguments of Byers, set out below. Indeed, Resolution 1373 deals mostly with preventing the financing of terrorism. In his statement of 8 October 2001, Kofi Annan, Secretary-General of the United Nations, said:

> Immediately after the 11 September attacks on the United States, the Security Council expressed its determination to combat, by all means, threats to international peace and security caused by terrorist acts. The Council also reaffirmed the inherent right of individual or collective self-defence in accordance with the Charter of the United Nations. The States concerned have set their current military action in Afghanistan in that context.

Also on 8 October, the President of the UN Security Council, Richard Ryan (Ireland), issued a press statement following a meeting called at the request of the USA and UK, to inform Security Council members regarding the military action. According to him, the UK and US permanent representatives made it clear that 'the military action that commenced on 7 October was taken in self-defence and directed at terrorists and those who harboured them', and stressed that every effort was made to avoid civilian casualties. It appears that the members of the Council were 'appreciative' of the presentation made by the US and UK, but were deeply concerned at the humanitarian situation in Afghanistan.

Thus, it is clear that the Security Council neither endorsed nor authorised the military action, merely noted that it is taking place, with a justification of self-defence. The Secretary-General's careful formulation is particularly interesting.

Michael Byers notes that there were at least four possible legal justifications

---

92 Shea (2002).   93 Shea (2002) p. 76.

for the use of force against Afghanistan: Chapter VII of the UN Charter (for example, Iraq), intervention by invitation (for example, Grenada), humanitarian intervention (for example, Kosovo), and self-defence. 'It is significant that the US relied solely on the last justification.'[94] However, Byers takes the view that Resolution 1373 contains language – buried away in the provisions on freezing terrorist assets – that arguably constituted an almost limited mandate to use force. Thus:

> The Security Council . . .
> Acting under Chapter VII of the Charter of the United Nations . . .
> 2. Decides also that all States shall . . .
> (b) Take the necessary steps to prevent the commission of terrorist acts, including . . .

According to Byers: '. . . it provides better evidence of a Chapter VII authorisation than either the "material breach" argument used to justify the no-fly zones in Iraq, or the "implied authorisation" argument used to justify the 1999 Kosovo intervention.'[95] He notes that in future China or Russia could invoke Resolution 1373 and block any attempts to clarify or rescind it – which would explain why it was adopted unanimously. Byers' conclusion, while more measured in tone than his LRB piece in 1991, contains an equally stark warning: 'The events of 11 September have set in motion a significant loosening of the legal constraints on the use of force, and this in turn will lead to changes across the international legal system. Only time will tell whether these changes to international law are themselves a necessary and proportionate response to the shifting threats of an all too dangerous world.'[96]

It is plain that the Security Council would indeed have abdicated all authority and responsibility if it had really issued such an unlimited and unrestricted permission to use force. But the reality is even less appealing. The Security Council, and, in effect, the whole of Charter and customary law on the use of force and self-defence, have been jettisoned in the name of the war against terrorism. Once again Thomas Franck articulated the likely reasoning of the Bush administration. The *AJIL* as usual witnessed a fierce exchange of contrary views[97] between Jonathan Charney and Thomas Franck. While Charney argued strongly that the Security Council could and should have remained involved, Franck's conclusion took his own position several steps closer to a repudiation – contrary to his previous positions – of the role of the Security Council altogether: 'As a matter of law, however, there is no requirement whatever that a state receives the blessing of the Security Council before responding to an armed attack. Were this not so, how many

94 Byers (2002a) p. 401.   95 Byers (2002a) p. 402.   96 Byers (2002a) p. 414.
97 Charney (2001); Franck (2001).

states would deliberately agree to subordinate their security to the Council's assessment of the probity of the evidence on which they based their defensive strategy of self-preservation.'[98]

Finally, Slavoj Žižek makes the obvious but vitally important point: 'Is today's rhetoric not that of a global emergency in the fight against terrorism, legitimising more and more suspensions of legal and other rights? The ominous aspect of John Ashcroft's recent claim that "terrorists use America's freedom as a weapon against us" carries the obvious implication that we should limit our freedom in order to defend ourselves.'[99] This foreboding has been expressed also from a human rights universalist viewpoint, Jack Donnelly:

> First, anti-terrorism, whether good or bad, is not humanitarian intervention. There are many different forms of evil in the world for which we have developed different international legal norms and political practices. Second, I am doubtful that the international political world has been radically transformed. But, third, to the extent that it has, the consequences (for national and international) human rights are likely to be negative. More generally, appalling as these events were, it would be a further tragedy if they diverted (already scarce) international attention and resources away from more important and widespread moral and humanitarian concerns such as malnutrition, grinding poverty, genocide, pervasive repression, systematic political misrule, and the regular indignities and human rights violations that most people suffer daily in most of the contemporary world.[100]

Thus, the rejection of international law has as its corollary the undermining of the safeguards of domestic law.

Human rights – the villain of the piece?

For Chandler, more debatably, the villain of the piece is human rights ideology, or at least the version of human rights propounded by Geoffrey Robertson QC.[101] But what is at stake is not, as Chandler seems to suggest, the baleful influence of the ideology and discourse of human rights, undermining the gains of international law. I would like to adopt his more persuasive arguments set out in *New Left Review*:

> The 1945 settlement, preserved in the principles of the UN Charter, reflected a new international situation, transformed by the emergence of the Soviet Union as a world power and the spread of national liberation

---

98 Franck (2001) p. 843.   99 Žižek (2002).   100 Donnelly (2002) note 1, p. 105.
101 Robertson (2001).

struggles in Asia, the Middle East and Africa . . . sovereign equality was given technical recognition in parity of representation in the General Assembly and lip-service to the principle of non-interventionism, setting legal restrictions on the right to wage war.[102]

What is at stake is the decisive 1945 break with the Westphalian system, a new order of law which has been held together by the principle of sovereign equality. As he argues, it is 'not sovereignty itself but sovereign equality – the recognition of the legal parity of nation-states, regardless of their wealth or power – which is being targeted by the new interventionists. Yet such equality has been the constitutive principle of the entire framework of existing international law and of all attempts, fragile as they may be, to establish the rule of "right" over "might" in regulating inter-state affairs.'[103]

Conclusion

International law has certainly been dragged through the mire. Consummation followed by seduction then rejection is a squalid and pitiful sequence. Of course, scholars should have known better: they should not have greeted the apparent apotheosis of Security Council control in 1990 with such enthusiasm, knowing as they did the contempt with which the UK and US treated the United Nations and its mechanisms in 1986. The purported creation of new custom in 1999, to justify the bombing of Serbia, was inevitably followed by the rejection of the Security Council and of the UN itself following September 11. Any deployment of the rhetoric of human rights since 1991 has now been decisively undermined by the reality of UN administration in Kosovo (and Bosnia). Thus, it is wrong to argue, as does Chandler, that human rights are in some way responsible for what has befallen international law.

Instead, there is an uncompleted project to hand. As argued above, the UN and its principles and mechanisms came to life and acquired content during the period of decolonisation. The issues of global social justice which fired the campaigns for the rights to self-determination and development have not left the agenda. The question before the great majority of the world's population is how to reclaim the UN.

This chapter has analysed the history since 1986 of the systematic attack on international law and subversion of human rights by the USA and UK. The remainder of this book seeks both to redeem the promise of a substantivist account of human rights; and to show how a revolutionary conservatism in international law can provide a structure for a reasoned counter-attack. The next chapter analyses the illegality of the invasion and occupation of Iraq, and the commission of war crimes.

102 Chandler (2002) p. 58.   103 Chandler (2002) p. 55.

Chapter 3

The legality of the invasion and occupation of Iraq

Introduction

I have examined in the previous chapter the state of international law in the period immediately before the Iraq War which started on 20 March 2003. It might appear that international law has been thoroughly trashed by the actions of the USA and UK.

However, in this chapter I will seek to show that my arguments for revolutionary conservatism in international law are strengthened, not weakened, by what has happened. State sovereignty, the prohibition of the use of armed force except in self-defence or with the express authorisation of the Security Council, the rights of peoples to self-determination: each of these fundamental principles of the post World War II legal order has acquired new relevance and indeed substance.

I am not alone in these assertions. Much recent scholarship tends in this direction. Thus, in his wonderfully entitled article 'Arguments of Mass Confusion',[1] Dino Kritsiotis shows convincingly that from the viewpoint of international law the UK and US cannot be taken to have been seeking to advance arguments based on any purported doctrine of pre-emptive self-defence – at least, not legal arguments. To do so he adopts the analysis of the International Court of Justice in the *Nicaragua* case.[2] As he shows, the Court '. . . considered it imperative in its examination of the lawfulness of intervention to proceed on the basis of the legal justification advanced by the United States, and not on the basis of political arguments framed as justifications . . .'.[3] For this reason, he focuses on the communications filed by the US and UK on 20 March 2003 to notify the Security Council of their actions, and also to 'mark out the legal basis for their action'.

The United States considered that Operation Iraqi Freedom was '. . . authorised under existing Council resolutions, including its Resolutions 678

---

1 Kritsiotis (2004).   2 *Nicaragua v United States of America* ICJ Reports (1986) 14.
3 Kritsiotis (2004) p. 236.

(1990) and 687 (1991)', and that Iraq had decided '. . . not to avail itself of its final opportunity under Resolution 1441 (2002) and has clearly committed additional violations [and that] in view of Iraq's material breaches, the basis for ceasefire [in Resolution 687 (1991)] has been removed and the use of force is justified under Resolution 678 (1990)'.[4]

The United Kingdom in its turn asserted that '. . . Iraq has failed, in clear violation of its obligations [under Resolution 687 (1991)] to disarm and that in consequence Iraq is in material breach of the conditions of the cease-fire at the end of hostilities in 1991 as laid down by the Council in its Resolution 687 (1991)'.[5]

Even though the ICJ has not had the opportunity to pronounce on the invasion of Iraq, it is, Kritsiotis argues, appropriate to consider that these representations are '*the* legal justification provided for the intervention, because, even though they were made outside the court-room and within the undisputed political context of the Security Council, they occurred as part of a formal exercise of making justifications to defend the application of force under international law'.[6]

For my purpose, the great interest of these communications is that they are firmly based on the 'classical' principles of Charter law to which I referred in Chapter 1: the prohibition on the use of force in Article 2(4) save in the exceptional circumstances of self-defence (Article 51) or cases of authorisation by the Security Council (under Chapter VII).[7] They also, as Kritsiotis points out, rely on a detailed interpretation of Resolutions 678 (1990), 687 (1991), and 1441 (2002), and the use of legal terms such as 'authorisation', 'material breach' and 'ceasefire', as well as precedent.[8]

The only reference to 'self-defence' in the United States' communication is in the final sentence, where there is a mention of 'necessary steps' taken 'to defend the United States and the international community from the threat posed by Iraq *and* to restore international peace and security in the area'. As Kritsiotis points out, this passing reference to self-defence stands in stark contrast with the previous practice of the United States in the situations in which it has invoked self-defence as its legal justification: in Iraq in 1993, or Operation Infinite Reach against Afghanistan and Sudan (August 1998), or Operation Enduring Freedom against Afghanistan (October 2001).[9] Thus, as a matter of law, both the US and the UK argued that the authorisation contained in Resolution 678 (1990) was suspended and not terminated in Resolution 687 (1991), and was revived by Iraq's 'material breach' of its obligations.

---

4 UN Doc. S/2003/351 (21 March 2003).   5 UN Doc. S/2003/350 (21 March 2003).

6 Kritsiotis (2004) p. 242; see also Warbrick (2003).   7 Johnstone (2003).

8 Kritsiotis (2004) p. 244, and see footnotes 46–49.

9 Kritsiotis (2004) p. 251, and see footnotes 85–87.

Kritsiotis does not answer the question of legality directly. But he launches a series of precision-guided questions which destroy the credibility of the justification offered by the 'coalition'.[10] The central question is as follows: who should determine whether there had been a material breach? The Security Council? Any member of the Security Council? Or only any Permanent Member? Or any member of the United Nations? Or only the United States? Or just the United Kingdom? Or the United States, but only when acting with the United Kingdom? 'But what role then for the reports of the United Nations weapons inspectors set out in Resolution 1441 (2002)?'

It is significant that the *legal* justifications of the US and UK in May 2003 were firmly based on Charter law. But there is no doubt that both the UK and US dearly wish to achieve respectability for a new doctrine of 'preventive or pre-emptive attack'. Anthony Carty believes that the '. . . arguments used by political elites to drive the institutions of the states into motion' are really decisive in constituting the actions of a state.[11] Analysing recent work by commentators and close advisers to the Blair Government, he comes to the conclusion that the UK had indeed committed itself to set a precedent for pre-emptive attack, in a context in which the threat and use of force 'are becoming once again an integral part of UK national policy'.[12] Reviewing the recent book *The Breaking of Nations* by Robert Cooper,[13] a close adviser to Tony Blair, Carty explains that Cooper 'formulates a general principle for dealings with non-Western states which is incompatible with the international law of the Charter. It is based upon an openly imperialist anthropology that, not surprisingly, he sees to be as much a part of European as of American elite mentalities.'[14] At the same time, he criticises McGoldrick[15] for apparently taking the Government's legal arguments at face value.[16]

And, finally, it needs to be repeated: the invasion and occupation of Iraq were (and are at the time of writing) illegal, and the fact of their illegality makes a difference. While Christopher Greenwood[17] has made a brave attempt to construct the only possible legal justification for the invasion – and the justification adopted by the UK government – Gerry Simpson shows in detail that the 'war was illegal, and that this illegality matters'.[18] In his recent impassioned article he sets out a series of reasons why to him international law matters.[19] He ends his article with these words:

> And, every so often, someone, somewhere, in the midst of brutality, disorder and lawlessness, stands up and says, as the US prison guard who handed over evidence to US authorities in January 2004 said: 'There are

---

10 Kritsiotis (2004) pp. 267–269.   11 Carty (2005).   12 Carty (2005) p. 146.
13 Cooper (2004).   14 Carty (2005) p. 148.   15 McGoldrick (2004).
16 Carty (2005) p. 151.   17 Greenwood (2003).   18 Simpson (2005) p. 167.
19 Simpson (2005) pp. 185–186.

some things going on here that I can't live with.' International law mattered to him and it should matter to us.[20]

In their recent, provocatively lucid polemic, Goldsmith and Posner have sought to argue that states act as they do for prudential reasons, but never because of the constraints of international law or human rights. For them, '. . . human rights law fades into the background'.[21] The whole of my book has sought to make a realist case for the contrary view.

Individual responsibility: war crimes by Blair and others

In late 2003 and early 2003 I had the honour to chair an Inquiry conducted by a panel of eight distinguished international lawyers from four countries.[22] We heard evidence and prepared a report, which is at the present time under consideration by the Prosecutor at the International Criminal Court.[23] We found ample evidence that war crimes within the meaning of Article 8 of the Rome Statute of the International Criminal Court were committed by UK forces.

The primary evidence was that of the use of cluster bombs, referred to previously in this book. The UK and US were condemned out of their own mouths. The British Armed Forces Minister declared during an interview with the BBC that cluster weapons had been used against concentrations of military equipment and Iraqi troops in and around built-up areas around Basra, Iraq's second largest city.[24] In addition, the United States in its air and ground operations used considerably more cluster weapons, including many reported uses during the prolonged bombing campaign of Baghdad. Some US air attacks were carried out using British platforms, in which case the UK was required to give its approval of both the target and weapon selection.[25]

---

20 Simpson (2005) p. 188.   21 Goldsmith and Posner (2005) p. 134.

22 Upendra Baxi, Professor of Law, University of Warwick; Bill Bowring, Professor of Law, London Metropolitan University; Christine Chinkin, Professor of International Law, London School of Economics and Political Science; Guy Goodwin-Gill, Senior Research Fellow, All Souls College, Oxford; Nick Grief, Steele Raymond Professor of Law, Bournemouth University; René Provost, Professor of Law, McGill University, Canada; William Schabas, Professor of Law, National University of Ireland, Galway and Director of the Irish Centre for Human Rights; Paul Tavernier, Professor of Law, Faculté Jean Monnet and Director of Centre de recherches et d'études sur les droits de l'Homme et le droit humanitaire at the University Paris-Sud, France.

23 Peacerights (2004).

24 Armed Forces Minister Adam Ingram's BBC Radio 4 Interview, Item 28, Evidence Bundle 2, in the possession of the author.

25 Testimony of Air Marshal Burridge Q251–253 (Item 3, Bundle 2). General Myers confirmed that cluster munitions were used against 'many' military assets in populated areas: US Dept. of Defense Press Briefing, 25 April 2003 (quoted in House of Common Research Paper 03/50 at 75 – Item 1, Bundle 2).

Cluster weapons are not prohibited per se by the law of armed conflict. The Report considered whether their use against military objectives located in urban areas violates either the prohibition of intentionally targeting civilians (Article 8(2)(b)(i) ICC Statute) or the prohibition of attacks causing disproportionate incidental loss of life or injury to civilians (Article 8(2)(b)(iv) ICC Statute), thus providing the elements of war crimes.

Article 8(2)(b)(i) provides that 'intentionally directing attacks against the civilian population as such' constitutes a violation of the laws and customs of war and, in turn, a war crime subject to the jurisdiction of the ICC. While there is no credible information that UK forces meant specifically to target civilians, the intent requirement under this provision covers cases in which the perpetrator is aware that 'a consequence will occur in the ordinary course of events' (Article 30 ICC Statute).

Evidence presented to the Inquiry by weapons experts suggested that cluster weapons disperse their bomblets over a wide area that cannot be precisely targeted: bomblets can drift up to three kilometres away from the intended target. Bomblets used in the Iraq campaign were never 'smart' or 'precision guided'.[26] This type of weapon, when used in an urban setting, can reasonably be described as indiscriminate. In its *Advisory Opinion on the Legality of the Threat or Use of Nuclear Weapons*, the International Court of Justice stated that:

> The cardinal principles contained in the texts constituting the fabric of humanitarian law are the following. The first is aimed at the protection of the civilian population and civilian objects and establishes the distinction between combatants and non-combatants; States must never make civilians the object of attacks *and must consequently never use weapons that are incapable of distinguishing between civilian and military targets* [emphasis added].[27]

The prohibition against indiscriminate attacks is given precise meaning by Article 51(4) of 1977 Additional Protocol I, which provides that such attacks include those which employ a method of combat which cannot be directed at a specific military objective and, as a result, 'are of a nature to strike military objectives and civilians or civilian objects without distinction'. The International Criminal Tribunal for Yugoslavia, in the Review of the Indictment against Milan Martić, found that, given their accuracy and striking force, the use of cluster bombs against targets in Zagreb could not be designed to hit

---

26 Testimony by Landmine Action experts David Taylor and Richard Lloyd; *Briefing: Indiscriminate Attack? The Potential Use of Landmines and Cluster Bombs in Iraq* (Item 17, Bundle 1).

27 ICJ Reports 1996, p. 226, para. 78.

military targets and was as such contrary to customary and conventional international law.[28]

Given the inaccurate nature of cluster weapons, their use by UK forces or under UK approval provided evidence that violations of Article 8(2)(b)(i) ICC Statute – that is, war crimes – may have occurred and should be investigated by the ICC Prosecutor.

The Report broke new ground by considering the possibility of charging UK politicians and soldiers with the commission of war crimes committed as part of a criminal joint enterprise:

> . . . to the extent that acts perpetrated by US troops constituted crimes against humanity or war crimes, in violation of Articles 7 and 8 ICC Statute, the ICC can prosecute nationals of the UK who ordered, solicited, induced, aided or abetted or otherwise assisted in their commission or attempted commission, including providing the means for their commission. It is, however, necessary to prove that the UK nationals had knowledge that these acts were being perpetrated.[29]

This led us to consider the crime of aggression. The ICC Statute, in Article 5(1), identifies aggression as one of the crimes within its jurisdiction. Of course, Article 5(2) says that the ICC shall not exercise its jurisdiction over aggression until a definition has been adopted, and until the conditions under which it may be exercised have been agreed to.

The Report argued that: 'The waging of aggressive war was held to be an international crime in the Charter of the Nuremberg Tribunal in 1945, which was adopted by the United States of America, the UK, France and the Soviet Union. These countries cannot now argue that the waging of aggressive war is not prohibited as a crime under international law.'[30] Thus in concluding that aggression had been committed, the ICC would not be exercising jurisdiction over aggression, as it would not be attempting to actually hold any person accountable for the crime. It would merely be reaching the view that the criminal enterprise of waging aggressive war had been committed as a preliminary circumstance to the prosecution of criminal acts over which it may exercise jurisdiction – namely crimes against humanity and war crimes. This would appear to be what is foreseen in Article 25(3)(d) ICC Statute, which imposes liability upon a person who:

> (d) In any other way contributes to the commission or attempted commission of such a crime by a group of persons acting with a

---

28 *The Prosecutor v Martič* (Case no. IT–95–11–R61, para. 31) Review of the Indictment Pursuant to Rule 61, 8 March 1996.

29 Peacerights (2004) para. 3.22.   30 Peacerights (2004) para. 3.24.

common purpose. Such contribution shall be intentional and shall either:

(i) Be made with the aim of furthering the criminal activity or criminal purpose of the group, where such activity or purpose involves the commission of a crime within the jurisdiction of the Court; or

(ii) Be made in the knowledge of the intention of the group to commit the crime;

This led us inexorably to the following conclusion:

> These legal provisions, applicable under the ICC Statute but familiar to most if not all criminal justice systems, including those currently in force within the UK, are designed to promote deterrence. Those who participate in criminal activity with others whose values are perhaps not set at quite as high a threshold as their own, may be held liable for the acts of their 'partners in crime'. Accomplices should not be able to resist liability for crimes committed as part of a collective venture by merely claiming that the most evil of the acts were the responsibility of their associates.[31]

Conclusion

The question of war crimes committed in the invasion and occupation of Iraq, and the liability not only of UK politicians for war crimes, but of the UK as a state for human rights violations, leads me to my next chapter.

---

31 Peacerights (2004) para. 3.26.

Chapter 4

After Iraq – international human rights law in crisis

Introduction

The invasion and occupation of Iraq have placed international law as a whole and human rights law in particular under extraordinary stress. In the face of brute and lawless force all normativity may appear to have evaporated from the international scene. Nevertheless, it is highly likely that in due course the European Court of Human Rights (ECtHR) will be called upon to adjudicate on complaints arising from the conduct of the United Kingdom, and possibly other European states of the 'Coalition of the Willing'. My argument in this chapter is that significant normative and legal resources already exist in the jurisprudence of the ECtHR, and that through the cases decided over the years, especially the Chechen cases, a wholly positive clarification of the relationship between International Humanitarian Law (IHL) and International Human Rights Law (IHR) is already taking place. However, this process, on my account, can only be understood in the context of colonial and post-colonial armed struggles.

In order to show this, I engage with two points of – apparently – positive legal doctrine; and a more general problem of human rights confronted by gross, widespread and systematic violations.

The first point of doctrine is the question of the extra-territorial reach of human rights law. This question is far from technical in the current context. It is the question whether the UK can be condemned in the European Court of Human Rights (ECtHR) for some of its actions in Iraq – specifically, for those actions which violate the European Convention on Human Rights (ECHR). It is significant but not surprising that legal doctrine on this question has been developed in relation to Turkey and Russia.

My second point of doctrine joins Vladimir Putin and Tony Blair in an unholy coupling. The technical issue is that the war in Iraq, like Russia's own wars in Chechnya, throws into sharp relief a hitherto latent tension between the international law of human rights (IHR) and international humanitarian law (IHL), the international law of armed conflict. Is IHL a *lex specialis* which displaces IHR in the context of international or internal armed conflict?

The general problem in question is the following. The ECHR and ECtHR were elaborated as an ideological instrument in the context of the onset of the Cold War.[1] The UK was very reluctant to accept the creation of a court capable of interfering in internal affairs and rendering obligatory judgments, but finally agreed in a spirit of solidarity against the threat of Communism.[2] For the first three decades of the work of ECHR mechanisms the Court was for the most part called upon to deal with lapses, more or less inadvertent, by Western European states in which the rule of law and adherence to generally understood principles of democracy were not seriously in doubt. Even the many Northern Irish cases against the UK did not present as the result of serious armed conflict. Only in the 1990s, with the tidal wave of Turkish Kurdish cases, especially those concerning village destruction, followed by the many Chechen cases against Russia, has the Court been obliged to confront the human rights consequences of armed conflict. The question is whether the concepts and systems developed in a quite different context half a century ago are remotely effective or indeed legitimate when the UK invades and occupies Iraq.

It will be recalled that United Kingdom has been in Iraq before. As Joel Rayburn points out, the UK seized the provinces of Basra, Baghdad and Mosul from the Ottoman Empire at the end of World War I and formally took control of the new country in 1920, under a mandate from the League of Nations. In 1920, a large-scale Shiite insurgency cost the British more than 2,000 casualties, and domestic pressure to withdraw from Iraq began to build. The UK's premature pullout in 1932 led to more violence in Iraq, the rise of a dictatorship, and a catastrophic unravelling of everything the British had tried to build there.[3] It may be that history repeats itself as farce; but this time there is an international mechanism which may see the UK called to account for its actions.

Extra-territorial effect

The question of extra-territorial applicability of IHR has recently been the subject of intense scholarly engagement.[4] The key cases have arisen in the context of the application of the European Convention on Human Rights (ECHR). This is because the consequences of the post-colonial if not imperial behaviour of Turkey, of the Russian Federation, and of the UK, have been adjudicated upon by judicial instances at the international level, and now in domestic courts as well. These are the cases where the armed forces of a state are alleged to have violated human rights outside the national territory.

---

1 Brownlie and Goodwin-Gill (2006) p. 609.   2 See Council of Europe (1975–1985).
3 Rayburn (2006).
4 See Hampson and Salama (2005) pp. 19–22; Lubell (2005) pp. 739–741; Leach (2005a).

In this area, at least, international law demonstrates its resilience. Since the early 1990s, states have not, on balance, done well. Thus, Turkey lost in respect of its occupation of North Cyprus in the *Loizidou* case,[5] the UK together with other NATO members in the ECHR system had a close shave regarding the bombing of Serbia in the *Bankovic* case,[6] Russia has been condemned for its alleged occupation of part of Moldova[7] in *Ilascu v Moldova and Russia*, and Turkey was once more found to be responsible for violations in neighbouring territory in *Issa v Turkey*.[8] The *Bankovic* case has been described, by a leading judge of the Strasbourg Court, Loukis Loucaides, as 'a set-back in the effort to achieve the effective promotion of and respect for human rights . . . in relation to the exercise of any State activity within or outside their country'.[9] The UK's occupation of Iraq is at the time of writing under scrutiny in the domestic courts in *Al-Skeini*[10] and *Al-Jedda*.[11] Writing in 2003, Vaughan Lowe suggested that in view of the principles set out in the *Loizidou* and *Bankovic* cases 'the UK may in principle incur liability under the ECHR in respect of its conduct in areas where it is in military occupation and exercising governmental powers'.[12] The crucial principle at stake is whether a state party to the ECHR can be in 'effective control' outside its own territory or indeed outside the overall territory of the Council of Europe states so that the actions of its state agents can engage Convention rights.

It should also be noted that the UN Human Rights Committee has interpreted this aspect of the International Covenant on Civil and Political Rights (ICCPR). In its *General Comment No 31*, 'The Nature of the General Legal Obligation Imposed on States Parties to the Covenant', which it adopted on 29 March 2004, it restated the relevant part of Article 2(1) of the ICCPR and continued, at para. 10:

---

5 *Loizidou v Turkey (Preliminary Objections)* 40/1993/435/514, paras 62–64.

6 *Bankovic and others v Belgium and 16 other states*, Application no. 52207/99, judgment of 12 December 2001.

7 *Ilascu and others v Moldova and the Russian Federation, Romania intervening*, Application no. 48787/99, judgment of 8 July 2004.

8 *Issa and others v Turkey*, Application no. 31821/96, admissibility decision of 30 May 2000; judgment of the second Chamber, 16 November 2004.

9 Loucaides (2006) At note 2, p. 392, Loucaides cites the large number of scholarly articles strongly criticising the decision.

10 *R (Al-Skeini and others) v Secretary of State for Defence*, High Court 14 December 2004, Court of Appeal 21 December 2005, [2005] EWCA Civ 1609; [2006] HRLR 7; [2007] UKHL 26, 13.06.07.

11 *R (Hilal Abdul-Razzaq Ali Al-Jedda) v Secretary of State for Defence*, Court of Appeal 20 March 2006, C1/2005/2251, [2006] EWCA CIV 327; [2007] UKHL 58, 12.12.07.

12 Lowe (2003) p. 869.

This means that a state party must respect and ensure the rights laid down in the Covenant to anyone within the power and effective control of that state party, even if not situated within the territory of that state party . . . This principle '– of applicability to all individuals who may find themselves subject to the jurisdiction of the state party –' also applies to those within the power or effective control of the forces of a state party acting outside its territory, regardless of the circumstances in which such power or effective control was obtained, such as forces constituting a national contingent of a state party assigned to an international peace-keeping or peace-enforcement operation.[13]

The question why there is a problem of the application of the ECHR at all is to be answered by reference to the history of the institution which gave birth to it, the Council of Europe.

The Cold War origins and post-colonial destiny of the Council of Europe

The Council of Europe (CoE), which now comprises 47 states (since Montenegro voted to separate from Serbia), with a total population of some 850 million people, exemplifies one of the most poignant ironies of history. It was founded in 1949 in London, by the 10 Western European states which signed its Statute, as, quite self-consciously, 'a sort of social and ideological counterpart to the military aspects of European co-operation represented by the North Atlantic Treaty Organisation'.[14] The three 'pillars' of the CoE, which are exemplified in its more than 200 binding treaties are pluralist democracy, the rule of law, and protection of individual human rights. By promulgating the ECHR, and creating the ECtHR, the first international court with powers to interfere in the internal affairs of states and to render obligatory judgments against them, the CoE showed it was truly serious about the 'first generation' of civil and political rights, especially personal liberty, freedom of expression, the right to compensation for deprivation of property, the right to free elections. It is notable that the list of rights contained in the ECHR does not depart significantly from the list in the French Revolution's Declaration of the Rights of Man and of the Citizen of 1789. It contained no social, economic or cultural rights, largely at the insistence of the UK. The content of the ECHR contrasted strongly with the human rights guaranteed in the constitutions of the USSR and its subject states, all of which gave pride

---

13 CCPR/C/21/Rev.1/Add.13, of 26 May 2004. See also the International Court of Justice in the recent Advisory Opinion on the *Legal Consequences of the Construction of a Wall in the Occupied Palestinian Territory* (2004) ICJ Reports, p. 136 at paras 108 and 109.

14 These are the words of Professor Ian Brownlie, in Brownlie and Goodwin-Gill (2006) at p. 609.

of place to the right to work, followed by rights to social security, healthcare, education and housing. These states could show that they were serious about the social and economic rights enshrined in their constitutions and, by and large, delivered them in practice. Indeed, not only did every person of working age have work, but it was a crime, the crime of 'parasitism', not to work.

It should be no surprise that the UK was strongly resistant to the principle of obligatory judicial decisions at the international level. It remained determined that even if there was to be a Convention, there would be no court, at least for the UK. Thus, when, on 7 August 1950, the Committee of Ministers adopted a draft convention, weakened as a result of UK pressure, it made the right of individual petition conditional on a declaration of acceptance by the State Party, and the jurisdiction of the ECtHR optional.[15] The UK's Attorney-General, Shawcross, stated on 4 October 1950 that: '. . . we should refuse to accept the Court or the Commission as a Court of Appeal and should firmly set our faces against the right of individual petition which seems to me to be wholly opposed to the theory of responsible government.'[16] On 18 October 1950 there was a Ministerial Meeting of the ministers most directly concerned, and Shawcross advised that the ECHR was in essence a statement of the general principles of human rights in a democratic community, in contrast with their suppression under totalitarian government. There had been strong political pressure on the UK government to agree to the Council of Europe Convention, and he felt that the wisest course was to accept it.[17]

Why was the UK so reluctant to submit to such interference? Part of the answer, still relevant for my purposes, lies in the concerns that the ECHR might bring colonial matters under international scrutiny. This was borne out in two of the first cases decided against the UK which directly concerned its colonial past.[18]

One of the first such cases, decided in 1973, involved events taking place outside the UK, and indeed far from Europe.[19] The UK's East African colony Uganda had an Asian population of many thousands, the descendants of Asians who had been brought by the British Empire from India, and who served as civil servants and ran shops and businesses. Uganda was granted independence in 1962. However, in January 1971 the elected President, Apolo Milton Obote, was overthrown by his army commander, Idi Amin Dada. The following year, as part of a policy of 'Africanisation', Amin gave all Asians in

---

15 Trav. Prep. (*ibid*) Vol. V, p. 56.   16 LCO 2/5570 [3363/22].
17 CAB 130/64 [EN. 337/1st Meeting].
18 See also the earlier case *Kingdom of Greece v United Kingdom* App. no. 176/56, Commission decision of 26 September 1958, rejecting the complaints by Greece arising out of the conflict in Cyprus. It will be noted that the complaint by Greece was made, and the Commission decided, before the UK recognised – in 1966 – the right of individual petition.
19 *East African Asians v United Kingdom* App. no. 4403/70 – 4429/70 and others, Commission Report adopted on 14 December 1973.

Uganda 90 days to leave the country, claiming that God had ordered him to do so in a dream.[20] The UK refused them entry. As the government advisers had feared, a number of the Asians complained to Strasbourg. They could not do so under Protocol 4, but, advised by Anthony Lester, argued that deprivation of their right of entry to the UK had caused them humiliation and distress amounting to 'inhuman and degrading treatment' in violation of Article 3. On 14 December 1973 the (former) European Commission on Human Rights found that the enactment of the Commonwealth Immigrants Act 1968 had breached Article 3 of the Convention. The case did not have to go to the Court, since the UK conceded.

The second case was extraordinarily embarrassing for the UK: an inter-state complaint brought by the Republic of Ireland, alleging that suspected terrorists held in administrative detention in Northern Ireland had been sub-jected to torture. The then Commission agreed; the Court held that the use by the UK of the methods of psychological pressure known as the 'five tech-niques' amounted to inhuman and degrading treatment, again a violation of Article 3.[21]

Both these cases therefore concerned the imperial – or at any rate colonial – past of the UK, in a way which threw into sharp relief the real reasons why the UK was so reluctant to make application to the ECtHR a reality (and in fact failed to incorporate the ECHR in domestic law until the Human Rights Act 1998 came into force in 2000).

UK occupation of Southern Iraq

The issue of extra-territorial jurisdiction has resurfaced in relation to the invasion and occupation of Iraq. On 7 April 2004 the Armed Forces Minister, Adam Ingram, stated that:

> the ECHR is intended to apply in a regional context in the legal space of the Contracting States. It was not designed to be applied throughout the world and was not intended to cover the activities of a signatory in a country which is not signatory to the Convention. The ECHR can have no application to the activities of the UK in Iraq because the citizens of Iraq had no rights under the ECHR prior to the military action by the Coalition Forces.[22]

This assertion has now been fully discredited. In October and December 2005

---

20 Wairgala Wakabi 'Idi Amin just won't go away', 30 April 1999, The Black World Today, www.blackworldtoday.com/views/feat/feat1142.asp.

21 *Republic of Ireland v United Kingdom* App. no. 5310/71, judgment of 18 January 1978.

22 Rt Hon Adam Ingram MP, Ministry of Defence, Letter to Adam Price MP, 7 April 2004.

the Court of Appeal heard appeals in *Regina (Al-Skeini and others) v Secretary of State for Defence (The Redress Trust and another intervening).*[23] These were applications for judicial review brought by relatives of Iraqi citizens who had been killed in incidents in Iraq involving British troops. Five of the deceased had been shot by British troops, and a sixth, Baha Mousa, had died while being held in a British detention facility. The claimants sought judicial review of a failure by the Secretary of State for Defence to conduct independent inquiries into or to accept liability for the deaths and the torture. On the hearing of preliminary issues the Divisional Court declared that the ECHR and the Human Rights Act 1998 did not apply in the cases of the first five claimants, but that in the case of the sixth claimant the 1998 Act did apply and the United Kingdom's procedural duties under Articles 2 and 3 of the Convention had been breached. The Court held that a state can be held to have 'effective control' of an area only where that area is within the territory or 'legal space' – *espace juridique* – of the Convention, and therefore only where the area occupied was that of another State Party to the ECHR. Accordingly, since Iraq was not within the regional space of the ECHR, the claimants' cases were not within the jurisdiction of the UK.

The Court of Appeal dismissed the applicants' appeals, and held that the jurisdiction of a State Party to the ECHR was essentially territorial; that if a Contracting State had effective control of the territory of another state, it had jurisdiction within that territory under Article 1 of the ECHR and an obligation to ensure Convention rights and freedoms; but that since none of the victims in the first five cases were under the actual control and authority of British troops at the time when they were killed, and since it was impossible to hold that the United Kingdom was in effective control of that part of Iraq which its forces occupied or that it possessed any executive, legislative or judicial authority outside the limited authority given to its military forces there, neither the Convention nor the 1998 Act applied. The government's appeal with respect to Mr Mousa was also dismissed.

Nevertheless, the Court of Appeal disagreed with the Divisional Court as to *espace juridique*. Lord Justice Brooke answered the question whether the ECHR could have extra-territorial effect as follows:

> It was common ground that the jurisdiction of a contracting state is essentially territorial, as one would expect. It was also common ground that: (i) if a contracting state has effective control of part of the territory of another contracting state, it has jurisdiction within that territory within the meaning of article 1 of the ECHR, which provides that 'the high contracting parties shall secure to everyone within their jurisdiction the rights and freedoms defined in section 1 of the Convention'; (ii) if an

---

23 [2005] EWCA Civ 1609; also reported at [2006] 3 WLR 508.

agent of a contracting state exercises authority through the activities of its diplomatic or consular agents abroad or on board craft and vessels registered in or flying the flag of the state, that state is similarly obliged to secure those rights and freedoms to persons affected by that exercise of authority.[24]

The first of these he referred to as 'ECA' (effective control of an area) and the second 'SAA' (state agent authority). For the purposes of SAA he held that none of the first five claimants were under the control and authority of British troops at the time when they were killed.[25] For the purposes of ECA he asked: '[w]as the United Kingdom in effective control of Basra City in August–November 2003?' He held that it was 'quite impossible to hold that the UK, although an occupying power for the purposes of the Hague Regulations and Geneva IV, was in effective control of Basra City for the purposes of ECHR jurisprudence at the material time'.[26]

  Philip Leach[27] argues (and Brooke LJ appears not to disagree) that until 28 June 2004 when the Iraqi Interim Government assumed full responsibility and control for governing Iraq[28] the UK was an occupying power as defined by the Hague Regulations of 1907 and the Fourth Geneva Convention of 1949. Thus, in his view: '. . . it is very clear that the exercise of authority or control by the United Kingdom over parts of southern Iraq in 2003–4 was extensive. For the purpose of the Strasbourg "effective control" test, it cannot be sensibly or convincingly distinguished from the control which Turkey has been found to exercise over northern Cyprus.'[29] Ralph Wilde has made similar arguments.[30] Loucaides cites with approval the words of Sedley LJ in *Al-Skeini*:

> I do not accept Mr Greenwood's submission that Bankovic is a watershed in the Court's Jurisprudence. Bankovic is more accurately characterised, in my view, as a break in the substantial line of decisions, nearly all of them relating to the Turkish occupation of northern Cyprus, which hold a member state answerable for what it does in alien territory following a de facto assumption of authority.[31]

That, in my view, is the correct approach. The House of Lords has now pronounced on both cases, on 13 June and 12 December 2007. However, the fundamental issues are not resolved, and the litigation will continue to Strasbourg if necessary.

---

24 [2005] EWCA Civ 1609, para. 48.   25 Ibid. para. 101.   26 Ibid. para. 124.
27 Leach (2005) p. 457.   28 UN Security Council Resolution 1546.
29 *Cyprus v Turkey* (2002) 35 EHRR 30.   30 Wilde (2005).
31 Loucaides (2006) p. 401; *Al-Skeini* ibid. para. 193.

Tension between international humanitarian law and the law of international human rights

My starting point in this section is a history of struggle and of disputed doctrine. The anti-colonial struggles were largely aimed at securing independence within defined, overseas, territories – that is, the 'salt-water self-determination', in respect of territories separated from the colonial metropolis by seas and oceans to which the UN declaration of 1960 was directed.[32] The non-state protagonists were the 'national liberation movements'. The legal issues arising from the use of force by these movements, and the right or otherwise of other states to render support, including intervention, usually by the USSR, were explored in detail, almost at the end of the Cold War, by Julio Faundez, writing in the first issue of the first international law journal published in French and English and aimed at Africa,[33] and Heather Wilson, with a background in the US armed forces.[34] That was the period, up to the collapse of the USSR, when the use of force by self-determination movements – National Liberation Movements – was not, as is so often the case today, characterised as 'terrorism'.

International humanitarian law had been substantially updated and codified following World War II, in the four Geneva Conventions, dealing with wounded and sick, shipwrecked, prisoners of war, and civilians in the power of an opposing belligerent and civilians in occupied territory. These conventions were adopted in 1949 at the initiative of a private organisation, the International Committee of the Red Cross.[35]

As Hampson and Salama point out, there was no successful attempt to update the rules of conduct of hostilities until 1977, when two Additional Protocols were promulgated. They suggest that 'this may have been partly attributable to the reluctance, after both the first and second world wars, to regulate a phenomenon which the League of Nations and later the United Nations were intended to eliminate or control'.[36] However, these distinguished authors appear to miss the significance of the two Additional Protocols to the Geneva Conventions, adopted in 1977. It is of course the case, as they note, that Protocol I dealt with international armed conflicts, updating provisions on the wounded and sick, and formulating rules on the conduct of hostilities, while Protocol II dealt, for the first time, with high-intensity non-international armed conflicts. In this, they follow Doswald-Beck and Vité, in whose view the most important contribution of Protocol I 'is the careful delimitation of what can be done during hostilities in order to spare civilians as much as possible'.[37]

---

32 UN General Assembly Resolution 1514(XV).
33 Faundez (1989).   34 Wilson (1990).
35 For a useful brief summary of the history of IHL see note 16 in Hampson and Salama (2005) pp. 25–26.
36 Hampson and Salama (2005) n. 16, p. 26.   37 Doswald-Beck and Vité (1993) p. 9.

However, of a number of scholars recently publishing on the tension (or clash) between IHR and IHL, only William Abresch notes correctly that the Additional Protocols aimed to extend the reach of the existing treaties governing international conflicts to internal conflicts: 'thus, Protocol I deemed struggles for national liberation to be international conflicts'.[38] In other words, if an armed conflict is a struggle for national liberation against 'alien occupation' or 'colonial domination' it is considered an 'international armed conflict' falling within Additional Protocol I.[39]

This, I suggest, is the key to understanding the significance of both Additional Protocols. They were the response of the ICRC, and then the overwhelming majority of states which have ratified the Protocols, to the new world of 'internationalised' internal conflicts, in the context of armed struggle for self-determination by National Liberation Movements.

International Humanitarian Law and internal armed conflicts

Additional Protocol II provides for non-international internal armed conflicts in which the State Party is confronted by a well-organised armed group which controls part of its territory.[40] It therefore requires the existence of a high intensity civil war in which the armed groups are 'under responsible command' and 'exercise such control over a part of [the state's] territory as to enable them to carry out sustained and concerted military operations'.[41]

For this reason it could not apply to the conflict in Northern Ireland, but most certainly applied to the First Chechen War from 1994 to 1997. In the cases of the United Kingdom (Northern Ireland), Turkey (South-Eastern Turkey), and the Russian Federation (Chechnya), the state concerned has been at pains to deny the existence of an 'armed conflict', but has instead characterised the events as 'terrorism', 'banditry' or simply organised crime. However, it is also clear that for the purposes of Protocol I, the international community has given no shred of recognition to the situation of the Irish Republicans, the Turkish Kurds or the Chechens as involving 'alien domination' or 'colonial occupation', whatever the claims to self-determination of the Irish, Kurds and Chechens. The Irish and Kurds never exercised sufficient control over territory to justify the application of Additional Protocol II. The Irish Republicans for years demanded the ratification by the UK of the additional protocols, and UK ratification was delayed, despite the fact that, as pointed out, the protocols could have had no application.

---

38 Abresch (2005) p. 742.
39 Additional Protocol I, Article 1(4), and see Abresch (2005) p. 753.
40 See Bennoune (2004) p. 177, n. 18.
41 Additional Protocol II, Article 1(1), and see Abresch (2005) p. 753.

However, it should be noted that the Good Friday Agreement, which brought the Northern Irish conflict to an end, at least to the present day, recognised the 'right to self-determination of the people of the Island of Ireland', a long-standing demand of Sinn Fein. But this does not affect the general point made.

The Chechen exception

The conflict in Chechnya provides the essential context to the question of the tension between IHL and IHR. This was highlighted in a judgment of the Bow Street Magistrates Court in London.[42] In his judgment of 15 November 2003 in the extradition case *Government of the Russian Federation v Zakayev*,[43] Senior District Judge Timothy Workman held as follows:

> The Government maintain that the fighting which was taking place in Chechnya amounted to a riot and rebellion, 'banditry' and terrorism. The Defence submit that it is clear beyond peradventure that this was at the very least an internal armed conflict and could probably be described as a war . . . I am quite satisfied that the events in Chechnya in 1995 and 1996 amounted in law to an internal armed conflict . . . In support of that decision I have taken into account the scale of fighting – the intense carpet bombing of Grozny with in excess of 100,000 casualties, the recognition of the conflict in the terms of a cease fire and a peace treaty. I was unable to accept the view expressed by one witness that the actions of the Russian Government in bombing Grozny were counter-terrorist operations . . . this amounted to an internal armed conflict which would fall within the Geneva Convention.[44]

Another relevant feature of the First Chechen War was highlighted in 1996 by Professor Paola Gaeta.[45] On 31 July 1995 the Constitutional Court of the Russian Federation delivered its decision on the constitutionality of President Yeltsin's decrees sending Federal forces into Chechnya.[46] The Court was obliged in particular to consider the consequences of Russia's participation

---

42 The author provided written expert evidence for this case, but not on the point of internal armed conflict.
43 Full text at http://www.hrvc.net/west/15–11–03.html.
44 Transcript of the judgment on file with the author.
45 Paola Gaeta, 'The Armed Conflict in Chechnya before the Russian Constitutional Court' (1996) 7:4 *European Journal of International Law* 563–570.
46 An unofficial English translation of this judgment was published by the European Commission for Democracy through Law (Venice Commission) of the Council of Europe, CDL-INF (96) 1.

in the 1977 Additional Protocol II (AP II) to the 1949 Geneva Conventions.[47] As Gaeta pointed out:

> The Court determined that at the international level the provisions of Protocol II were binding on both parties to the armed conflict and that the actions of the Russian armed forces in the conduct of the Chechen conflict violated Russia's international obligations under Additional Protocol II to the 1949 Geneva Conventions. Nonetheless, the Court sought to excuse this non-compliance because Protocol II had not been incorporated into the Russian legal system.

The Court clearly spelled out that the provisions of AP II were binding upon *both* parties to the armed conflict, i.e. that it confers rights and imposes duties also on insurgents. This statement was, in Gaeta's view, all the more important in the light of the fact that, at the Geneva Conference, some states expressed the opposite view, since they were eager to keep rebels at the level of criminals without granting them any international status.[48] This view had also found support in the legal literature.[49]

Gaeta rightly emphasised the importance of the determination by the Court that the Russian Parliament had failed to pass legislation to implement AP II, and that this failure was one of the grounds – probably even the primary ground – for non-compliance by Russian military authorities with the rules embodied in the Protocol. In its determination of the case, the Court expressly directed the Russian Parliament to implement AP II in Russian domestic legislation, thus showing how much importance it attached to actual compliance with that treaty. Secondly, the Court underscored that, according to the Russian Constitution and the UN's ICCPR, victims of any violations, crimes and abuses of power shall be granted efficient remedies in law and compensation for damages caused.

The Second Chechen War and the Council of Europe

Russia's failure to obey the clear instructions of the Constitutional Court as to the implementation of AP II has not been remedied to date, and the start

---

47 The Russian Federation is a party to the 1949 Geneva Conventions. The Soviet Union ratified both the 1977 Additional Protocols on 29 September 1989 to become effective on 29 March 1990. The Russian Federation deposited a notification of continuation on 13 January 1992.

48 See Antonio Cassese, 'The Status of Rebels under the 1977 Geneva Protocol on Non-International Armed Conflict' (1981) 30 *International and Comparative Law Quarterly* 415.

49 On Protocol II see, among others, R. J. Dupuy and T. Leonetti, 'La notion de conflit armé à caractère non international', in Antonio Cassese (ed.), *The New Humanitarian Law of Armed Conflict* Volume I (1979) p. 272.

of the Second Chechen War was accompanied by an equally egregious manifestation of non-concern by the Russian authorities in relation to compliance with the ECHR.

On 26 June 2000 the Council of Europe published the 'Consolidated report containing an analysis of the correspondence between the Secretary General of the Council of Europe and the Russian Federation under Article 52 of the ECHR'.[50] This report was prepared, at the request of the Secretary General, by three experts, Tamas Bán, Frédéric Sudre and Pieter Van Dijk, who were asked to analyse the exchange of correspondence between himself and the Russian Federation 'in the light of the obligations incumbent on a High Contracting Party which is the recipient of a request under Article 52 of the European Convention on Human Rights'. The first request was dated 13 December 1999. The experts were asked to focus in particular on the explanations that the Secretary General was entitled to expect in this case by virtue of Article 52 and to compare that with the content of the replies received. They concluded that the reply given by the Russian Federation did not even meet the minimum of the standard that must be considered to be implied in Article 52 in order to make the procedure effective, and remarked:

> For example, it would have been legitimate to expect, as a minimum, that the replies would provide information, in a concrete and detailed manner, about issues such as the instructions on the use of force under which the Federal forces operated in Chechnya, reports about any cases under investigation concerning any human rights violations allegedly committed by members of the Federal forces, the detention conditions of persons deprived of their liberty by the Russian authorities and their possibilities for effectively enjoying the rights guaranteed by Article 5 of the Convention, the precise restrictions which have been put in place on freedom of movement in the area, et cetera. However, even after clarification by the Secretary General of what was expected, the replies lacked any such details . . . We conclude that replies given were not adequate and that the Russian Federation has failed in its legal obligations as a Contracting State under Article 52 of the Convention.[51]

The dubious role of the UK

The United Kingdom has played a questionable role in apparently assisting President Putin to deflect international condemnation of his actions in

---

50 Document SG/Inf(2000)24, at http://www.coe.int/T/E/Human%5Frights/cddh/2.%5FTheme-%5Ffiles/03.%5FArticle%5F52/01.%5FDocuments/01.%5FChechnya/SG%20Inf%282000%2924%20E%20-%20SG%20report.asp#TopOfPage.

51 Document SG/Inf(2000)24, ibid. – no page numbers in the web version.

Chechnya, especially after 11 September 2001. Tony Blair visited Moscow on 4 October 2001, and Putin was especially grateful to him – for the fact that Blair was one of the few European leaders who had taken the initiative to assist Russia in April 2000, when Russia was coming under especially fierce criticism for its conduct of the war in Chechnya.

On 6 April 2000 the Parliamentary Assembly of the Council of Europe (PACE) received a report by its Rapporteur on Chechnya, Lord Frank Judd, condemning Russian actions.[52] PACE considered that '. . . the European Convention on Human Rights is being violated by the Russian authorities in the Chechen Republic both gravely and in a systematic manner', and voted to recommend to the CoE's Committee of Ministers that 'should substantial, accelerating and demonstrable progress not be made immediately in respect of the requirements set out in paragraph 19,[53] [it should] initiate without delay, in accordance with Article 8 of the Statute, the procedure for the suspension of the Russian Federation from its rights of representation in the Council of Europe'.[54] Most painfully for Russia, it appealed for an inter-state complaint of human rights violations to the European Court of Human Rights by other Council of Europe members.[55]

This vote did not affect the cordial relationship Blair and Putin had already established. Just 10 days later, on 16 April 2000 Putin visited London, despite the fact that he was still not formally President of Russia – he was only sworn in on 7 May 2000.[56] His programme included tea with the Queen at Buckingham Palace. At a joint press conference on 17 April 2000, Blair welcomed Putin's commitment that all reports of human rights violations would be looked into by Russia. Referring to Putin as 'Vladimir', he rejected suggestions that Britain should distance itself from Russia because of events in Chechnya. Putin in turn stated that they had agreed on joint responses to problems of organised crime and narcotics.

Thus, said Putin on 4 October 2001, Tony Blair had been instrumental in creating a new situation. He said:

---

52 PACE Doc. 8697, 4 April 2000, 'Conflict in Chechnya – Implementation by Russia of Recommendation 1444 (2000)', Report, Political Affairs Committee, Rapporteur: Lord Judd, United Kingdom, Socialist Group, at http://assembly.coe.int//main.asp?link=http://assembly.coe.int/Documents/WorkingDocs/doc00/EDOC8697.HTM.

53 These included '. . . immediately cease all human rights violations in the Chechen Republic, including the ill-treatment and harassment of civilians and non-combatants in the Chechen Republic by Russian federal troops, and the alleged torture and ill-treatment of detainees', and 'seek an immediate cease-fire'.

54 Recommendation 1456 (2000)[1], 'Conflict in the Chechen Republic – Implementation by the Russian Federation of Recommendation 1444 (2000)', at http://assembly.coe.int/main.asp?-Link=/documents/adoptedtext/ta00yerec1456.htm.

55 Reuters, 6 April 2000; via Johnson's Russia List.

56 See BBC 'Putin flies into legal battle' 16 April 2000 at http://news.bbc.co.uk/2/hi/europe/714998.stm.

... it was just as important for us that the Prime Minister took his initial initiative and established his first contacts with the Russian leadership, with myself personally, we felt and we saw and we knew that our voice was being heard, that the UK wanted to hear us and to understand us and that indeed we were being understood and this was a very good basis upon which together we managed to work jointly and quite effectively to neutralise international terrorism in this instance in Afghanistan.[57]

He was referring to April 2000. Action against Russia could only have been taken by the Council of Europe's Committee of (Foreign) Ministers. Britain is a founder and leading member of the Council. Putin recognised, and expressed his gratitude, for the fact that the invitation extended to him so promptly made it absolutely clear that no action would be taken.

Thus, Russia has added a new dimension of obduracy, or even downright non-compliance, to the relationship between the Council of Europe and its mechanism for human rights protection – and one of its largest and newest members.

What really happened in Chechnya?

A sobering commentary on the situation in Chechnya was provided by the parallel session, co-sponsored by the International Federation for Human Rights (FIDH) and the International League for Human Rights (ILHR), which took place on 30 March 2005 during one of the last sessions of the UN Human Rights Commission.[58] Several of the authoritative opinions expressed, by leading Russian actors as well as NGO representatives, are of special note.

A Chechen victim of gross violations, Libkan Bazayeva (she was one of the applicants in the first six Chechen cases at the Strasbourg Court, referred to below), provided some striking casualty statistics. She used, for reference, the roughly 200,000 dead or missing after the Asian tsunami in December 2004. Not long before the start of the First Chechen War, Chechnya's population passed the one million mark. During the 10 years of the two wars, she estimates that between 100,000 and 200,000 civilians have died, although she admitted that estimates vary considerably due to the difficulty getting accurate data. The official 2002 census claimed that the population was 1,088,000, which she called a blatant falsification. She believed that the current population is now less than 800,000.[59] There was further disturbing information, from an independent source. As of 31 March 2005, a total of 32,446 internally

---

57 http://www.number–10.gov.uk/output/Page1679.asp.
58 Record of the Parallel Session, at http://www.ngochr.org/view/index.php? basic_entity= DOCUMENT&list_ids=378.
59 Presentation by Libkan Bazaeva, in the Record, ibid. (no page numbers on the website).

displaced persons (IDPs) from Chechnya (7,227 families) were registered for assistance in Ingushetia in the database of the Danish Refugee Council (DRC). Of this total, 12,064 persons (2,617 families) were in temporary settlements, and 20,382 persons (4,610 families) in private accommodation.[60]

Anna Neistat, the Director of the Moscow office of Human Rights Watch, estimated that between 3,000 and 5,000 civilians had disappeared over the previous five years.[61] Official Russian estimates of 2,000 for the same period, although more conservative, were still significant, she said. In the past, most abducted civilians were men between the ages of 18 and 40 and the abductions were usually carried out by Russian forces. That was changing: more women and elderly are being targeted. The 'Chechenisation' of the conflict had transferred responsibility to the Chechen authorities and other Chechen groups that are pro-Moscow. With multiple groups involved in abductions, it was difficult to know where to enquire when a friend or relative disappears.

All participants were perturbed by the fact that the European Union, which had in previous years introduced a resolution on Chechnya at the Commission, had declined to do so in 2005. Rachel Denber, acting executive director of Human Rights Watch's Europe and Central Asia Division said:

> It is astounding that the European Union has decided to take no action on Chechnya at the Commission. To look the other way while crimes against humanity are being committed is unconscionable. Thousands of people have 'disappeared' in Chechnya since 1999, with the full knowledge of the Russian authorities. Witnesses now tell us that the atmosphere of utter arbitrariness and intimidation is 'worse than a war.'[62]

Human Rights Watch had also published a 57-page briefing paper which documented several dozen new cases of 'disappearances' based on their research mission to Chechnya.[63]

Many participants were frustrated by the apparent lack of interest by the international community. Tatyana Lokshina, founder of the Demos human rights information service, the best of its kind in Russia,[64] accused organisations like the United Nations, the Commission on Human Rights and the Organisation for Security and Cooperation in Europe (OSCE) of not taking adequate measures. Particularly disappointing was the absence of any resolution at the Commission in 2005 condemning human rights abuses in Chechnya, although in her view the absence did not come as a total surprise.

---

60 http://www.reliefweb.int/rw/RWB.NSF/db900SID/EGUA–6BLKXS?OpenDocument.
61 Presentation by Anna Neistat, in the Record, ibid. (no page numbers on the website).
62 Presentation by Rachel Denber, in the Record, ibid. (no page numbers on the website).
63 http://hrw.org/english/docs/2005/03/21/russia10342.htm.   64 See www.demoscenter.ru.

The last resolution was tabled in 2001, before 9/11. Since then, Russia has been seen as a valuable partner in the war on terror. Therefore major players were looking the other way, and allowing Russia to claim that Chechnya was an internal matter, or that it was also another front in the war on terror.[65]

Action of a different kind was, however, being taken at that time, with significant results later in 2005. Both Libkan Bazayeva and Tatyana Lokshina were part of it.

Making use of the Council of Europe's mechanism for protection of human rights

In early 2000 the author began to work with the Human Rights Centre of the leading Russian human rights NGO *Memorial*, preparing applications for the European Court of Human Rights (ECtHR) at Strasbourg. Russia had ratified the ECHR in 1998. One of the first applicants was Libkan Bazayeva. Her case is described below. In March 2001 the author applied for a grant from the European Commission's European Human Rights and Democracy Initiative to provide resources and support for the Strasbourg applications. In December 2002 a new litigation project, the European Human Rights Advocacy Centre (EHRAC), was founded with a grant of 1 million Euro from the EC. It works in partnership with *Memorial*, and with the Bar Human Rights Committee of England and Wales. The author is Chair of its International Steering Group, and Tatyana Lokshina is one of its members.[66] EHRAC is now assisting more than 100 Russian applicants, about half of them Chechen, before the Strasbourg Court, as well as conducting cases against Azerbaijan, Georgia and Latvia. The project employs nine lawyers and support staff in Russia,[67] including the Vice-Chair of the Steering Group, the Chechen lawyer Dokka Itslaev, who works with extraordinary courage from the Chechen town of Urus Martan.

On 24 February 2005 the First Section of the European Court of Human Rights delivered three resounding judgments in the first six cases to be brought against the Russian Federation in relation to the current conflict in Chechnya. On 6 July 2005 the Court rejected Russia's application to the Grand Chamber, and the judgments became final.[68]

These applications were lodged at the Court in early 2000, and communicated to the Russian government in April 2000. They were given 'fast track'

---

65 Presentation by Tatyana Lokshina, in the Record, ibid. (no page numbers on the website).
66 See, for full details, Bulletins, and case information, http://www.londonmet.ac.uk/ehrac; and the Russian site http://www.ehracmos.memo.ru.
67 As well as four staff in London, including the Director, Philip Leach, author of *Taking a Case to the European Court of Human Rights* (2006) (2nd edn, Oxford: Oxford University Press).
68 See Bowring (2005).

status, but nonetheless it was six years before judgments became final.[69] This was not perhaps so surprising given the extraordinary load which Russian membership has now placed on the ECHR system.[70]

All three of the judgments in the first six Chechen cases concern the deaths of the children and other relatives of the six applicants as a result of Russian military action at the end of 1999 and the beginning of 2000. The applicants argued that the Russian government had violated their rights under Article 2 (the Right to Life), Article 3 (the Prohibition on Torture) and Article 13 (the Right to an Effective Remedy) of the ECHR.

The bombing of the refugee column

The first case[71] concerned three Chechen women, Medka Isayeva, Zina Yusupova and Libkan Bazayeva – mentioned above, who were victims of the bombing by the Russian airforce of the 1000-vehicle civilian convoy which had been given permission by the Russians to leave Grozny by a 'humanitarian corridor' on 29 October 1999. The Russian government did not dispute that its aircraft bombed and killed the applicants' children and relatives, but argued that its use of force was justified as 'absolutely necessary in defence of any person from unlawful violence' under paragraph 2(a) of Article 2. The Court doubted whether there was such 'defence', in the absence of any corroborated evidence that any unlawful violence was threatened or likely. The Court found that the applicants' right to life had been violated since, even if the Russian military were pursuing a legitimate aim in launching at least a dozen powerful S-24 missiles, the operation had not been planned and executed with the requisite care for the lives of the civilian population.

Furthermore, the Court held that the Russian authorities should have been

---

69 A six-year delay would in any domestic legal system constitute a violation of the Article 6 right to a judicial decision within a reasonable period. This is completely inexcusable in the context of the facts of the cases.

70 On 21 April 2005 Anatoly Kovler, the Russian judge on the European Court of Human Rights, told a conference in Yekaterinburg that more than 22,000 Russian citizens have sent applications to the Court. This figure is now much larger (see www.rferl.org/newsline/2005/04/1-RUS/rus–210405.asp). According to the Court's Survey of Activities for 2004 (see http://www.echr.coe.int/Eng/EDocs/2004SURVEY(COURT).pdf), just 13 judgments were delivered against Russia in 2004, and while 6,691 applications were lodged, 374 were declared inadmissible, 232 were referred to the government, and 64 were declared admissible. Statistics published on 25 January 2005 showed that the Court delivered 718 judgments in 2004, of which 588 gave rise to a finding of at least one violation of the Convention. The Court also declared inadmissible a total of 20,348 applications. The number of cases terminated increased by around 17.5 per cent compared with 2003. In addition, it was estimated that the annual number of applications lodged with the Court rose to about 45,000 in 2004, an increase of approximately 16 per cent. It is known that about 96 per cent of all applications are declared inadmissible; this percentage rises to 99 per cent in the case of Russia.

71 *Isayeva, Yusupova and Bazayeva v Russia*, Application nos. 57947/00, 57948/00 and 57949/00, 24.02.05.

aware that they had announced a humanitarian corridor, and of the presence of civilians in the area. Consequently they should have been alerted to the need for extreme caution regarding the use of lethal force. The pilots' testimony, that they attacked two isolated trucks, did not explain the number of casualties and was inconsistent. The attack took place over a period of up to four hours and was not a single attack. The weapons used were extremely powerful in relation to whatever aims the military were seeking to achieve.

It is notable that the Russian judge, Anatoly Kovler, voted with the rest of the Court in these three cases. There was no dissent.

The massacre in a Grozny district

In the case of Magomed Khashiyev and Roza Akayeva[72] the applicants' relatives were killed in disputed circumstances, while the Russian forces were in control of the Staropromyslovskiy district of Grozny, in which the applicants resided. At the end of January 2000 the applicants, who had fled, learned that their relatives had been killed. The bodies of the deceased showed signs that they had been killed by gunshots and stabbing.

The Court found that where such deaths lie wholly or mainly within the exclusive knowledge of the authorities, just as in the case of persons in detention, strong presumptions of fact will arise in respect of injuries and deaths occurring. The burden of proof is on the authorities to provide a satisfactory and convincing explanation. Despite its strongly worded request, the Court never received the full case files and no explanation was ever provided. The Court found that it could draw consequential inferences.

Although the government never concluded an investigation and those responsible were never identified, in fact the only version of events ever considered by the Russian investigators was that put forward by the applicants. The documents in the investigation file repeatedly referred to the killings as having been committed by military servicemen. The Court concluded that, on the basis of the material in its possession, it was established that the victims had been killed by the Russian military. No ground of justification had been relied on by the government and accordingly there had been a violation of Article 2.

The bombing of a Chechen village

The case of Zara Isayeva[73] concerned the indiscriminate bombing of the village of Katyr-Yurt on 4 February 2000. The Russian government did not

---

72 *Khashiev and Akayeva v Russia*, Application nos. 57942/00 and 57945/00, 24.02.05.
73 *Isayeva v Russia*, Application no. 57950/00, 24.02.05.

dispute that the applicant and her relatives were bombed as they tried to leave their village through what they perceived as a safe exit. It was established that a bomb dropped from a Russian plane exploded near the applicant's mini-van killing the applicant's son and three nieces. The government again argued that the case fell within Article 2, paragraph 2(a). The Court accepted that the situation in Chechnya at the relevant time called for exceptional measures. However, the Court noted that it was hampered in that no evidence had been produced by the government to explain what was done to assess and prevent possible harm to civilians in Katyr-Yurt. There was substantial evidence to suggest that the Russian military expected, and might even have incited, the arrival of a group of armed insurgents in Katyr-Yurt.

The Court held that nothing was done to warn the villagers of the possibility of the arrival of armed insurgents and the danger to which they were exposed. The Russian military action against the insurgents was not spontaneous but had been planned some time in advance. The Russian military should have considered the consequences of dropping powerful bombs in a populated area. There was no evidence that during the planning stage of the operation any calculations were made about the evacuation of civilians. The use of FAB–250 and FAB–500 bombs in a populated area, without the prior evacuation of civilians, is impossible to reconcile with the degree of caution expected from a law enforcement body in a democratic society.

No effective remedy in Russia

In all three cases the Court found that the Russian government had violated the applicants' rights under Article 13 (the right to an effective remedy). In cases such as these, where there were clearly arguable violations of the applicants' rights under Article 2 and Article 3, the applicants were entitled to 'effective and practical remedies capable of leading to the identification and punishment of those responsible'. The criminal investigations into the suspicious deaths of the applicants' relatives had lacked 'sufficient objectivity and thoroughness'. Any other remedies, including civil remedies suggested by the government, were consequently undermined and the government had failed in its obligations under Article 13.

Each of these cases was a microcosm of the large-scale violations of human rights committed by Russia in Chechnya. In each case the EHRAC lawyers argued that the use of force by the Russian government was disproportionate, and that there were no effective domestic remedies which the applicants could have pursued. Their arguments were founded exclusively on the principles of European Human Rights Law.[74]

---

74 These were the first six cases – the Russian counterpart of *Akdivar and others v Turkey* (Application no. 21893/93, Judgment of 19 October 1994), in view of the importance of

How the Chechen cases highlighted the tension between IHR and IHL

One striking difference between IHL and IHR, which for some reason is not the subject of comment in the scholarly literature on the tension between them which I now review, is that while IHL deals with the personal responsibility and criminal liability – under domestic and international law – of military commanders and politicians, IHR is exclusively concerned with state responsibility.

That is, while the victims of violations of the laws of war, grave breaches of the Geneva Conventions – the relevant part of IHL for the purposes of my argument – may be individuals or groups, only individuals may be prosecuted and punished. In this regard, IHL is unique in international law, of which states are traditionally the only subjects. It may be asserted that while IHR is characterised by methodological individualism in that its subjects, even for minority rights law, are individuals, or the persons who make up relevant groups, it is rigorously collectivist when it comes to its objects. Whatever the post-modernist or 'globalisation' arguments as to the weakening or disappearance of the state, the state must in every case answer to allegations of violations of IHR. This vitally important distinction, I would suggest, is the source of the many radical differences between IHL and IHR, manifested first of all in the many differences of terminology.

As I noted above, William Abresch has analysed the implications of the Chechen judgments for the relationship between IHL and IHR.[75] As he points out, the generally accepted doctrine has been that in situations of armed conflict, humanitarian law serves as *lex specialis* to human rights law. He does not notice, apparently, that the consequences of the application of one regime or the other would be quite different.

This doctrine is apparently supported by the International Court of Justice in its 1996 Advisory Opinion on the *Legality of the Threat or Use of Nuclear Weapons*.[76] The Court stated that it:

> observes that the protection of the International Covenant on Civil and Political Rights (ICCPR) does not cease in time of war . . . In principle, the right not arbitrarily to be deprived of one's life applies also in hostilities. The test of what is an arbitrary deprivation of life, however, then falls to be determined by the applicable *lex specialis*, namely, the law applicable in armed conflict which is designed to regulate the conduct of

these decisions as test cases – and there are many more. The Court's judgments provide a firm foundation for the work of EHRAC and others in enabling victims of gross violations of human rights to obtain an authoritative finding as to what befell them and their families, and to secure reparation.

75 Abresch (2005).   76 Advisory Opinion, 8 July 1996, *ICJ Reports 1996*.

hostilities. Thus whether a particular loss of life . . . is to be considered an arbitrary deprivation of life contrary to Article 6 of the Covenant, can only be decided by reference to the law applicable in armed conflict and not deduced from the terms of the Covenant itself.[77]

What is the meaning of the Latin maxim *lex specialis derogat lex generali*? In his paper analysing the 'fragmentation' of international law Martti Koskenniemi pointed out that the rule described by this maxim is usually considered as a conflict rule, where a particular rule is considered to be an exception to rather than an application of a general rule.[78] The point of the maxim is to indicate which rule should be applied, whether as an application of or an exception to the general law. The other way in which such conflicts are dealt with, he continues, is through the 'doctrine of self-contained regimes'.[79] The latter is the situation in which a set of primary rules relating to a particular subject matter is connected with a special set of secondary rules that claim priority to the secondary rules provided by general law.[80] He gives as an example the fact that human rights law contains well-developed systems of reporting and individual complaints that claim priority to general rules of State responsibility. For Koskenniemi, the rationale for the rule is that the *lex specialis* takes better account of the subject matter to which it relates.[81]

Nevertheless, he insists that '[a]ll rules of international law are applicable against the background of more or less visible principles of general international law'.[82] These include 'sovereignty', 'non-intervention', 'self-determination', 'sovereign equality', 'non-use of force', and the prohibition of genocide. The reader will recall my argument that the third of these, now recognised as part of *jus cogens*, acquired the status of such a principle, of a right in international law, as a consequence of the decolonisation struggles of the national liberation movements. Thus, I have no problem with Koskenniemi's general statement. I maintain, however, that IHL and IHR inhabit quite different moral universes; IHL was historically and remains a limitation on the use of lethal force, irrespective of the legality of the use of force. I cannot agree with Hampson that 'the ultimate object of the two regimes is broadly similar, but they seek to attain that object in radically different ways', although she accurately distinguishes the vitally important differences of result.[83]

Noam Lubell notices that IHL and IHR appear to be quite different languages: teaching IHL to human rights professionals or discussing human

---

77 Advisory Opinion, paras 24–25; see also ICJ *Advisory Opinion on Legal Consequences of the Construction of a Wall in the Occupied Palestinian Territory*, 9 July 2004, paras 102, 105.
78 Koskenniemi (2003) p. 4; see also the finalised version – Koskenniemi (2007).
79 Koskenniemi (2003) p. 8.   80 Koskenniemi (2003) p. 8.
81 Koskenniemi (2003) p. 10.   82 Koskenniemi (2003) p. 7.
83 Hampson and Salama (2005) p. 13.

rights law to military personnel can seem like speaking Dutch to the Chinese or vice versa.[84] But he seems not to notice either that individuals or groups will rarely make claims under IHL; it is not that kind of procedure. But they are drawn, despite all the limitations, to seek to make use of human rights mechanisms.

However, Abresch is interested in which rules are being and will be followed in the European Court of Human Rights, which now, in his view, applies the doctrines it has developed on the use of force in law enforcement operations to high intensity conflicts involving large numbers of insurgents, artillery, and aerial bombardment.[85] He remarks that for IHL lawyers the law of international armed conflict would be the ideal for internal armed conflict. He calls this an 'internationalizing trajectory'.[86] However, the Strasbourg Court has broken from such a trajectory, in order to derive its own rules from the 'right to life' enshrined in Article 2 of the ECHR. Abresch's optimistic prognosis is that:

> ... given the resistance that states have shown to applying humanitarian law to internal armed conflicts, the ECtHR's adaptation of human rights law to this end may prove to be the most promising base for the international community to supervise and respond to violent interactions between the state and its citizens.[87]

This assessment differs sharply from that of Hampson, who clearly considers that the Strasbourg Court should take IHL into account, and believes that despite the fact that the Court has never referred to the applicability of IHL, 'there is an awareness of the type of analysis that would be conducted under IHL'.[88] In this she follows the 'classical' model of Doswald-Beck and Vité, who considered that 'the obvious advantages of human rights bodies using [IHL] is that [IHL] will become increasingly known to decision-makers and the public, who, it is hoped, will exert increasing pressure to obtain respect for it'.[89] Similarly, Reidy considered that in the Turkish cases the Strasbourg Court was 'borrowing language from [IHL] when analysing the scope of human rights obligations. Such willingness to use humanitarian law concepts is encouraging.'[90] She too saw this development as 'certainly welcome in so far as it contributes to a stronger framework for the protection of rights'.[91]

Using the Chechen cases in which I participated as the centre-piece, I have sought to show that the European Court of Human Rights, despite the first

---

84 Lubell (2005) p. 744.   85 Abresch (2005) p. 742.   86 Abresch (2005) p. 742.
87 Abresch (2005) p. 743.   88 Hampson and Salama (2005) p. 18; see also Heintze (2004).
89 Doswald-Beck and Vité (1993) p. 108.   90 Reidy (1998) p. 521.
91 Reidy (1998) p. 521.

generation limitations of the instrument it interprets and enforces, has been obliged to respond to circumstances in which applicants, representing themselves and groups of which they are part, have brought renewed symbolic and material content to human rights. I have insisted that IHL and IHR do indeed speak quite different languages, for reasons which are entirely obvious. IHL itself has been obliged to respond to the anti-colonial struggles and use of force by national liberation movements in the post World War II period, but is extremely unlikely to find application in the strictly internal context of Northern Ireland, South-Eastern Turkey or Chechnya. In this regard, the Balkan conflicts are an exception, since the ICTY was able to treat them as international conflicts.

The problem of gross and systematic violations

The final question concerns the scale of the potential violations committed by the United Kingdom in Iraq. Does the ECHR system have the capacity to deal with gross and systematic contraventions of human rights standards?

The first four decades of the work of the European Court of Human Rights, in the context of the member states of Western Europe, were for the most part concerned with mistaken or negligent government behaviour, even in the case of Northern Ireland. The conflict in Northern Ireland, including heinous acts of terrorism (rightly called by that name) by the IRA on the UK 'mainland', was always a conflict of relatively low intensity,[92] and the UK was clearly taking considerable trouble to combat terrorism and protect the lives and security of ordinary members of society without violating human rights. This, it is asserted, was not the case in Iraq. In my view, British actions in Iraq have considerably more in common with the campaigns conducted by Turkey against the Kurds, and Russia against the Chechens. What these two conflicts did not have in common with the UK in Iraq is that both took place within the territory of the state concerned. I have explored above the issue of extra-territoriality.

The focus of this section is, therefore, 'systematic' violations, or, rather, 'gross and systematic violations', as they are described in Menno Kamminga's 1994 article,[93] to which I return below.

'Gross and systematic violations' should be distinguished from 'systemic' violations, which have been analysed by Philip Leach in the context of the recent practice of the European Court of Human Rights.[94] These are the 'clone' cases, the 'repeat offenders' which the Protocol 14 reforms to the European Convention on Human Rights are intended, in part, to address. In their Resolution of May 2004 the Council of Europe's Committee of Ministers urged the European Court of Human Rights to take further steps to assist

92 See Kitson (1971).   93 Kamminga (1994).   94 Leach (2005).

states by identifying underlying problems – 'as far as possible to identify . . . what it considers to be an underlying systemic problem'.[95]

The issue of gross and widespread violations has been brought to a head by the conflict in Chechnya, and will without doubt rear its head in relation to Iraq, especially if cases like *Al-Skeini* find their way to Strasbourg; although it was noticed in the scholarly literature as a result of the cases decided by the Strasbourg Court from the early 1990s against Turkey.

It goes without saying that only a minimal range of – almost exclusively civil and political – rights are protected by the ECHR. And although both groups and individuals (as well as legal persons) may apply to the ECtHR, the Court has proved itself incapable of responding adequately to the claims made on it. This became starkly apparent in the 1990s, in relation to the Turkish Kurdish cases.

The Strasbourg Court's inherent weakness in dealing with gross violations

The Kurdish cases exemplify the Strasbourg Court's difficulty in engaging with circumstances of generalised armed conflict. During the early 1990s the conflict between the Turkish government and the Kurdish Workers Party (PKK) reached new levels of intensity. The government declared a state of emergency in South Eastern Turkey, in the course of which, in order to deny bases and territorial support to the PKK, state forces destroyed thousands of villages, and three and a half million rural Kurdish inhabitants became refugees in their own country. In 1993, the London-based Kurdish Human Rights Project (KHRP)[96] began sending an impressive series of test cases to Strasbourg. The most important of these, the basis for many of the later victories, *Akdivar and Others v Turkey*,[97] was decided in 1994.

The problem inherent in bringing such cases was identified early on. In 1994, Professor Menno Kamminga warned: 'During the past four decades, the Convention's supervisory system has generally responded disappointingly to gross and systematic violations of human rights.'[98] He pointed out that '[t]he problem with gross and systematic violations is not so much that they are more complicated from a legal point of view. Rather, the problem is that their consideration tends to give rise to less cooperation from the offending state. This makes it more difficult to establish the facts.'[99]

He foresaw that as a result of Protocol 11, which stipulated that inter-state applications go straight to the Grand Chamber, states might be even more

---

95 Resolution Res(2004)3, 12 May 2004.
96 Founded by Professors Kevin Boyle and Françoise Hampson of Essex University.
97 Application no. 21893/93, Decision of 19 October 1994.   98 Kamminga (1994) p. 153.
99 Kamminga (1994) p. 161.

reluctant than in the past to resort to the procedure. He therefore recommended reforms which would enable the Court to consider situations of gross and systematic violations of human rights *proprio moto*, that is, on information supplied by NGOs.

In 1997, Aisling Reidy, Françoise Hampson, and Kevin Boyle, all three of whom represented Kurdish clients through KHRP, published what was in effect a follow-up to Kamminga's article.[100] They correctly pointed out that '[a] pattern of systematic and gross violation of human rights does not occur in a vacuum, or as a result simply of negligence or default on the part of governmental authorities. Rather such a pattern requires the sanction of the state at some level.'[101] They posed the question which haunts EHRAC and its Chechen cases as well: 'one can question whether the use of an individual petition mechanism is suited to addressing the nature of complaints arising out of such a conflict.'[102]

Their answer was that recourse to international legal procedure can influence a political situation. They listed the 'fruits' of engaging legal proceedings:

- a determination of facts which are disputed or denied by the perpetrators;
- an objective assessment of the accountability of the perpetrators of the violations;
- the establishment of recommendations or steps (enforceable or otherwise) to be taken to remedy the situation;
- the determination of the legal standards being violated and therefore the identification of the standards of behaviour which a political resolution will be required to incorporate;
- the creation of an effective tool for political leverage;
- the prevention of the continuation of the scale of abuses as a result of the public and authoritative exposure of the situation.

They argued that:

> By using legal methods to investigate a situation of gross violation the perpetrators' ability to act with impunity can be limited. Those in authority can be exposed and held accountable for their actions and hindered in their ability to continue such practices.[103]

They recognised of course that the extent of any impact would depend on the effectiveness of the legal norms and mechanisms engaged.

All of these considerations have of course informed the strategy of the

100 Reidy, Hampson and Boyle (1997).   101 Reidy et al. (1997) p. 162.
102 Reidy et al. (1997) p. 162.   103 Reidy et al. (1997) p. 163.

partnership of EHRAC and *Memorial*. It was plain that the Chechen applicants in the first six cases were not interested in money, especially since the
cases take so long. These extraordinarily courageous applicants were primarily interested in obtaining, from the highest court in Europe, an authoritative
account of the events through which they lived (and their families died), and
recognition of the gross violations they had suffered. In addition, they
wanted to lay the basis for the prosecution of the individuals responsible. In
their application for individual and general measures in the enforcement proceedings currently before the Committee of Ministers, they insist that the
Russian government should investigate with a view to the prosecution of
Generals Shamanov and Nedobytko, in whose cases the Court's findings of
fact amount to the circumstances of war crimes.

The three authors also highlighted the difficulties individual applicants
faced in proving gross and systematic violations, especially where they claim
that there is no domestic remedy, and that there has been no effective internal
investigation. In many of the Turkish Kurdish cases the Commission (later,
the Court) was obliged to carry out fact-finding in Turkey. In January 1997
Mrs Thune, a member of the Commission, reported that there had already
been 27 fact-finding investigations, involving 12 members of the Commission, hearing 216 witnesses over 39 days (302 hours) of hearings, generating
6,400 pages of transcripts.[104]

Despite this extraordinary effort by the Commission and the Court, applicants found it impossible to establish an 'administrative practice' in which,
first, such violations frequently occur, and second, there is an absence of
effective remedies, often coupled with impunity for offenders: a 'practice', in
particular, of torture. This amounts to deliberate violation by the State,
authorised at the highest levels, rather than mere inadvertence or a failure of
discipline in an individual case.

It was the former European Commission of Human Rights which first
coined the description 'administrative practice' during its deliberations at the
admissibility stage; this became 'practice' at the merits stage. The Commission found the principle to be applicable in individual cases, for example in
1975 in *Donnelly & others v UK*.[105] The Court finally dealt with the issue at the
merits stage in 1978 in the notorious inter-state case concerning violation of
Article 3 of the ECHR, *Ireland v UK*.[106]

However, in *Aksoy v Turkey*[107] neither the Commission nor the Court

---

104 Verbatim Record, Case of *Mentes and Others v Turkey*, European Court of Human Rights,
   22 January 1997. The author took part in two fact-finding hearings in Ankara, in the cases
   of *Aktas v Turkey* (App. no. 24351/94, judgment of 24 April 2003) and *Ipek v Turkey* (App.
   no. 25760/94, judgment of 17 February 2004).
105 App. no. 5577–5583/72, Admissibility Decision of 15 December 1975, 4 D&R 4.
106 Judgment of 18 January 1978.
107 100/1995/606/694, judgment of 18 December 1996.

addressed the question of the practice of torture, which had been pleaded by the applicant, citing the lack of evidence produced by them, despite the fact that the reports of the UN Committee Against Torture and the European Committee for the Prevention of Torture were before it. Reidy, Hampson and Boyle ask:

> How then can an applicant adduce the kind of evidence required to establish practice? . . . a single applicant or group of applicants is put in a position of providing evidence they simply do not have the resources to deliver.[108]

For obvious reasons, the issue of 'administrative practice' was raised by the individual applicants in many of the Kurdish cases from south-east Turkey. The Commission never found it necessary to deal with the issue. As a result, in not one of the Turkish cases was there a finding of fact on the basis of which the Court could decide that there had indeed been an 'administrative practice'. This was despite the fact that in many of the decisions the Court found an absence of effective domestic remedies, thereby absolving the applicants from seeking to exhaust them, in circumstances which were tantamount to 'administrative practice', and otherwise inexplicable. 'Administrative practice' was also pleaded, using the same arguments, in the first six and subsequent Chechen cases, but has been similarly ignored by the Court.

In essence applicants face the problem of persuading the Court that the government in question, Turkey or Russia, is guilty not only of individual violations, but also of 'administrative practice' as defined by the Court. Of course, the Court is reluctant to take such a bold step, since a finding of 'administrative practice' would amount to a finding that a state is deliberately violating human rights.

But then the evidence in the *Al-Skeini* case (and evidence adduced in the associated courts martial[109]) tends to show that the decision to inflict such harsh treatment on Iraqi detainees, leading to the death of one of them, was taken at a much higher level than the soldiers who found themselves prosecuted.

In her Study for the Council of Europe on human rights protection during situations of armed conflict,[110] Hampson also noted the fact that the former Commission had recognised that the issue of repeated violations – which could also properly be described as 'systemic' violations – raised distinct issues apart from, although linked to, 'administrative practice'. Among other

---

108 Reidy et al. (1997) p. 171.
109 See the *Guardian*, Leader: 'Army on trial', 15 March 2007, at http://www.guardian.co.uk/ Iraq/Story/0,,2034335,00.html.
110 Hampson (2002).

things, the fact that repeated violations could only occur as a result of deliberate government policy meant that domestic remedies were necessarily ineffective.

It is highly likely that this will become an issue when Iraq cases against the UK begin to find their way to Strasbourg. I have already mentioned the sorry story of the courts martial following the murder of one Iraqi detainee and the systematic ill-treatment of others.

Conclusion

The Strasbourg Court is today in deep crisis, overwhelmed by the tidal wave of complaints coming from Russia.[111] Russia's refusal on 20 December 2006 to ratify Protocol 14 of the Convention,[112] on reform of the procedure of the Court, when every other Council of Europe member state has done so, appears to threaten the very future of the Court. The question posed by this chapter is whether the legitimacy of the Convention system is now in doubt. Will the Court have the capacity and intellectual resources to measure up to the challenge of cases relating to Iraq?

This chapter has answered with a qualified 'yes'.

First, the Court has now, despite a setback in the *Bankovic* case, developed a strong line of cases showing quite clearly that a member state can indeed be held responsible for violations of Convention rights committed outside its territory. This has now proved highly disagreeable for a number of states, especially those with a colonial past. There is an excellent recent example. On 11 January 2007 President Putin of Russia was asked by the former Constitutional Court judge and leading human rights promoter Tamara Morshchakova specifically about the refusal to ratify Protocol 14. Putin replied:

> Unfortunately, our country is coming into collision with a politicisation of judicial decisions. We all know about the case of Ilascu, where the Russian Federation was accused of matters with which it has no connection whatsoever. This is a purely political decision, an undermining of trust in the judicial international system. And the deputies of the State Duma turned their attention also to that . . .

We can expect similar protests in future from the United Kingdom.

Second, the Chechen cases discussed in detail above show that the Court

---

111 Now some 25 per cent of the Court's case-load, 19,000 in all in the past year. See also Bowring (2005b).
112 'Russia "gives it" to the European Court', *Kommersant* daily newspaper at http://www.kommersant.com/p732043/r_500/State_Duma_European_Court.

will refrain from applying IHL to complaints by civilians of violations by members of armed forces committed in the context of armed conflict. IHL is predicated upon the existence of a state of war, in which casualties are inevitable, and it is to be expected that civilians will suffer. By applying to these cases the rich jurisprudence through which it explained and extended Article 2 (on the right to life), the Court has shown that states will be held to account under the very much more stringent standards according to which a state must show that it has taken every possible precaution to protect the lives and welfare of civilians.

Third, I have sought to answer the question whether the Court now shows itself to be paralysed in the face of gross and systematic violations of human rights, especially those committed in the context of armed conflict, of an internal or international nature. Again, the Chechen cases, despite the fact that decisions followed almost six years after the violations in question, show that the Court is capable of adjudicating in a decisive and creative manner.

Whether of course it will have the courage to do so in the case of the United Kingdom is an open question; but there are already a number of first-rate precedents.

Chapter 5

Ideology in international law, and the critique of Habermas

Introduction

This chapter has two purposes, as I move from the poignant facticity of human rights practice, to a critique of the theoretical underpinnings of international law and human rights.

First, to ask the question: Why is it important to practise ideology critique in international law? I reflect on the work of Susan Marks, an outstanding contemporary Marxist international legal theorist, and author of a well-known book and several important shorter texts on ideology critique.[1]

Second, to subject to respectful criticism the great German philosopher Jürgen Habermas – attractive, inclusive and engaged though he is – for his increasingly conservative and ideologised position. I argue that he is not so much the source of a potential solution, as himself a problem. This, I suggest, is the case both in relation to his derivation of human rights from his ethical and political conceptions, and his influential notion of 'deliberative democracy'.[2]

I want to suggest that Habermas' problem as described is symptomatic of a significant tendency in theorising about human rights, especially as human rights have become an increasingly important component part of international law. Specifically, locating human rights in language, rhetoric, even intersubjective ethics, strips them of the content which I suggest they have, historically and in the present.

Why should we do ideology critique in international law?

Why should we do ideology critique? Susan Marks cites the words of Martti Koskenniemi, who more than most international legal scholars combines theory and practice, to the effect that they (we) would be better advised to search for 'more concrete forms of political commitment' which might 'engage them in actual struggles, both as observers and participants, while

1 Marks (2000) p. 112; Marks (2000a).   2 For example, Wheatley (2003).

also taking the participants' self-understanding seriously'.[3] That is, he and Susan Marks pose the possibility of politics in inauspicious times. There is one brute fact, the context of the degradation of international law, which I have explored in this book and elsewhere,[4] and in respect of which the UN Secretary General has recently issued a dire warning. But this must be balanced against the hope, as Michael Byers expresses it, that '[a]lthough law is necessarily the result and reflection of politics, law nevertheless retains a specificity and resistance to short-term change that enables it to constrain sudden changes in relative power, and sudden changes in policy motivated by consequentially shifting perceptions of opportunity and self-interest'[5] – and the fact that the UN is the only place where non-hegemonic (i.e. weak) states can have a voice.

In order to pursue this project, Susan Marks published a few years ago her PhD thesis, under the title *The Riddle of All Constitutions: International Law, Democracy and the Critique of Ideology*.[6] In this work and in her various articles, she undertakes a thorough exploration of ideology – through an exploration of, for example, Eagleton, Foucault, Derrida, and my own favourite, Slavoj Žižek. Ideology, in her understanding, as set out in the article which followed her book, and developed and further clarified its arguments, is 'not an inherent property of particular ideas or a characteristic of particular ideational systems, but it is rather a function of the way meaning is generated, conveyed, apprehended and appropriated in different contexts.'[7]

Furthermore, ideology refers to the 'ways in which meaning serves to establish and sustain relations of domination',[8] the ways in which words (and other symbolic forms) support inequalities of power.[9]

She identifies five strategies ideology usually employs:

- *universalisation*: 'Through processes of universalisation, social and political institutions are made to seem impartial, inclusory and rooted in considerations of mutual interest. In this way, an illusory unity may be conferred on societies, and differential levels of social power may be masked.'[10]
- *reification*: This concept is familiar from Marx's use of it – 'the process by which human products come to appear as if they were material things, and then to dominate those who produced them. Thanks to strategies of reification, men and women may cease to recognise the social world as the outcome of human endeavour, and begin to see it as fixed and unchangeable, an object of contemplation rather than a domain of action.'
- *naturalisation*: '. . . contested arrangements appear obvious and self-

---

3 Koskenniemi (1996) at Marks (2000) p. 141.   4 Bowring (2002).
5 Byers (2002) p. 35.   6 Marks (2000a).
8 Thompson (1990) p. 56.   9 Scott (1994).   7 Marks (2000) p. 112.
                                                              10 Marks (2001) p. 112.

evident, as if they were natural phenomena belonging to the world "out there".'

- *rationalisation*: '. . . through the construction of a chain of reasoning of which the *status quo* is the logical conclusion, it may be made to seem as if there are good reasons why things are as they are. Change may thus come to seem irrational.'
- *narrativisation*: '. . . the telling of stories which set particular developments in the context of a history . . . practices and institutions may be made to seem worthy of respect and perpetuation, whether because they are venerable or because they represent progress.'

Bronwen Morgan, in a thoughtful essay on William Lucy's work, has also taken account of Susan Marks' contribution by way of a strong contrast.[11] She too notices Marks' definition of ideology as 'ways in which meaning . . . serves to establish and sustain relations of domination'. What is important for Morgan is that this:

> retains a critical edge but not one that depends on epistemological or value determinacy . . . the deceptive aspect of ideology for her lies in its claim to represent the 'general good' when the material reality of assymetrical power relations in particular social contexts means that benefits in fact accrue to a limited subsection of society . . . Marks' definition, by adding a material analysis of the comparative power of actors affected by ideological moves, lends a critical edge to the universalisation dimension by constantly interrogating the 'fit' between claimed benefits and actually accruing benefits. If 'truth' is involved, it is not an epistemologically determinate system of truth, but the constantly dynamic empirical actuality of social facts invoked in the service of such an immanent critique.[12]

Truth is not abandoned in this analysis: far from it. Instead, truth is located in reality rather than in language or in formal logic.

Morgan correctly identifies the importance of the dynamic in Marks' analysis – and her description of immanent critique is close to that of Theodor Adorno, to whom I turn below. For me, the most significant of these aspects of ideology as so identified is the respect in which change becomes unthinkable, irrational. And I will suggest, *pace* Morgan, that some greater epistemological determinacy is warranted.

But a more radical view can be taken of the conditions of possibility of change, and what presently stifles and inhibits change. Analysis of this crucial problem can be found in the recent work of Alain Badiou,[13] and Slavoj Žižek, who argues: 'This is what the distinction between "formal" and "actual"

---

11 Morgan (2002).   12 Morgan (2002) pp. 528–529.   13 Badiou (2001).

freedom ultimately amounts to: "formal" freedom is the freedom of choice *within* the co-ordinates of the existing power relations, while "actual" freedom designates the site of an intervention which undermines these very co-ordinates.'[14] And: 'What this means is that the "actual freedom" as the act of consciously changing this set occurs only when, in the situation of a forced choice, one acts *as if the choice is not forced* and "chooses the impossible".'[15]

Some targets of ideology critique

As Susan Marks herself notes, ideology critique in international law has some fairly easy targets.

First, there is Immanuel Kant's cosmopolitan manifesto, most recently finding its place in John Rawls' concerned liberalism.[16] This is thoroughly dissected – ideology critique by another name – by John Tasioulas.[17] Second, the work of Thomas Franck, a dominant figure in Anglo-American international legal theory, with his books and articles on the right to democratic governance, and *Fairness in International Law and Institutions*.[18] Third, Francis Fukuyama, whom Susan Marks devastatingly critiques.[19] Fourth, and most with the greatest success in the post-War academy, the New Haven school, the policy oriented scholars who so frequently find themselves in line with US policy.[20] Nevertheless, Susan Marks is rightly concerned to prepare the foundations for a more general critique; my own attempt here is to criticise Habermas and Loughlin.

In the next sections of this chapter, I will seek to show how, through a reflection on its intellectual antecedents, Marks' strategy can fruitfully be applied to the problem of human rights.

Critique in Hegel and Marx

I want at this point to explore the inspiration Susan Marks draws from Marx, and by necessary implication, from Hegel. The title of her book is taken from Marx's *Contribution to a Critique of Hegel's Philosophy of Right*[21] – actually, the passage in which Marx is discussing Hegel's (re)construction of the principles of monarchy. The passage is as follows:

> Democracy is the solved riddle of all constitutions. Here, not merely *implicitly* and in essence but *existing* in reality, the constitution is

---

14 Žižek (2001) p. 122.   15 Žižek (2001) p. 121, and see Žižek (2002).

16 Rawls (1999).   17 Tasioulas (2002).   18 Franck (1990); Franck (1995).

19 Marks (2000).   20 See, for example, Scobbie (2006); and Chimni (1993).

21 Marx (1975) written in spring and summer of 1843, first published in Marx/Engels, *Gesamtausgabe*, Abt. 1, Bd 1, Hb. 1, 1927.

constantly brought back to its actual basis, the *actual human being*, the *actual people*, and established as the people's own work.[22]

There is an important aspect of Marx's text which is often overlooked. Marx by no means rejects Hegel's analysis out of hand. His 'Contribution' is not, as is often crudely assumed, simply a radical critique of Hegel, not just an unmasking of Hegel's reconciliation with actuality.

In three passages Marx identifies a respect in which Hegel's theory of law and the state exposes radical contradictions within the heart of law and the state, and is in this way more dynamic and more critical than Habermas' imposing *Between Facts and Norms*,[23] to which I will return. Gillian Rose's wonderful *Hegel: Contra Sociology*[24] shows to my mind conclusively that Hegel is far more radical than is usually supposed, especially in the following passage:

> In the case of the proposition that the actual is rational, what has been overlooked is the explanatory coda that the truth of this proposition must be sought – 'in dem *Scheine* des Zeitlichen', in the illusion of the temporal, of history. The proposition has been misread as if it equated natural law with positive law, as if it *justifies* existing law, when it summarises Hegel's critique of natural law. For it is natural law theory which takes the illusions or relations of bourgeois private property as the rational principle of the whole society. It is natural law theory which *justifies* bourgeois positive law which it 'derives' from the fictional state of nature. Hegel is precisely drawing attention to the illusions (relations, difference) of bourgeois society.[25]

Or, as Robert Fine beautifully expressed the same point:

> The *Philosophy of Rights* represented the dialectic of freedom and necessity in modern society. It laid the *foundation* for the critique of juridic forms based on contradiction between form and content, concept and experience. Hegel does not tell us where resolution lies, but how could he? He wrote at the *dawn* of the modern state, whereas such knowledge arises like the owl of Minerva 'at the falling of the dusk'.[26]

Marx himself recognised the often implicit – rather than explicit – critique at the heart of Hegel's enterprise, and I demonstrate this by citing three important passages.

First, Marx wrote: 'However, we recognise the profundity of Hegel precisely

22 Marx (1975) p. 29.   23 Habermas (1997).   24 Rose (1995).
25 Rose (1995) p. 81.   26 Fine (1993) p. 59.

in the fact that he everywhere begins with and lays stress on the *opposition* between attributes (as they exist in our states).'[27]

Second: 'It shows Hegel's profundity that he feels the separation of civil from political society as a *contradiction*.'[28]

Third: 'Here the antitheses have assumed an entirely new and very material form such as we would scarcely have expected in the heaven of the political state. As expounded by Hegel, the antithesis is, expressed in all its sharpness, the antithesis of *private property* and *wealth*.'[29]

Here there is a vivid contrast between Hegel's profundity – the fact that his method always brought him to be confronted by contradiction, the root of all criticism – and Habermas' commitment to the Enlightenment and social democracy, combined however with a deep conservatism, derived, I would argue, from his 'linguistic turn', and departure from the traditions of historical materialism.

Habermas as critic – or as apologist for the contemporary state

Habermas plays a central role in the argument of this paper as the most important contemporary representative of critical theory, and the key ideologist of a particular and influential take on human rights. It is no surprise to me, therefore, that Susan Marks is drawn to the early, radical, Habermas of *Knowledge and Human Interests*,[30] rather than to his later and more conservative work. She summarises his (then) position as follows: '. . . critical social science is concerned not simply to predict, nor indeed to comprehend. Rather, it intends to transform.'[31]

There is indeed a deep divide between Habermas' works of the 1970s, and those of the 1990s. Susan Marks takes her inspiration from *Erkenntnis und Interesse*, written in the context of the events of 1968 (it was published in English as *Knowledge and Human Interests* in 1971).[32] Her next reference is to *Faktizität und Geltung. Beiträge zur Diskurstheorie des Rechts und des demokratischen Rechtsstaates* (which should be rendered literally as *Facticity and Validity. Contribution to the Discourse Theory of Law and of the Democratic Rule of Law State*), published in Germany in 1992, and translated – I would say misleadingly – into English as *Between Facts and Norms: Contributions to a Discourse Theory of Law and Democracy* in 1997.[33]

The full German title of *Faktizität und Geltung* says it all. Already in

---

27 Marx (1975) p. 54.   28 Marx (1975) p. 75.   29 Marx (1975) p. 98.

30 Habermas (1987).   31 Marks (2000) p. 129.

32 She does not – does not need to – refer to the most traditionally Marxist of his works, *Legitimationsprobleme im Spätkapitalismus*, published in Germany in 1973 (published in English as *The Legitimation Crisis in Late Capitalism* in 1975).

33 Habermas (1997).

Theorie und Praxis. Sozialphilosophische Studien (Theory and Practice), published in 1963, and republished in 1971, Habermas rejected one of Marx's key concepts: his 'Hegelian-inspired concept of labor as humankind's self-creative activity'. According to Nancy S. Love, Habermas considers instead that 'it is social interaction that is our distinctively human capacity'.[34] Between 1973 and 1992 Habermas comprehensively abandoned the tradition of historical materialism, the foundation of the Frankfurt School, in favour of a 'linguistic turn', and the development after 1981 (the publication of *Theorie des kommunikativen Handelns* (Bd.1: *Handlungsrationalität und gesellschaftliche Rationalisierung*, Bd. 2: *Zur Kritik der funktionalistischen Vernunft*) – in English the *Theory of Communicative Action*) of his discourse ethics, which now underpins all his work on law, political theory, and human rights.

The Habermas of *Faktizität und Geltung* is much more conservative than Hegel. Impressively monumental in architecture and synthetic achievement as it is, this work really amounts to a neo-Kantian transcendental deduction of the conditions of necessity of the contemporary German constitutional state. That is, the state – by any reckoning a remarkably successful organism – is taken as the starting point, whose actuality is not to be questioned, and Habermas' versions of discourse ethics and human rights are shown to be the conditions of its existence. There is very little if any criticism, much less immanent critique, and no sense of the dynamism of the historical production of constitutional forms, least of all the possibility of change. It is for this reason that Habermas first undertakes, in this work, the deduction of fundamental human rights from the ethical presuppositions of human communication.

This critique can be further demonstrated by two more recent works. The first is *The Postnational Constellation: Political Essays* published in English in 2001,[35] and in particular the essay 'Remarks on Legitimation through Human Rights'. This is a text which I require my students of the 'History and Theory of Human Rights' to analyse, as a remarkably pithy and persuasive set of representative arguments. Habermas has in mind the legitimation of the Western European states, and in particular their legitimation through classical European human rights. He tells us that: 'Political theory has given a twofold answer to the question of [state] legitimacy: popular sovereignty and human rights . . . The classical human rights . . . ground an inherently legitimate rule of law.'[36] This leads him to the conclusion that: 'For the Western style of legitimation, the co-originality of liberty rights and the rights of citizens is essential.'[37] What he means by 'Western' is shown in the following passage: 'The conception of human rights was the answer to a problem that once confronted Europeans – when they had to overcome the political consequences

34 Love (1995) pp. 49–50.   35 Habermas (2001).   36 Habermas (2001) pp. 115–116.
37 Habermas, (2001) p. 118.

of confessional fragmentation – and now confronts other cultures in a similar fashion.'[38] That is, it would appear that the Western model of state legitimation through this version of human rights will present itself as the only possible model for all other societies – a classic move for ideology as defined by Susan Marks.

The second recent work by Habermas is an essay, 'Constitutional Democracy: A Paradoxical Union of Contradictory Principles?', published in the journal *Political Theory* in 2001.[39] Here Habermas restates his position in *Faktizität und Geltung* in the following terms:

> First, only those outcomes can count as legitimate upon which equally entitled participants in the deliberation can freely agree – that is, outcomes that meet with justified consent of all under conditions of rational discourse. Second . . . the participants commit themselves to modern law as the medium for regulating their common life. The mode of legitimation through a general consent under discursive conditions realises the Kantian concept of political autonomy only in connection with the idea of coercive laws that grant equal individual liberties.[40]

Habermas is quite clear that this is the model of justification of his subject matter in the article – the United States and the German Federal Republic.

Habermas and deliberative democracy – for minorities and their rights

That this method can rightly be described as an ideology in precisely the sense defined by Susan Marks can be shown by the way 'deliberative democracy'[41] has been put to use in a thoughtful article in the *EJIL* by Steven Wheatley.[42] Wheatley states that: 'The pure deliberative model, outlined by Jürgen Habermas in *Between Facts and Norms*, assumes that given sufficient time and goodwill, it is always possible to reach a consensus.' He recognises that there are times when a consensus cannot be reached for ethno-cultural minorities, so democratic deliberation 'should not aim to establish uniform rules in all areas of public life, but to determine a constitutional arrangement that will guarantee the cultural security of the minority group'. He concludes that: 'Government policy on minorities will be fairer and enjoy a greater degree of legitimacy in the eyes of both majority and minority populations promoting a greater degree of justice and internal and external peace and security, as differences are channelled into democratic institutions and mechanisms and resolved without recourse to violence.'[43]

---

38 Habermas (2001) p. 128.   39 Habermas (2001).   40 Habermas (2001) p. 772.
41 See also Oquendo (2002).   42 Wheatley (2003).   43 Wheatley (2003) p. 527.

It is my contention, with respect to Wheatley, that his model, and the mobilisation of some version of Habermas' prescriptions, cannot provide any valuable insight into the many cases of historical and contemporary injustice with respect to minorities. A recent example to have confronted me in my own work has been that of the Meskhetian Turks, expelled by order of Stalin from the border of Georgia (then part of the USSR) nearest to Turkey in 1944 for alleged collaboration with the Nazis and deported to central Asia, relocated to the area of Chernobyl in Ukraine and Belarus, and finally settling, prior to the final collapse of the USSR, in Krasnodar Krai, now one of the regions of the Russian Federation. Despite their long settlement in the area, they are treated as temporary migrants by the racist – in the person of the former Governor Kondratenko even fascist – regional authorities, denied registration, passports, or any relaxation of constant harassment. The present Governor, Tkachev, is no better. In March 2002 he said that 'the Turks must be deported in airplanes!' Their Soviet passports are about to expire, and when they apply to court to vindicate their right in Russian law to a Russian passport, the court refuses to recognise them as subjects of the law. On 11 September, the local authorities, supported by police, 'withdrew' the (USSR) passports of some 800 Meskhetian Turks, relying on a recently enacted local law that plainly violates constitutional as well as human rights norms.[44]

Deliberative democracy cannot provide the answer to their problems, nor does it provide the means of analysing and recognising their predicament.

Going beyond Habermas – and Susan Marks

I therefore recognise that Susan Marks goes far beyond Habermas. Her immanent critique allows her to push from inside the prevailing ideologies. This was a crucial part of Marx's method – to recognise the power of the work of Smith, Ricardo, and Hegel (himself influenced in his early days by English political economy[45]) and to locate and exploit their limits; and to refuse ever to seek to provide models for the future. Immanent critique is not at all the sole prerogative of Marxists. There is a nice example of its use by a liberal theorist in (the liberal) Jeremy Waldron's *The Right to Private Property*, in which he takes the theories of Locke, Hegel and Nozick, and pushes them from the inside to expose the fact that, taken to their logical conclusions, each must hold that every person is entitled to some property. In other words, a kind of communism.[46]

Nevertheless, I would like to suggest that Marks does not go far enough. In

44 See 'The Meskhetian Turks are having their passports withdrawn in Krasnodar Krai', *Polit.Ru*, 11 September 2003.
45 Lukacs (1975) especially Part II, Chapter 6.   46 Waldron (1990).

her view, progressive change, the radical democracy for which she argues, is – redistributive social change. By this she means: democracy as a 'principle of democratic inclusion',[47] and 'a kind of bias in favour of popular self-rule and equal citizenship'.[48] These objectives are noble and desirable. But how are they to be instantiated?

The problem faced by Susan Marks can, it seems to me, be posed as follows. How does the scholar or activist make the transition from immanent critique of the ruling ideologies of international law, to reasons for engagement and action? This is Martti Koskenniemi's challenge, to which I referred at the start of this chapter. In order to answer the question, it is, I believe, important to return once more to Marx, and his definition of 'science', as well as his understanding of reality, which Bronwen Morgan paraphrased in the passage cited above. Immanent critique is not only the means of pointing out the inconsistency and inadequacy of prevailing ideologies: for Marx, his theoretical enquiries led him to real discoveries. In this regard, he followed Hegel. Science, in an Hegelian, or Marxist sense, or – to avoid those intimidating names – *realist* sense is the contrary of empiricism. For Hegel, the task of the science of right (law), the subject matter of his *The Philosophy of Right* '. . . is to develop the Idea – the Idea being the rational factor in any object of study – out of the concept, or, what is the same thing, to look on at the proper immanent development of the thing itself'.[49]

Marx himself referred to the importance of 'grasping the inner nature of capital'. More recently, the philosopher of critical realism, Roy Bhaskar, has explained that:[50] 'explanatory structures, generative mechanisms or (in Marx's favoured terminology) *essential relations* are (a) ontologically distinct from, (b) normally out of phase with and (c) perhaps in opposition to the phenomena (or phenomenal forms) they generate.' Marx himself asserted that '. . . all science would be superfluous if the outward appearances and essences of things directly coincided'.[51] Science in this sense therefore rejects representation, or (as the sociologist Margaret Archer has explained 'representation'[52]) a one-dimensional reality coming through the senses: a social science implies a stratified social world including non-observable entities. Social structures really exist, and have emergent causal powers.

Adorno and immanent critique – and deracinated human rights

The most powerful representative of critical theory – more pessimistic but with far more of a sense of critical engagement than Habermas – was Theodor

---

47 Marks (2000) p. 109.   48 Marks (2000) p. 111.   49 Hegel (1967) p. 14.
50 Bhaskar (1991).   51 Marx (1971) p. 817.   52 Archer (1995).

Adorno, especially in his *Negative Dialectics*,[53] published in 1966 in Germany, and in 1973 in England. It is particularly striking that Habermas' critique of Adorno and Horkheimer in *The Philosophical Discourse of Modernity* almost entirely misses the point about each of them.

Adorno explained the specificity of the method of Marx and Hegel as follows: 'The name of dialectics says no more, to begin with, than that objects do not go into their concepts without leaving a remainder, that they come to contradict the traditional norm of adequacy. Contradiction . . . indicates the untruth of identity, the fact that the concept does not exhaust the thing conceived.'[54] Further: 'Aware that the conceptual totality is mere appearance, I have no way to break immanently, in its own measure, through the appearance of that identity . . . Dialectics is the constant sense of non-identity.'

A little further there is an extraordinary passage, which provides me with the bridge to the concluding part of this paper. 'Through Hegel, philosophy had regained the right and the capacity to think *substantively* instead of being put off with the analysis of cognitive forms that were empty and in an emphatic sense, null and void.'[55] Thinking substantively is something which Hegel, Marx and Adorno all inherited from Aristotle, of whom more below.

Therefore, to recapitulate, what I am arguing is that dialectics, with its method of immanent critique, is the opposite of the *identity thinking*, derived from the philosophy of Kant, which Adorno so mercilessly exposes.[56] Dialectics provides the bridge from critique, to engagement in the real world.

What does this mean for the theoretical study of human rights?

My position is that human rights are not simply rhetoric, and equally not a set of ethically neutral procedures, nor the deracinated empty forms proposed by Habermas. This is the way Habermas puts it in his 2001 essay:[57]

> A system of positive and compulsory law with such an individualistic quality can come about only if three categories of rights are concomitantly introduced. If we consider that the capacity for general consent is a requirement of legitimacy, these categories are as follows:
>
> i. basic rights (whatever their concrete content) that result from the autonomous elaboration of the right to the greatest possible measure of equal individual freedom of action for each person
> ii. basic rights (whatever their concrete content) that result from the autonomous elaboration of the status of a member in a voluntary association of legal consociates

---

53 Adorno (1996).   54 Adorno (1996) p. 5.   55 Adorno (1996) p. 7.
56 See also Norrie (2000), and especially Norrie (2005), in which he answers an objection by me in a review of his 2000 book, with a penetrating analysis of Adorno's antinomies.
57 Habermas (2001) p. 777.

    iii. basic rights (whatever their concrete content) that result from the autonomous elaboration of each individual's right to equal protection under law, that is, that results from the actionability of individual rights

    iv. basic rights (whatever their concrete content) that emerge from the autonomous elaboration of the right to an equal opportunity to participate in political law-giving.

It is immediately apparent that rights on this account, if they have no particular concrete content, have no content at all. Phrases like 'freedom of action' become meaningless except as elements in a purely linguistic construction, or as an entirely abstract formula for political procedure. Habermas fails to provide us either with an explanation for political struggle, or with a reason for political engagement. Why should anyone bother?

Here also is the version of Martin Loughlin – in an essay which is the only response to the question whether human rights discourse has any foundations, in a volume of 'sceptical' essays on human rights:

> Modern natural rights theorists have therefore engaged in a search for the authority of these rights in some ethical scheme that can be shown to be ingrained in the structure of reason . . . but this quest, one which stretches from Kant to Rawls, has never been able to produce a compelling account of rights which comes anywhere near satisfying the canons of objectivity . . . we are left with the contention that such rights are fundamental essentially because they command general support . . . the authority accorded basic rights rests on political consensus.[58]

I am not sure, with respect to Loughlin, how the 'canons of objectivity' may themselves be identified. But the outcome of his approach is much the same as Habermas' deracinated account. Basic rights, for Loughlin, have no content other than that given to them by those in power, depending on purely contingent subjective factors. It follows that human rights can be nothing but rhetoric.

In the next chapter, I argue for a substantive account of human rights.

---

58 Loughlin (2001) p. 45.

Chapter 6

A substantive account of human rights

How can human rights be other than rhetoric? For example, Alan Norrie reads Adorno as having a positive side which comes rather close to Douzinas' thesis of the 'end' of human rights with which I engage in Chapter 8. For Norrie, Adorno also speaks of:

> . . . a social and historical evolution of the quality of being human. Such a vision of the human condition, latent and unfulfilled, speaks through the limits of the existing forms in which freedom is expressed. What lies underneath those forms and is signalled by their presence is the promise of a real autonomy. This presses at the limits of what is expressed or understood as actually existing autonomy, as something inchoate within the present: something already there, but also still 'to come'.[1]

I disgree with this position just as I disagree with Douzinas. Human freedom, human autonomy, human rights – all these are the subjects and objects of real struggles in the real world.

So, what would it mean to think *substantively* about human rights (or for that matter about other categories and concepts which find their place at the centre of international law, for example the right of states to non-interference in their internal affairs, or the right of peoples to self-determination)?

A human rights nihilist?

I start from Alasdair MacIntyre's notorious remarks about human rights in *After Virtue*, and cite a number of leading human rights scholars, each of whom would appear to have misread the text entirely, in startlingly different ways. These authors and others have missed the point about MacIntyre. My own take on MacIntyre is also highly selective, and not at all consistent with the general tenor of his thought. My reason is that I wish to develop an

---

1 Norrie (2005) p. 176.

account of human rights which is substantive rather than procedural. That is, a case can be made for an Aristotelian, substantive account of human rights; a case that is thoroughly historicised, but restores human rights to their proper status as always scandalous, the product of, and constantly reanimated by, human struggle. I have found a number of points in MacIntyre's work at which, for reasons consistent with his Aristotelian frustration with the emptiness of contemporary rights talk, he provides strong support for my contentions. I recognise, however, that in his more recent work he tends to an increasingly conservative set of conclusions, consistent with his Catholicism. But my own feeling is that not only has MacIntyre been misunderstood by his human rights critics: in an important sense, he has more and more misunderstood himself.

My strategy in this chapter is first to refer briefly to the critics already referred to. Next, I outline MacIntyre's own core positions as I see them. This takes me to an account of the thinking about human rights of two contemporary Aristotelians, James Griffin and John Tasioulas. Finally, I attempt a sketch of what an Aristotelian Marxist account of human rights might look like.

MacIntyre's *After Virtue*, and his human rights critics

In *After Virtue* Alasdair MacIntyre famously assaulted the contemporary discourse of 'rights attaching to human beings simply *qua* human beings'. He selected Gewirth (*Reason and Morality*, 1978), and Dworkin (*Taking Rights Seriously*, 1976), in order to show that 'there are no such rights, and belief in them is one with belief in witches and in unicorns'.[2] He specified that by 'rights' he did not mean those rights conferred by positive law or custom on specified classes of person. 'I mean those rights which are alleged to belong to human beings as such and which are cited as a reason for holding that people ought not to be interfered with in their pursuit of life, liberty and happiness.'

MacIntyre points to the fact that prior to the eighteenth century, where such rights were spoken of as 'natural rights' or 'rights of man', there was no expression in any ancient or medieval language correctly translated by the modern expression 'a right'. This of course does not mean that there were no such rights – only 'that no one could have known that there were'.

In a rather later explicitly Christian text MacIntyre referred to '. . . the inadequacy and the sterility of the modern idiom and rhetoric of rights'.[3]

As a result of these arguments, MacIntyre has become something of a straw man for human rights theorists/apologists. Michael Freeman selects MacIntyre as someone who asserts that human rights doctrine is false; the belief in human rights is an ontological error.[4] According to Freeman,

2 MacIntyre (1985) pp. 68–69.   3 MacIntyre (1991) p. 110.
4 Freeman, M. (1994) pp. 491–514, at p. 498.

'MacIntyre misses his target, and the target he misses is a non-foundationalist defense of rights.' In his more recent textbook,[5] he contends that MacIntyre's mistake is to think of 'human rights' as 'things' that we could 'have' as we have arms or legs. Freeman's answer is that rights are not *things*, but *just claims or entitlements*. Thus, this '. . . defeats MacIntyre's objection that belief in human rights is superstitious, for there is nothing superstitious in thinking what human beings may be entitled to'. But that is not MacIntyre's objection. Upendra Baxi characterised MacIntyre's position as 'human rights weariness – a kind of moral fatigue with rights languages and logics, marked by an ethical disposition that contests the very notion of human rights as a moral language and rhetoric'.[6] Conor Gearty, in the recent Hamlyn Lectures, says: 'I think MacIntyre was wrong to hanker after a now impossible Aristotelian virtue but he was right that something needs to be done.'[7] It does indeed. Finally, in her book *Who Believes in Human Rights?*,[8] Dembour simply classes MacIntyre, with herself (!), as a 'human rights nihilist or discourse scholar'.

MacIntyre's Aristotelian starting point

In fact, MacIntyre was very far from being a nihilist. Instead, he argued for 'socially embodied moral concepts'.[9] Aristotle, for him, had the following position: '. . . that it was only within a particular type of political and social order that rationally practical and moral concepts could be socially embodied.'[10] This was in fact his position from at least 1967. In *A Short History of Ethics*, he wrote: 'Moral concepts are embodied in and are partially constitutive of forms of social life.'[11] Steven Lukes described MacIntyre as '. . . developing a "social ideological", quasi-Aristotelian view . . .'.[12]

Susan Stephenson summarises MacIntyre's 'reworked Aristotelianism' as having three central terms – practices, narratives and traditions. 'Practices' he defines as 'any coherent and complex form of socially established human activity through which goods internal to that form of activity are realised in the course of trying to achieve those standards of excellence which are appropriate to, and partially definitive of, that form of activity with the result that human powers to achieve excellence, and human conceptions of the ends and goods involved, are systematically extended.'[13] He defines 'tradition' as '. . . an historically extended, socially embodied argument, and an argument precisely in part about the goods which constitute that tradition . . .'.[14] However, MacIntyre has also criticised conservative thinkers, such as Burke, who wanted to counterpose tradition and reason and tradition and revolution. He

5 Freeman, M. (2002) pp. 5–6.   6 Baxi (2002) pp. 51–52.
7 Gearty (2006) pp. 57–58.   8 Dembour (2006) p. 258.   9 MacIntyre (2006) p. 111.
10 MacIntyre (2006) p. 111.   11 MacIntyre (1967) p. 1.   12 Lukes (1981) p. 334.
13 MacIntyre (1985) p. 187.   14 MacIntyre (1985) p. 222.

makes a very profound remark: 'Yet, if the present arguments are correct, it is traditions that are the bearers of reason, and traditions at certain periods actually require and need revolutions for their continuance.'[15] He is referring to the 'great revolution' – the French Revolution.

It will be seen from these quotations which MacIntyre it is that speaks to me most directly. He is plainly arguing for a substantive rather than a procedural understanding of ethics, one that is socially embodied and located in history. Indeed, Kelvin Knight, who establishes 'how little MacIntyre shares with the likes of Gadamer and how much he shares with the likes of Marx ...',[16] correctly observes that 'whereas Gadamer is a hermeneuticist through and through, MacIntyre is a realist'.[17]

Of course, MacIntyre is commonly categorised as a 'communitarian', although he declared his dislike for '[c]ontemporary communitarians, from whom I strongly dissociate myself whenever I have had an opportunity to do so', because they '. . . advance their proposals as a contribution to the politics of the nation state'.[18] However, he has also stated that: '. . . Aristotle gave us excellent reasons for believing that both rational enquiry in politics and ethics and rationality in action require membership in a community which shares allegiance to some tolerably specific overall conception of the ultimate human good.'[19]

In *Whose Justice? Which Rationality*, exploring Aristotle's legacy, he wrote:

> Aristotle's presupposed social context is one in which evaluation is primarily in terms of the achievement of the ends of activity; Hume's is one in which evaluation is primarily in terms of the satisfaction of consumers. The individual envisaged by Aristotle engages in practical reasoning not just *qua* individual, but *qua* citizen, of a *polis*; the individual as envisaged by Hume engages in practical reasoning *qua* member of a type of society in which rank, property, and pride structure social exchanges.[20]

This passage is highly characteristic of MacIntyre, who has always been an anti-capitalist, if not always a communist. MacIntyre has also said:

> The conclusion to which the argument has so far led is not only that it is out of the debates, conflicts and enquiry of socially embodied, historically contingent traditions that contentions regarding practical rationality and justice are advanced, modified, abandoned or replaced, but that there is no other way to engage in the formulation, elaboration, rational justification, and criticism of accounts of practical rationality and justice

15 MacIntyre (2006) p. 12.   16 Knight (2007) p. 102.   17 Knight (2007) p. 103.
18 MacIntyre (1994) p. 302.   19 MacIntyre (1991) p. 99.
20 MacIntyre (1988) p. 298.

except from within some one particular tradition in conversation, cooperation, and conflict with those who inhabit the same tradition.[21]

This is what Charles Taylor has described as MacIntyre's distinction between 'substantive notions of ethics' and 'procedural notions of ethics' – the latter in a powerful tradition from Bentham through Kant to Rawls, Dworkin and Habermas.[22] Taylor says that for the former '. . . you have to start for your theory of justice from the kinds of goods and the kinds of common practices organised around these goods that people actually have in a given society.'[23]

At this point MacIntyre provides for me a significant resource in seeking to find a non-liberal, non-procedural account of human rights. In 1995 he gave several reasons why 'political liberalism is to be rejected'. He points out that: 'The self-image of the liberal is after all that of a protagonist of human rights and liberties.' First, by working only for betterment within the confines imposed by capitalism and parliamentary democracy, they would destroy themselves. Second, liberalism is the politics of a set of elites; liberalism 'ensures the exclusion of most peoples from active and rational participation . . .'. And third, 'the moral individualism of liberalism is itself the solvent of participatory community . . .'.[24] I do not follow MacIntyre from Marxism to Thomian Catholicism; but his critique of liberalism is infinitely superior, in intellectual and human terms, to that of Carl Schmitt.

However, it seems to me that the more religious MacIntyre has allowed himself to view rights as only and always 'admirably suited to the purposes of individuals or groups who believe themselves restricted or restrained in any way by religious institutions or authorities'. The very conservative tendency of this line of thought may be seen in the passage which follows on the same page:

> Generally and characteristically [rights] are used to present continually renewed challenges to what is taken by those who present them to be the institutional *status quo*, challenges designed to dissolve the bonds, and undermine the authority, of all institutions intermediate between the individual on the one hand and the government and the justice system on the other: such institutions as, families, schools and churches.[25]

Human rights as substantive rather than procedural

So, what would it mean to think *substantively* about human rights (or for that matter about other categories and concepts which find their place at the

21 MacIntyre (1988) p. 350.   22 Taylor (1994a) p. 27.   23 Taylor (1994a) p. 31.
24 MacIntyre (2006a) p. 153.   25 MacIntyre (1994) p. 105.

centre of international law, for example the right of states to non-interference in their internal affairs, or the right of peoples to self-determination)?

At this point I have drawn particular inspiration from a pair of articles in the *European Journal of Philosophy*, the first by James Griffin, the second, 'Human Rights, Universality and the Values of Personhood: Retracing Griffin's Steps', by John Tasioulas.[26] Both draw on a substantive account of human rights, developed by Wayne Sumner.[27] Griffin states that: 'We need a substantive account of human rights. By a "substantive" account I mean one that adds enough content to the notion of "human" in the term "human rights" to tell us, for any proposed such right, whether it really is one – one that thereby supplies what I shall call "existence conditions" for a human right.'[28] The reader will note that this is what is entirely missing in Habermas' (or Loughlin's) account. Griffin contrasts this with a 'structural' or 'conceptual' account – the accounts of Feinberg, Dworkin, Rawls, or Hohfeld. In order to supply a substantive account, he prefers a 'bottom-up approach' – which starts with '. . . human rights as used in our actual social life by politicians, lawyers, social campaigners, as well as theorists of various sorts, and then sees what higher principles one must resort to in order to explain their moral weight . . .'.[29] For him, human rights are grounded in 'personhood' – with the constraint that they are rights not to anything that promotes human *good* or *flourishing*, but merely what is needed for human *status*.[30]

John Tasioulas argues for a broadening out of Griffin's approach, for a 'pluralist' account – he means a pluralism of values. This follows from his notion of 'temporal relativity' – '. . . on this view, human rights would be possessed by humans *qua* human, but not necessarily at all times and all societies throughout history. Instead, they would be possessed by all in certain broadly defined historical contexts.'[31] His substantially Aristotelian conclusion is that '. . . if we were to reduce the pluralist account to a slogan, it would be that human rights are to certain minimum conditions of a good life . . .'.[32]

More recently Tasioulas has specifically criticised MacIntyre for overlooking Tasioulas' own understanding of rights – 'that in order to "complete the Enlightenment project" of human rights we need to go back beyond the Enlightenment to an Aristotelian tradition of thought about the human good and the special protection it merits.'[33]

I would agree to that, especially since, as Terry Eagleton reminds us: 'For Aristotle, ethics and politics are intimately related. Ethics is about excelling at being human, and nobody can do this in isolation. Moreover, nobody can do it unless the political institutions that allow you to do it are available. This kind of moral thinking was inherited by Karl Marx.'[34]

26 Griffin (2001); Tasioulas (2002).   27 Sumner (1987).   28 Griffin (2001) p. 307.
29 Griffin (2001) p. 308.   30 Griffin (2001) p. 312.   31 Tasioulas (2002) p. 87.
32 Tasioulas (2002) p. 96.   33 Tasioulas (2003) p. 26.   34 Eagleton (2003).

A sketch of another account

At this point I want to focus on the importance of 'temporality' as identified by John Tasioulas. I have already referred to the scandal attaching to the concept of human rights from the very first declarations of fundamental rights. For me, the delight of teaching human rights is that they problematise themselves at every step.

For the purpose of my attempt at a substantive account of rights, I now turn to the schema – much criticised and perhaps primarily of pedagogical value – of 'three generations' of human rights, developed in the 1970s by Karel Vasak of UNESCO.[35] It is interesting that this model gained currency as part of the fierce debate concerning a concept which has always been controversial, which, in the 1980s, was on the crest of a wave, but is now largely disowned – the concept of people's rights.

The 'first generation', the civil and political rights, together with the right to private property, have temporal origins: they sprang from the French Revolution in 1789, and the American Revolution of the same period. I have already mentioned the horror inspired by the Declaration in England. However, Marx a little later provided the most devastating critique of the 'first generation' of rights, the civil and political rights. In his short polemic *On the Jewish Question*,[36] written at the same time as the *Contribution to the Critique of Hegel's Philosophy of Law*, he engaged with the rights set out in the French Declaration of Rights of Man and of the Citizen, and the Constitutions of 1793 and 1795. Marx stated:

> Liberty, therefore, is the right to do everything that harms no one else. The limits within which anyone can act *without harming* someone else are defined by law, just as the boundary between two fields is determined by a boundary post. It is a question of the liberty of man as an isolated monad, withdrawn into himself . . . the right of man to liberty is based not on the association of man with man, but on the separation of man from man. It is the right of this separation, the right of the *restricted* individual, withdrawn into himself . . . The practical application of man's right to liberty is man's right to private property.

Marx's critique of 'first generation' rights was and remains incisive, indeed definitive. What he could not anticipate was the increasing importance, as a direct result of political events and struggles, of the 'second' and 'third' generations, especially social and economic rights, and peoples' rights. I suspect his response would have been rather different.

---

35 Vasak (1977); discussed in Rich (1988) p. 41.
36 Marx (1975a) written in 1843, published in 1844.

The temporality of the recognition in international law of the 'second generation' of human rights, social and economic rights, *as* human rights can also be dated very accurately. These rights achieved the status of legal rights, and, most important, became available as instruments of legitimation and struggle, as a direct consequences of the events of 1917, more specifically in the creation of the International Labour Organisation in 1919. The ILO remains the most important source and mechanism for protection of social and economic rights. These rights have recently become much more concrete, in the context of the collapse of the USSR, by way of the Council of Europe's 1996 *Revised Social Charter*,[37] which came into force in 1999, with its mechanism for collective complaints, by trade unions and NGOs, to the European Committee of Social Rights.

The 'third generation' – the peoples' rights to self-determination, to development, to a clean environment, to peace – were recognised as rights in international law following the colonial struggles of the 1960s, specifically with the coming into force of the two great UN Covenants on Human Rights in 1976. They have lost none of their relevance in the context of the continuing cruel injustice of the global economy.[38]

Conclusion

This chapter has therefore taken forward my account of international law and human rights, through an engagement with the meaning and effect of ideology in perpetuating a kind of thinking about theory which robs the objects of thought of all their material efficacy and scandalous power. I now return to the history and context of self-determination, a key principle of international law; and, in particular, attempts to construct a Marxist theory of international law.

---

37 ETS No. 163.
38 See in addition to Crawford's (1988) collection, the much more sceptical Alston (2001).

Chapter 7

Human rights as the negation of politics?

Introduction

In the last chapter I provided a sketch of the theoretical foundations for my substantive account of human rights. However, do the discourse and practice of human rights have any right themselves to exist? This chapter investigates one response to the burning question of our present conjuncture: are politics possible? And a subsidiary question: are 'human rights' a resource only for stasis and reaction?

In his *Ethics: An Essay on the Understanding of Evil*[1] Badiou declares that the 'return to the old doctrine of the natural rights of man is obviously linked to the collapse of revolutionary Marxism, and of all forms of progressive engagement that it inspired'.[2] It is immediately apparent that Badiou does not share my dialectical understanding of human rights. For him, human rights discourse is a symptom of failure. But this is clearly not the main theme of his book, which is of extraordinary interest.

To take the title first, it should be pointed out that Badiou defines 'ethics' and 'evil' radically, within a political problematic – the problem how, in the twenty-first century, is it possible to be political? For Badiou, '. . . the term "ethics" relates above all to the domain of human rights'[3]. What then is the role of 'ethics', so understood?

For Badiou, 'ethics', that is 'human rights', is a block, 'in the name of Evil and of human rights' on the 'event'. For Badiou, an 'event' 'is purely haphazard, and cannot be inferred from the situation';[4] it is unprecedented and unexpected, a pure beginning, which always resembles an instance of (laicised) grace. Examples given by Badiou are the Copernican 'event' of calling the solar system 'heliocentric' against the established body of knowledge claiming the sun circled the earth; the 'event' of the French Revolution within the situation of the *ancient regime*; the 'event' of special relativity within the immutable laws of Newtonian physics.

---

1 Badiou (2001); first published in French in 1998.   2 Badiou (2001) p. 4.
3 Badiou (2001) p. 4.   4 Badiou (2005) p. 215; Hallward (2003) p. 114.

In explaining the 'event', Badiou identifies three major dimensions of a 'truth-process' – the event, the fidelity, and the truth.[5] The 'event' is that which 'brings to pass "something other" than the situation' – Marx is, for Badiou, an event for political thought; the 'fidelity' is the 'name of the process . . . an immanent and continuing break'; the 'truth' is 'what the fidelity gathers together and produces'. Later, he specifies that the Revolutions of 1792 and 1917 were 'true universal events'. St Paul's proclamation of the Resurrection was another.[6]

Thus, Badiou asserts (and I enthusiastically agree) that the twentieth century was not a century of promises, but of accomplishment, of victorious subjectivity.

> This victorious subjectivity survives all apparent defeats, being not empirical but constitutive . . . 'Revolution' is one of the names of this motive. The October revolution in 1917, then the Chinese and the Cuban revolutions, and the victories by the Algerians or the Vietnamese in the struggles of national liberation, all these serve as the empirical proof of the motive and defeat the defeats; they compensate for the massacres of June 1848 or the Paris Commune.[7]

That is, for Badiou, 'ethics' or 'human rights' has the malign effect of blocking 'the positive prescription of possibilities . . . it accepts the play of necessity as the objective basis for all judgments of value'. Badiou's diagnosis of 'ethics' (or 'human rights') is precise: '. . . from the beginning it confirms the absence of any project, of any emancipatory politics, or any genuinely collective cause.'[8]

As Barker correctly explains, this leads Badiou to reject entirely the contemporary orthodox doctrine of universal or natural human rights. This is part and parcel of the ideology of liberal humanitarianism and the law of the global market, which appears to have triumphed following the failure of the revolutionary project of Marxism.[9]

I repeat that the possibility of politics is, for Badiou, the 'event'.

Badiou identifies two further blocks. One is Levinas' 'ethics of alterity' (and, for that matter, 'culturalism'), for which he has no patience. Badiou says: 'No light is shed on any concrete situation by the notion of the "recognition of the other".'[10] The other is the 'natural law' conception of Ernst Bloch's (and Costas Douzinas') 'not yet' – the demand that human dignity is 'not yet'. For Badiou, 'The Immortal exists only in and by the mortal animal. . . . There is no History other than our own; there is no true

---

5 Barker (2002) p. 67.   6 Badiou (2003).   7 Badiou (2007) p. 9.
8 Badiou (2001) p. 31.   9 Barker (2002) p. 135.   10 Badiou (2001) p. 27.

world to come. The world as world is, and will remain beneath the true and the false.'[11]

The texts in the later *Infinite Thought* do not address human rights as such, nor, explicitly, does *Being and Event*, or its successor volume, *Logiques des Mondes*.[12] Does this represent a disjuncture in Badiou's thought? It should be recalled that *Infinite Thought* is a varied collection of texts from before to shortly after *Ethics*.[13] The 'event', as before, plays a crucial role – it is something in respect of which a wager is taken.[14] The 'event' is, however, closely linked to 'justice': '. . . once justice is conceived of as an operator of capture for egalitarian political orientations – *true* political orientations – then it defines an effective, axiomatic, and immediate subjective figure.'[15]

Badiou repeats that 'politics is also a thinking' – and cites Robespierre, Saint-Just, Lenin, Che Guevara, Mao[16] – and reminds us of Lacan's comparison between the relation Lacan–Freud and the relation Lenin–Marx.[17]

Indeed, Badiou is one of the few contemporary philosophers to think seriously about the 'collapse of revolutionary Marxism' mentioned above – and to engage with the question: what does the word 'communist' now signify? And what is philosophy able to think under this name? He adds in parenthesis – 'philosophy under the condition of a politics'. This for Badiou is '. . . the tenacious militant determination, set in motion by some incalculable event, to maintain, come what may, the proposition of a singularity without predicate, an infinity without determination or immanent hierarchy . . .'.[18]

Thus, in his final polemic, he asserts that the duty of philosophy is '. . . to rationally reconstitute the reserve of the affirmative infinity that every liberating project requires. Philosophy does not have . . . the effective figures of emancipation. That is the primordial task of what is concentrated in political doing-thinking. Instead, philosophy is like the attic where, in difficult times, one accumulates resources, lines up tools, and sharpens knives.'[19]

Badiou's take on human rights is clarified further in an interview published in 2001.[20] He states:

> Under the pretext of not accepting Evil, we end up making believe that we have, if not the Good, at least the best possible state of affairs . . . The refrain of 'human rights' is nothing other than the ideology of modern

---

11 Badiou (2001) p. 85.   12 Badiou (2006).
13 'Philosophy and desire' 1999; 'Philosophy and politics' 1999; 'Philosophy and psychoanalysis' 1999; 'Philosophy and art' 1992; 'Philosophy and cinema' 1999; 'Philosophy and the "death of communism" ' 1998; 'Philosophy and the "war against terrorism" ' 2001; 'Ontology and politics' 1999.
14 Badiou (2003) p. 62.   15 Badiou (2003) p. 72.   16 Badiou (2003) p. 79.
17 Badiou (2003) p. 85.   18 Badiou (2003) p. 130.   19 Badiou (2003) p. 163.
20 Cox and Whalen (2005).

liberal capitalism. We won't massacre you, we won't torture you in caves, so keep quiet and worship the golden calf. As for those who don't want to worship it . . . there's always the American army . . . to make them be quiet.

He insists that nothing in the concepts of human rights or democracy leads in the direction of the real emancipation of humanity. 'It is necessary to reconstruct rights, in everyday life as in politics, of truth and of the Good. Our ability to once again have real ideas and real projects depends on it.'

The 'human rights' which Badiou castigates are part of the block on politics. He insists that '. . . Politics is first the invention and the exercise of an absolutely new and concrete reality. Politics is the creation of thought.' On my reading, Badiou goes much further than his English commentator Peter Hallward would go. Hallward puts it this way:

> Since every truth springs from an exception to the rules, we must refuse, in principle, the idea of any automatic or inherent rights of Man. No less than Lacan and Žižek, Badiou displaces the facile emphasis on human rights from the centre of ethics by accepting that fidelity to truth need have 'nothing to do with the "interests" of the animal . . . and has eternity as its destiny.' Human rights, if they exist at all, can only be *exceptional* rights, asserted and affirmed in their positivity rather than deduced, negatively, from the requirements of survival.[21]

Otherwise, human rights would be no different, says Hallward, from animal rights. However, this account misses what is most radical in Badiou.

The question I pose, within Badiou's problematic, is whether the material effects of the theory and practice of 'human rights' could on the contrary have a political content, part of the 'fidelity' to the 'event'.

First, however, I want to explore briefly Žižek's take on Badiou. It was through Žižek that I began to read Badiou.

Badiou and Žižek

As is well known, Badiou's writing is an essential resource for Slavoj Žižek's engagement with the possibility of politics, and with the exemplary (for him) figure of Lenin.[22] Žižek affirms that: 'The Leninist answer to the postmodern multiculturalist "right to narrate" should thus be an unashamed assertion of the *right to truth*.'[23] This is pure Badiou!

And Žižek's condemnation of human rights is even more forthright: he

---

21 Hallward (2003) p. 258.   22 Žižek (2004).   23 Žižek (2004) p. 177.

views them as rights to break the Ten Commandments (what is a right to privacy but a right to commit adultery? the right to property but a right to theft? the right to religious freedom but a right to worship false gods?) – and rights to solicit or control enjoyment.[24]

One should, however, equally note Žižek's critique of Badiou, for his Jacobinism and idealism. Thus, Žižek writes that 'the "pure politics" of Badiou, Rancière and Balibar, more Jacobin than Marxist, shares with its great opponent, Anglo-Saxon Cultural Studies and their focus on struggles for recognition.' In Žižek's view these and other French or French-orientated theorists of the Political aim at '. . . the reduction of the sphere of the economy (of material production) to an "ontic" sphere deprived of "ontological" dignity'.[25]

In another text,[26] Žižek asserts that Badiou:

> . . . gets caught . . . in the proto-Kantian trap of 'spurious infinity': afraid of the potential 'totalitarian' terrorist consequences of asserting 'actual freedom' as *the direct inscription of the Event into the order of Being*, he emphasises the gap that separates them forever. For Badiou, fidelity to the Event involves the work of discerning its traces, the work which is by definition never done; in spite of all claims to the contrary, he thus relies on a kind of the Kantian regulative Idea, on the final end (the full conversion of the Event into Being) which one can only approach in an endless process.[27]

The important point for me is the point at which Žižek and Badiou meet, with plain consequences for a proper understanding of human rights as always scandalous and subversive. This can, I suggest, only mean that human rights as a scandal must always be political. Indeed, this is the only mode in which human rights can become universal. Žižek puts it this way: 'Against the cliché according to which politics tears people apart . . . we should claim that *the only real universality is the political one*: the universal link binding together all those who experience a fundamental solidarity, all those who become aware that their struggles are part of the very struggle which cuts across the entire social edifice.' To put it in Badiou's terms: universality (of the truth-procedure) can assert itself only in the guise of such a cut, of a radical division, at the very heart of the social body.

There is another way of understanding this point, namely that the universality of each of the 'generations' of human rights is precisely the consequence of the world-historical revolutionary events which gave birth to them, and of which they are the truth, whatever befell those revolutions in subsequent

24 Dean (2006) p. 100.   25 Žižek (2004) p. 271.   26 Žižek (2001).
27 Žižek (2001) p. 125.

developments. This is also why the universality of these human rights is guaranteed by their political content: each was entirely unpredicted or unpredictable. Furthermore, the specific rights which constitute each generation necessarily become mere procedural or technical formalism until re-invested with new political struggles.

Žižek clarifies his own point of view in one of his recent, intensely provocative, short essays.[28] The *New Left Review* essay was largely extracted from Žižek's latest book, the massive *Parallax View*.[29]

He puts it this way in the first paragraph of the article:

> Contemporary appeals to human rights within our liberal-capitalist societies generally rest upon three assumptions. First, that such appeals function in opposition to modes of fundamentalism that would naturalize or essentialize contingent, historically conditioned traits. Second, that the two most basic rights are freedom of choice, and the right to dedicate one's life to the pursuit of pleasure (rather than to sacrifice it for some higher ideological cause). And third, that an appeal to human rights may form the basis for a defence against the 'excess of power'.

This is actually quite accurate as a description of the general trend of human rights discourse, which Žižek accurately locates in the work of Michael Ignatieff – the 'depoliticised humanitarian politics of "Human Rights" as the ideology of military interventionism serving specific economic-political purposes'.[30] Human rights under this description is no more than moralising self-justification – for disengaged individualism or, which is often linked to it, for political inaction in the face of gross illegality and injustice.

Žižek does not return to the specific problematic of human rights until later in the article:

> At an even more general level, we might problematize the opposition between the universal (pre-political) human rights possessed by every human being 'as such' and the specific political rights of a citizen, or member of a particular political community. In this sense, Balibar argues for the 'reversal of the historical and theoretical relationship between "man" and "citizen" ' that proceeds by 'explaining how man is made by citizenship and not citizenship by man'.[31] Balibar alludes here to Arendt's insight on the condition of refugees: 'The conception of human rights based upon the assumed existence of a human being as such broke down at the very moment when those who professed to believe in it were for the

---

28 Žižek (2005) p. 115.
29 The passage cited at the previous note also appears at Žižek (2006) p. 340.
30 Žižek (2006) p. 339.   31 Balibar (2004) pp. 320–321.

first time confronted with people who had indeed lost all other qualities and specific relationships except that they were still human.'

This passage can be read as a merciless attack on any attempt to de-link human rights from the political events which gave birth to them. The irrational and a-historical fantasy of 'pre-political' human rights, attaching to persons by virtue of humanity only, already breaks down in the cases of young children, the demented elderly, persons in long-term coma and others. There can be no conclusion other than to recognise that a person taken out of their historical and social context is no longer a human being. The human being who can be a subject of human rights is also the person who partakes in what Marx referred to as 'species being'.

The passage just cited from Hannah Arendt leads, for Žižek:

> ... straight to Agamben's notion of *homo sacer*[32] as a human being reduced to 'bare life'. In a properly Hegelian dialectics of universal and particular, it is precisely when a human being is deprived of the particular socio-political identity that accounts for his determinate citizenship that – in one and the same move – he ceases to be recognized or treated as human. Paradoxically, I am deprived of human rights at the very moment at which I am reduced to a human being 'in general', and thus become the ideal bearer of those 'universal human rights' which belong to me independently of my profession, sex, citizenship, religion, ethnic identity, etc.[33]

I suspect that by 'determinate citizenship' Žižek does not mean the attribute of bearing constitutional rights. It is clear from the paragraph as a whole that he means a human being somehow located outside human society. Thus, he could readily (why does he not?) add to this list by citing historical context. On my own reading, the human being becomes truly human, part of the re-investment of human rights with their universal, political content, at the moment of participation in collective projects of emancipation.

Žižek cites Jacques Rancière's 'dialectical reversal':

> 'When they are of no use, one does the same as charitable persons do with their old clothes. One gives them to the poor. Those rights that appear to be useless in their place are sent abroad, along with medicine and clothes, to people deprived of medicine, clothes and rights.' Nevertheless, they do not become void, for 'political names and political places never become merely void'. Instead the void is filled by somebody or something else: if those who suffer inhuman repression are unable to

---

32 Agamben (1998).   33 Žižek (2005) pp. 126–127.

enact the human rights that are their last recourse, then somebody else has to inherit their rights in order to enact them in their place. This is what is called the 'right to humanitarian interference'—a right that some nations assume to the supposed benefit of victimized populations, and very often against the advice of the humanitarian organizations themselves. The 'right to humanitarian interference' might be described as a sort of 'return to sender': the disused rights that had been sent to the rightless are sent back to the senders.[34]

Characteristically, Žižek pursues this dialectic: 'So, to put it in the Leninist way: what the "human rights of Third World suffering victims" effectively means today, in the predominant discourse, is the right of Western powers themselves to intervene politically, economically, culturally and militarily in the Third World countries of their choice, in the name of defending human rights.'[35]

It is important to note here the phrase 'in the predominant discourse'. Žižek is fully aware of the fact that so far he has only been describing the bourgeois (mis)appropriation of the discourse of human rights. His conclusion is therefore tantalising in the extreme:

> Far from being pre-political, 'universal human rights' designate the precise space of politicization proper; what they amount to is the right to universality as such – the right of a political agent to assert its radical non-coincidence with itself (in its particular identity), to posit itself as the 'supernumerary', the one with no proper place in the social edifice; and thus as an agent of universality of the social itself. The paradox is therefore a very precise one, and symmetrical to the paradox of universal human rights as the rights of those reduced to inhumanity. At the very moment when we try to conceive the political rights of citizens without reference to a universal 'meta-political' human rights, we lose politics itself; that is to say, we reduce politics to a 'post-political' play of negotiation of particular interests.[36]

This passage can be read as arguing that there must be a revolutionary origin and content in human rights, which is their connection to politics and its possibility. Human rights emptied of their scandalous political content become merely the structure and limits of fair and efficient administration, politics without politics.

34 Rancière (2004) pp. 307–309.   35 Žižek (2005) p. 128.   36 Žižek (2005) p. 131.

Badiou and the event

From Žižek I return to Badiou. With all due respect to Žižek's formidable contribution, Badiou seems to me to be a defining philosopher of our epoch, a true descendant of Aristotle, Spinoza, Hegel and Marx. In parenthesis, I should emphasise that this genealogy, the thinkers whom I venerate, is quite different from, for example, that of Douzinas and Gearey, who would instead follow Plato, Nietzsche, Heidegger and Lacan.

I start with a characteristically lapidary passage (in fact from a meditation on Pascal), from Badiou's magnum opus, *Being and Event*, published in France as long ago as 1988, and in English translation in 2005. Badiou writes, in his chapter on Pascal:

> . . . what is at stake here is the militant apparatus of truth: the assurance that it is in the interpretative intervention that it finds its support, that its origin is in the event: and the will to *draw out* its dialectic and to propose to humans that they consecrate the best of themselves to the essential.[37]

This is the revolutionary impulse that lies at the heart of and is constantly re-invested in human rights.

The centre of attention for us, however, is his chapter entitled 'Meditation Nine: The State of the Historical-social Situation'. This is a short but rich and profound essay on the State. Badiou's problematic is the despair of Lenin and of Mao at the difficulty of attacking, much less destroying, the State, whatever they believed Marx to have predicted. As Badiou puts it:

> Scarcely five years after the October Revolution, Lenin, ready to die, despaired over the obscene permanence of the State. Mao himself, more phlegmatic and more adventurous, declared – after twenty-five years in power and ten years of the Cultural Revolution's ferocious tumult – that not much had changed after all.[38]

Badiou's analysis starts with Aristotle's realisation that all constitutions come to grief for the same reason, which prevents 'thinkable constitutions'. The same reason causes 'pathological' regimes (tyrannies, oligarchies and democracies) to prevail over the 'normal' (monarchies, aristocracies and republics). This reason is the existence of the rich and the poor. Thus, real states relate to their un-binding, their internal oppositions, so often expressed in the form of parties, constituted by the rich and the poor.[39] In this sense Aristotle is a proto-Marxist. Badiou considers that Marxism in turn marks a

37 Badiou (2005) p. 222. 38 Badiou (2005) p. 110. 39 Badiou (2005) p. 104.

great advance in understanding that the State is not concerned with the multiple of individuals, but with the multiple of classes of individuals. In Badiou's ontological language of set theory, this is the 'count-as-one' ensured by the State: the State's representation of society.[40]

The question of representation is of the greatest importance for Badiou. He distinguishes between 'normality', which is the condition of being presented and represented; 'singularity', which is to be presented but not represented; and 'excrescence', which is to be represented but not presented. He adds that '. . . what remains is the void, which is neither presented nor represented'.[41] This is the analytical basis on which he shows that there is a 'fatal ambiguity' in Engels, and following him, Lenin, when they underlined the separate character of the State, and showed that coercion is reciprocal with separation. That is why for them (and for Weber) the essence of the State is in the final analysis its bureaucratic and military machinery – 'armed bodies of men'. That is, in Badiou's language, 'its character of being monstrously excrescent', its *excess* over social immediacy.

Badiou's analysis of Engels' (and Lenin's) position goes as follows. For Engels, the bourgeoisie is a 'normal' term, since it is presented economically and socially, and re-presented by the State. The proletariat is a 'singular' term, since it is presented but not re-presented. Finally, the State apparatus is an 'excrescence'.[42] Badiou explains that on this basis it is possible to hope for the disappearance of the State; although Communism would on this account turn out in fact to be the 'unlimited regime of the individual'. One is reminded of Fine and Marks, discussed above.

This leads back to Badiou's pessimistic remarks about Lenin and Mao. For Badiou, the State is 'precisely non-political', and even if the direction of political change must be bordered by the State, the State cannot change, except in who is in charge. Politics 'stakes its existence' on a quite different relation both to the 'void' and to 'excess' than that of the State. A full explication of the terms 'void' and 'excess' is beyond the scope of this book: but Badiou makes it clear what he means. He notes that governments 'when an emblem of their void wanders about' – generally an inconsistent or rioting crowd – prohibit 'gatherings of more than three people'; and the excess, of classes or groups, beyond the control of the State, 'designates a potential place for the fixation of the void'.[43]

In this context Badiou's concluding statement makes complete sense. 'Rather than a warrior beneath the walls of the State, a political activist is a patient watchman of the void instructed by the event, for it's only when grappling with the event that the State blinds itself to its own mastery.'[44] This

---

40 Badiou (2005) p. 105.　　41 Badiou (2005) p. 108.　　42 Badiou (2005) p. 109.
43 Badiou (2005) p. 109.　　44 Badiou (2005) p. 111.

is a precise description, in Badiou's terminology, of the essential characteristic of Lenin's analysis and gamble in April 1917.[45]

Another account of human rights

To conclude this chapter, I wish to propose an alternative account, one which is already strongly implied in Badiou's thought cited above. For surely 'human rights' were integral to the 'events' whose honour Badiou defends. One of the most revolutionary products of the French Revolution, recognised as such with horror by Burke and Bentham among others, was the Declaration of Rights of Man and of the Citizen. Lenin in 1917 not only proclaimed the 'right of nations to self-determination', which became the battle-cry of anti-colonial struggles, but also the rights of the working people which have since become enshrined as social and economic rights.

There is another way of putting this – as a continuation of Hegel's critique of liberalism. As Steven B. Smith put it:

> Rights, then, are not simply given, but are part of a larger historical struggle of human beings to achieve, or to become worthy of respect or recognition. Without some account of the emergence of rights, the concept itself will remain insecure.[46]

Žižek also proposes that it is only '. . . by problematising democracy – by making it clear that liberal democracy a priori, in its very notion (as Hegel would have put it), cannot survive without capitalist private property – that we can become truly anti-capitalist'.[47] Thus rather than bare proceduralism (Habermas), or even political rhetoric or consensus (Loughlin), rights are shown to have a real, substantive content, which may be located temporally. This is not to relativise human rights. On my account, the concept of the universality of human rights on a foundation of natural law has no moral content. It cannot assist either in the critique of ideology or indeed actuality; nor can it provide the bridge which can indicate the actions we ought to take.

It is therefore my case that human rights are real, and provide a ground for judgment, to the extent that they are understood in their historical context, and as, and to the extent to which, they embody and define the content of real human struggles. That is also the meaning of the doctrine of the UN's Vienna World Conference on human rights in 1993, that all three generations of human rights are indivisible. This is – and in my own view will prove to be – much more subversive than at first glance it seems. This is also what Patricia Williams meant by 'alchemy' in her *The Alchemy of Race and Rights*.[48] Human

---

45 Žižek (2004).   46 Smith (1989) p. 114.   47 Žižek (2004) p. 273.
48 Williams (1992).

rights talk is often and increasingly the meaningless rhetoric of the powerful and the oppressor. But it becomes real when articulating the present, not the endlessly deferred, claims of the oppressed.

In this chapter I have tested my take on human rights, and have found that two of the most trenchant critics of human rights in reality can be taken to support my position. In the next chapter I go on the offensive, with a critique of two important contemporary post-modern scholars.

Chapter 8

'Postmodern' reconstructions of human rights

Introduction

The last chapter engaged with two scholars who have challenged human rights radically, that is, pulling them up by their roots. This chapter finds, perhaps surprisingly, less in common with two scholars working in the UK, who seek to rehabilitate human rights.

I interrogate recent work of Costas Douzinas[1] and – in complete contrast – Colin Perrin,[2] both of whom have rejected the possibility of foundations for human rights, while fully recognising the central importance of both human rights discourse, now so widespread, and the practice of human rights protection, as exemplified in the work of non-governmental organisations such as Amnesty International. Both are also engaged, in differing ways, in a critique of liberalism. In the latter project, as it is already plain, I concur with them. However, I do not follow their respective prescriptions.

Douzinas

Douzinas, as will be seen, has in a text which has become something of a classic, *The End of Human Rights*,[3] given human rights a utopian role, always deferred, but redeeming law through a purely discursive set of procedures. His points of reference were strange bedfellows – Martin Heidegger and the Marxist Utopian, Ernst Bloch. Perrin, on the other hand, prefers a more literary response to the question of foundation: following Maurice Blanchot, he argues that a 'foundation' for human rights may be traced to an impossibility of speaking at all.

Douzinas' impressive work *The End of Human Rights* was both a continuation and a reversal of his earlier writing, which moved from an enthusiastic reception of 'postmodernism', especially the work of Derrida, to a move

---

1 Douzinas (2000) and (2007); and Douzinas and Gearey (2005). 2 Perrin (2004).
3 Douzinas (2000).

'from Athens to Jerusalem', to the 'ethics of alterity' of Emmanuel Levinas, to a fascination with psycho-analysis, Lacan and Žižek. An important feature of this work was a consistent attempt to reclaim the possibility of politics, and a constant but wary attention to the legacy of Karl Marx.

However, Douzinas' work, and that of his collaborator Adam Gearey, were still described by them as 'postmodern', and I explore below the meaning they gave to this word.

Douzinas' latest work, *Human Rights and Empire*, with which I engage later in this chapter, represents another significant turn in his oeuvre. Bloch is hardly mentioned, and nor is Heidegger. Even Levinas has almost vanished. This time, the focal point of reference is Carl Schmitt.[4]

First, however, I look closely at *The End of Human Rights*. It is not simply a postmodern text.[5] It is the book in which Douzinas believed he had found his way to what was in effect a politics of law, or a law of politics, drawing from Bloch's Marxist utopianism. Douzinas' introduction contains a bold claim:[6]

> The hope is that by following the philosophical critics of liberalism, Kant's original definition of 'critique' can be revived and our understanding of human rights rescued from the boredom of analytical common-sense and its evacuation of political vision and moral purpose. This is a textbook for the critical mind and the fiery heart.

The first question for this chapter is whether Douzinas redeemed his promise. Has he laid the basis for the return of political vision and moral purpose?

Both his earlier works in the same territory (the first two volumes of what he described as a trilogy[7]) were essentially deconstructive, breaking down the possibility of an easy reconciliation with the claims of Law's Empire. *Postmodern Jurisprudence: the Law of the Text in the Texts of the Law*[8] contained at its centre a playful yet barbed attack on natural law, and *Justice Miscarried: Ethics, Aesthetics and the Law*[9] denounced the gulf between law and justice, in the name of a pre-theoretical, Levinasian insistence of the demands of the Other. The law itself provided no possibility of redemption. *The End of Human Rights* was different. Douzinas sought to persuade us that there is a role for law, at least when mediated by human rights.

Douzinas' writing is always characterised by an astonishing range of reference, high intelligence, fluency of writing and often startling perception. Moreover, *The End of Human Rights* was the most serious work on the theory of human rights yet to appear in the English language. Its only predecessor,

---

4 Schmitt (1985); (1996); and (2003).
5 The analysis which follows draws from the author's review – Bowring (2001).
6 Douzinas (2000) p. 4.   7 Douzinas (2000) p. vii.   8 Douzinas (1991).
9 Douzinas (1996).

on which it drew at a number of points, was Rolando Gaete's insufficiently noticed *Human Rights and the Limits of Critical Reason*.[10] However, in *The End of Human Rights*, Douzinas' postmodern playfulness had been replaced by a lucid eloquence, open to all readers.

Yet it is important to notice what Douzinas' *The End of Human Rights* is not, and why it provides no theoretical resources for my own attempts to find an adequate theory of human rights. There is practically no point at which his concerns intersect with what are for me the interesting debates in human rights law, as, for example, published in the *Human Rights Quarterly*, the most theoretically concerned of the many human rights journals. Douzinas is of course familiar with the leading textbook, Henry Steiner and Philip Alston's *International Human Rights in Context*, and the prominence given there to the familiar debate between universalism and cultural relativism.[11] Surprisingly, he dismisses the debate in the following terms:

> The universalism and relativism debate has replaced the old ideological confrontation between civil and political, and economic and social rights, and is conducted with the same rigour . . . The claims of universality and tradition, rather than standing opposed in mortal combat, have become uneasy allies, whose fragile liaison has been sanctioned by the World Bank.[12]

Unfortunately, these ringing words add nothing to our understanding of the inevitable tensions within human rights. The passage just cited is taken from a passionately argued section on 'humanitarian intervention' and the use of force in Kosovo/Yugoslavia. But Douzinas gives the reader no sense of the political roots or contemporary development of the dialectic (always more than simply a confrontation) between generations of rights. The realisation – the justiciability – of economic and social rights, and the irreducibility of group, especially cultural, rights, are among the burning issues of the day, and Douzinas passes them by. I hope I have given a better account of them in this book.

I note in particular the failure by Douzinas to engage with the issues concerning Islamic or other non-Western traditions in the historical or contemporary world. Neither of us analyses or criticises Samuel Huntingdon's influential thesis of the *Clash of Civilisations*, where Islam replaces the USSR's Evil Empire as the main opponent of Western, Christian civilisation.[13] I would point here to the important work of Abdullahi An-Na'im on cross-cultural approaches to human rights.[14] And mention should also be

---

10 Gaete (1993).   11 Steiner and Alston (2000) Chapter 4.
12 Douzinas (2000) p. 138.   13 Huntingdon (1993) p. 28.
14 See An-Na'im (1990); An-Na'im (1992); An-Na'im (2000).

made of Issa Shivji's polemical *The Concept of Human Rights in Africa*, with its conclusion that existing human rights ideology '. . . amounts to the production and reproduction of a human rights ideology which objectively buttresses the imperialist oppression of Africa on the one hand, and the authoritarian/military domination of its people on the other'.[15] My own engagement follows in Chapter 9.

I am still more critical of the fact that *The End of Human Rights* is in no sense inter-disciplinary. It treats questions of philosophy extensively, but from the standpoint of legal theory. The widely differing perspectives of the disciplines of political and social science, of anthropology and international relations are not taken into consideration. This is disappointing, in view of arguments that 'law should be removed from its hegemonic role in human rights studies, and relocated within a political science which is interdisciplinary between philosophy and social science, between the social sciences, and between political science and international relations'.[16] My response is that good writing about human rights is located in just such an interdisciplinary space. The reader of this text would remain ignorant of the nascent engagement between human rights and international relations.[17] And this gap – or aporia – is perhaps the reason for the weakness of the following assertion:

> When international politics are dominated by the rhetoric of rights, no moral argument can resist the desire of even small groups to acquire autonomy and statehood. . . . A world map in the form of a mosaic of statelets will be a natural extension of the aggressive logic of rights but at a huge distance from the cosmopolitan peace which Kant hoped rights would lead to.[18]

This is the only reference in *The End* to the burgeoning field of minority and group rights, and is startlingly simplistic. Again, it is my aspiration to provide at least a more serious engagement, and this follows in Chapter 9.

The focus of *The End of Human Rights* was much narrower than promised, and there could, in Douzinas' own terms, be a good reason for this. Douzinas had sought to write an immanent critique of the Western tradition of human rights. By an immanent critique, I mean, therefore, a critique of human rights, as it were from the inside, using the resources of Western philosophy – see my reflections on Michael Salter's work in Chapter 9. This kind of critique, as Marx has shown us, is often the best. So Douzinas is not to be condemned on these grounds. He put it somewhat differently: 'We will examine from liberal and non-liberal perspectives the main building blocks of the concept of human rights: the human, the subject, the legal person, freedom

---

15 Shivji (1989) p. 53.   16 Freeman (2001).   17 Forsythe (2000).
18 Douzinas (2000) p. 242.

and rights among others. Burke, Hegel, Marx, Heidegger, Sartre, psycho-analytical, deconstructive, semiotic and ethical approaches will be used, first, to deepen our understanding of rights, and then to criticise aspects of their operation.'[19] Note that 'liberal' and 'non-liberal' are both Western intellectual trends.

Douzinas' critique is not, therefore, centred on the problem of the legitimacy of human rights discourse as a 'dominant discourse', as a form of legal imperialism. Although in this text he is perfectly clear about the role of law in processes of globalisation: '. . . democracy and the rule of law are increasingly used to ensure that economic and technological forces are subjected to no other end from that of their continuous expansion.'[20] Instead, Douzinas was, in this book as in his earlier works, confronting the abyss which separates law and justice, the inexorable tendency of the law to erase human difference and immediacy in the name of abstraction and universalisation. The difference in this text is that he believed he had found a kind of redemption.

Douzinas employed an unusual method of organising his textbook. It was divided into two parts. The first part was entitled 'The Genealogy of Human Rights', and sought to explicate the historical development of natural law from the Greek classics to the transformation of natural law into human rights through and after the French and American revolutions. The second part was much more ambitious: 'The Philosophy of Human Rights'. This started, unsurprisingly, with Burke and Marx, in the roles of 'classical' critics of human rights, followed by Kant (treated for eight pages[21]) and Sartre on the subject of rights.

The reader might have expected Kant to be followed by his most cogent critic, Hegel. Hegel received 11 pages of discussion after a gap of 15 pages.[22] What did the intervening 15 pages contain? Here Douzinas once again displayed his (arguably commendable) lack of respect for intellectual chronology or development, and his taste for novelty and iconoclasm. The hero of the 15 pages[23] was none other than Martin Heidegger, not often considered a theoretician of human rights. Just what role the controversial philosopher of man as 'the Shepherd of Being' played in Douzinas' journey will be further explored below. But the key arguments of this part, Chapters 11 and 12,[24] were devoted to the application of psychoanalysis – especially the work of Lacan, Salecl, Žižek – to law and human rights. Readers of Douzinas' previous work already know that an earlier destination for Douzinas was Levinas' 'ethics of alterity'.

The real hero of the quest was much more unexpected, albeit, as is now apparent, a temporary point of reference for Douzinas: the Marxist utopian philosopher Ernst Bloch. Ernst Bloch's major influence has been in the

19 Douzinas (2000) p. 4.   20 Douzinas (2000) p. 7.
21 Douzinas (2000) pp. 188–195.   22 Douzinas (2000) pp. 263–273.
23 Douzinas (2000) pp. 201–216.   24 Douzinas (2000) pp. 297–342.

development of 'liberation theology'[25] in the 1960s – he is known as an 'atheist theologian'. Douzinas explained his choice as follows:

> His grandiose and eloquent utopianism, steeped in central European Jewish culture and German romantic values, remains unsurpassed although, after the collapse of communism, it is no longer fashionable or 'politically correct'. Bloch represents a genuine advance on Marx: he retains the main elements of his critique of rights but discovers in the tradition of natural law and right the historically variable but eternal human trait to resist domination and oppression and to imagine and fight for a society in which 'man will walk upright'.[26]

It is questionable whether this in fact surpasses Marx. But most importantly for Douzinas, Bloch's version of human rights 'takes the concrete form of a promise which anticipates a real humanity still to come'.[27] In Douzinas' own language, on his final page, this was translated as: 'Human rights are the necessary and impossible claim of law to justice . . . a concern with a political and ethical utopia, the epiphany of which will never occur but whose principle can stand in judgement of the present law.'[28] This is not the standard justification for human rights, and it is therefore necessary to look more closely and critically at Douzinas' arguments and procedures.

I have already noted that the first Part of Douzinas' book is the more straightforward. However, it often descends into rhetoric and wild assertion. As could be expected, Douzinas' accounts of Greek and Roman, and Aquinian, antecedents were brief but exemplary.[29] The closer he approached the present day, the more Douzinas opened himself to criticism. At times this was because of the rather narrow range of reference, already noted. Thus he noticed, while discussing Locke, that: 'The precondition of individual property rights is the absence of political and human rights, subjection the precondition of freedom. This is the tragedy of individualism, mitigated by the introduction of democracy but still present in the various forms of neoliberalism.'[30] The discussion would have been much richer with a consideration of C. B. Macpherson's theories of possessive individualism.[31]

Later assertions were unsubstantiated and on occasion apparently made for effect. Thus Douzinas asserted: 'If, according to Lenin, socialism was the combination of Soviet democracy and electricity, for President Carter, the first great exponent of a moral foreign policy, human rights are the combination of capitalism and the rule of law.'[32] Without holding a brief for Carter, one is entitled to ask: where did he say that? Further, Douzinas argued

---

25 Moltmann (1993).   26 Douzinas (2000) p. 176.   27 Douzinas (2000) p. 181.
28 Douzinas (2000) p. 380.   29 Douzinas (2000) pp. 47–56 and 56–61.
30 Douzinas (2000) p. 81.   31 Macpherson (1964).   32 Douzinas (2000) p. 91.

that the UN human rights declarations '. . . create and exhaust their own legitimacy in their act of enunciation . . . Human rights install the radical contingency of linguistic proclamation into the heart of constitutional arrangements.' It is hard to understand what this means, especially in the light of the much more nuanced discussion in the second part.

When Douzinas came to consider the actual human rights declarations, he was even more controversial. Thus he made a startling claim: 'If the (French) Declaration inaugurated modernity, it also started nationalism and all its consequences: genocides, ethnic and civil wars, ethnic cleansing, minorities, refugees, statelessness. Citizenship introduced a new type of privilege which was protected for some by excluding others.'[33] But what evidence is there to support this indictment of the 1789 Declaration? There are many serious theorists of nationalism who would take issue. And to what extent was exclusion new?

There was another significant aporia, in what was expressly intended to be a textbook. Douzinas demonstrated that he did not grasp (this was quite possibly a lack of inclination to find out) contemporary human rights mechanisms. He asserts that prior to 1998 politically controversial cases under the European Convention on Human Rights were left to the Council of Europe's Committee of Ministers.[34] This assertion is not only unsupported, but wrong. Moreover, on the same page, periodic reports to UN treaty bodies are said, again wrongly, to be about human rights violations: following that mistake, Douzinas cannot undertake a serious critique of the role of such mechanisms in protecting human rights. On the next page, there was another extraordinary, unsupported and, indeed, false claim: '. . . barristers appearing before international bodies such as the European Court of Human Rights quickly learn that it is better preparation to research the political affiliations of the government-appointed judges than to read the Court's case-law.'[35] Errors such as this undermine the value of the argument. I too am highly critical of contemporary human rights theory and practice – see Chapter 6 of this book, and my references to recent literature. But in order to criticise, it is first necessary to identify the target of criticism correctly.

This general disdain for international human rights mechanisms appeared to be contradicted in the second part of the book. Douzinas asserted: 'Indeed, the international law of human rights has emerged from the realisation that, if anything, people need to be protected most from their local custodians of legality.'[36]

---

33 Douzinas (2000) p. 103.   34 Douzinas (2000) p. 119.

35 The author has appeared on a large number of occasions before the Court, with some success, and has never undertaken this exercise; nor does he know of anyone who has. In any event, as Douzinas failed to ascertain, the first drafts of the judgments are written not by the judges, but by the Court's Registry lawyers.

36 Douzinas (2000) p. 155.

Furthermore, Douzinas' tendency to cite the *Guardian* as a source of information on human rights violations left his own outrage at the level of liberal indignation. Noam Chomsky, who has done this kind of work much more thoroughly, was only briefly mentioned. Perhaps this was why the conclusion to this part seems so thin, if it contains any significant meaning at all: 'Human rights, as the principle of hope, work in the gap between ideal nature and law, or real people and universal abstractions.'[37]

The second part also contained some breathtaking assertions. For example, at its start: 'Finally, postmodern approaches to law, influenced by the ethics of alterity associated with the philosophy of Levinas and Derrida, are critical of the rationalism of rights and emphasise their situated and embedded character. In this, they are not too removed from Burke's assertion that only individualised justice can protect freedom.' As Freeman reminds us 'what Burke called "the real rights of men" were not natural, but constituted by society. Burke opposed to the natural-law philosophical conception of natural rights a sociological account of rights.'[38] This is not what the postmodern Douzinas has in mind, surely.

Furthermore, Douzinas appeared to be caught in a rather crucial formal contradiction of himself.[39] First, he asserted that: 'Right operates as a critical function only against a future horizon, that of the (impossible) ideal of an emancipated and self-constituting humanity.' Further down the page this is followed by: 'But Marx neglected the possibility that the groundlessness of the discourse of rights and the non-determination of the concept of man – admittedly more asserted than real in the eighteenth century – would install indeterminacy in the heart of human identity and undecidability in politics and thus create the conditions of future self-realisation.' But surely this is for Douzinas an impossible ideal?

The most surprising assertions occurred in the passages on Heidegger. The first was breathtaking: 'Existentialism as a philosophical tradition lies behind Hegel's dialectics and Heidegger's ontology.'[40] Note the anachronism – even for Douzinas, existentialism must surely start with Kierkegaard and Nietzsche. Moreover, the exposition of Heidegger leaves the reader unsure what he has to do with human rights. For example: 'The subjective turn of modernity gives Heidegger the opportunity to reflect on the way in which metaphysical thought has waylaid humanity from its primordial destiny of 'caring for Being';[41] and 'Man's responsibility is to find in himself what befits the destiny of guarding the truth of Being because, unlike objects, "man is the shepherd of Being." '[42] Most readers would need considerable persuasion that such a 'destiny' plays a role in understanding human rights. The first and only indication of Heidegger's relevance is: 'Metaphysical humanism

---

37 Douzinas (2000) p. 145.   38 Freeman (2001) p. 125.   39 Douzinas (2000) p. 165.
40 Douzinas (2000) p. 200.   41 Douzinas (2000) p. 202.   42 Douzinas (2000) p. 206.

lies at the heart of an unprecedented colonisation of nature in its various meanings, as territory and physical landscape, as human or animal nature or, as the nature of the "naturals", the indigenous people. But aren't human rights a defensive shield against the self-destructive horrors of metaphysical arrogance?'[43] This should of course be contrasted with the passage noted above.[44]

I cannot resist at this point Badiou's comment on Heidegger: 'Heidegger holds that being "is as φύσυς".[45] We shall say, rather: being consists maximally as natural multiplicity, which is to say as homogenous normality. For the non-veiling whose proximity is lost, we substitute this aura-less proposition: nature is what is rigorously normal in being.'[46]

Douzinas was much more convincing in his discussions of the French post- (or neo-) Marxists Balibar, Lefort and Lyotard (in two passages in the discussion of Marx,[47] and following the exposition of Heidegger[48]) and the English critical theorist Jay Bernstein,[49] who wrote an exemplary paper on Marx's *Jewish Question*,[50] as well as the German critical theorist and intellectual heir of Habermas, Axel Honneth.[51] These are all subjected to criticism on the route to Douzinas' arrival at psychoanalysis and the ethics of alterity. There is not space here for a detailed deconstruction of Douzinas' argument, but it is notable that from this point to the passage where the treatment of psychoanalysis starts,[52] there is no sense of logical progression or transition.

Indeed, the last paragraph of Chapter 10,[53] which stands as a summing up of the Hegelian approach, contains what is to my mind the most convincing statement of the book:

> Thus rights protect the ability of people to participate in the life of the community as a whole, and the struggle for new rights is a struggle for changing the meaning of equal participation and extending it from political life to the workplace, to the environment and to the private domain. If the life of the law is not books but experience, the life of rights is not in the isolated individual but in the recognition of being with others.

This is Douzinas at his best, and much stronger than his earlier, apparently contradictory, passage in his newly discovered 'utopian' mode:

43 Douzinas (2000) p. 209.   44 Douzinas (2000) p. 242.
45 'Physis' – Badiou says, at (2005) p. 125, that *physis* is the authentic thought of being; for the Greeks, the work of art is founded on nature as *physis*.
46 Badiou (2005) p. 129.   47 Douzinas (2000) pp. 170–175.
48 Douzinas (2000) pp. 217–227.   49 Douzinas (2000) pp. 285–287.
50 Bernstein (1991).   51 Douzinas (2000) pp. 274–280.
52 Douzinas (2000) pp. 296–297.   53 Douzinas (2000) pp. 295–296.

Despite the problems, however, human rights are also the main tools we have against the cannibalism of public and private power and the narcissism of rights. Human rights are the utopian element behind legal rights. Rights are the building block of a liberal legal system. Human rights are its claim to justice and as such impossible and future looking. Human rights are parasites on the body of rights, judging the host. There is a poetry in human rights that defies the rationalism of law . . . [54]

Douzinas' 'textbook' did not, it is hoped, represent his final position on human rights, or on the gulf between law and justice. Despite the short-comings noted above, it was work of the greatest seriousness and importance. It was in no sense a textbook, but nevertheless a text no student of human rights, scholar or activist could afford to ignore. As Douzinas correctly asserts:[55] '. . . most human rights textbooks introduce their topic by present-ing the standard liberal theories of rights, as if there is no theory of human rights independent of rights theories.' Douzinas accepted this challenge, even if he did not find full success. Most vital of all, Douzinas was interrogat-ing, with much greater sophistication and range of reference than any other contemporary writer, the problem of finding a way back to politics, to human self-realisation. In his previous publications, Douzinas tended to dismiss human rights discourse as a Kantian mystification.[56] Now it is 'the necessary and impossible claim of law to justice', and Douzinas permits himself to assert: 'Human rights are the utopian futural aspect of law.'[57] However, I would argue that this position is implausible in the face of real struggles for human rights in the face of cruel and undiminishing oppression at the hands of repressive regimes and in the face of 'globalisation'. To fight to prevent and seek redress for violations of human rights is not to aspire to utopia. It is to struggle to provide the conditions here and now to become more human. Douzinas had arrived at a blind alley.

Douzinas' interpretation of Hegel's central dialectic of the struggle for recognition also disappoints. He appears to miss the point of the 'master–slave' dialectic, its bitter necessity in the appearance of consciousness as an attribute of human social being,[58] and this leads him to the surprising conclu-sion that there is a 'symmetrical reciprocity' between the two parties, and that the end of dialectics is the moment when 'the same becomes the synthesis of the same and the different'.[59] Hegel, and Habermas, are wrong if their con-clusion is an apotheosis of the Prussian, or indeed the German or European state. Honneth's attempted development can be criticised, as does Douzinas,

---

54 Douzinas (2000) p. 245.   55 Douzinas (2000) pp. 373–374.
56 On many occasions he playfully denounced this author as a Kantian.
57 Douzinas (2000) p. 250.   58 Douzinas (2000) p. 272.   59 Douzinas (2000) p. 345.

for its timid social democracy. Neverthless, Douzinas' exposition of Honneth seems to provide a way out of his own impasse:

> But if rights help constitute the subject through other-recognition, instead of being attributes of an atomic and isolated existence, they are deeply intersubjective. A second consequence is that rights, whether civil, economic or cultural, are deeply political: they presuppose logically and construct politically a community. Rights are not eternal, inalienable or natural.[60]

For me, this is Douzinas at his best. He does not need to move to his actual conclusion: 'Their function is to bestow social identity and community identity on their bearers.' Instead, the passage cited has perhaps laid the foundation for a new research project: of human rights, especially economic, social and cultural rights, as ineradicably intersubjective and political.

Five years later, Douzinas and his colleague Adam Gearey[61] returned to the theme of human rights in the context of a major work on *Critical Jurisprudence*, as 'The Political Philosophy of Justice'. Some passages in this text are taken verbatim from *The End of Human Rights*, especially when dealing with Bloch and Marx, to the advantage of the former and disadvantage of the latter.[62] What is more significant is the evolution of Douzinas' views on human rights.

The most interesting formulations of the new book develop out of a further new analysis of the dialectic of recognition, even if this time Axel Honneth does not figure, and the burden of interpreting Hegel falls to Charles Taylor. There is one formulation with which I agree unreservedly. That is that human rights have a 'deeply agonistic character'.[63]

In this text, in contrast to *The End of Human Rights*, the authors do have something to say about group rights. A not entirely convincing distinction is drawn between 'man' and 'human' in 'human rights', where, according to the authors, each word is empty of meaning, and can be attached to any concept – a 'floating signifier'; and the 'humanity' of human rights, which is not just an 'empty signified', but carries an enormous symbolic capital, '. . . endowed by the Revolutions and Declarations and augmented by every new struggle for the recognition of human rights'.[64] This is described as a 'symbolic excess' which somehow turns the 'human' again into a 'floating signifier' which participants in struggle will want to co-opt to their cause.

---

60 Douzinas (2000) p. 274.   61 Douzinas and Gearey (2005).
62 See p. 176 of *The End*, p. 99 of *Critical Jurisprudence*; p.181 of *TE*, p. 103 of *CJ*; p. 165 of *TE*, p. 215 of *CJ*.
63 Douzinas and Gearey (2005) p. 196.   64 Douzinas and Gearey (2005) p. 191.

But this agonism is placed in the context of individual recognition for the individual's unique identity. Thus, in a statement I find deeply problematic, but which closes the section on human rights: 'Human rights create selves in this intricate but paradoxical inter-twining with identity and desire.'[65]

It is against this background that it is possible to begin to understand an earlier formulation, in which the authors seek to develop Bloch's combination of natural law and social utopia 'in a postmodern perspective'. It is apparent that 'postmodern' here means the peculiarly Douzinasian mix of post-structuralist philosophy and Lacanian psychoanalysis.

The formulation in question is as follows:

> The utopia projected by the human rights imaginary would be a social organisation that recognises and protects the existential integrity of people expressed in their imaginary domain.[66]

But surely this is not only no concrete utopia, but no utopia at all. I much prefer Slavoj Žižek's appeal to utopia, when he writes:

> . . . although, as to their positive content, the Communist regimes were mostly a dismal failure, generating terror and misery, at the same time they opened up a certain space, the space of utopian expectations, which, among other things, enabled us to measure the failure of the really existing Socialism itself.[67]

And what is meant by a 'human rights imaginary'? The authors explain that for them human rights, or, more precisely, the discourse of human rights, supports a 'fantasy of integrity', which is inextricably bound with the desire of the other. A little later the authors refer to the 'redeeming feature of existential integrity', which is the work of the imaginary. This fantasy of integrity helps in turn to construct our radically inter-subjective selves.

This at first might appear to pile obscurity upon obscurity. However, it leads to a further explanation in an entirely different register. That is, according to the authors, when the struggle against injustice takes the form of human rights, that is, when people fight injustice using the language of human rights, human rights themselves 'become invested with' or acquire the content of, the energy and creativity of the fantasy, imaginary, or imagination, as it is variously described.

Despite my other criticisms, this is the point at which I find myself very

---

65 Douzinas and Gearey (2005) p. 197.   66 Douzinas and Gearey (2005) p. 104.
67 Žižek (2004a) p. 513.

close to these authors. It is my own case that human rights originate in and are invested with the revolutionary struggles in which they arise. I would locate the three generations of human rights fairly and squarely in the French Revolution, Russian Revolution, and the anti-colonial struggles of the 1960s. It is my case that the rights of each generation are re-invested with political – even revolutionary – content each time and only when they are re-appropriated in struggle. This is a philosophically realist perspective in which ideas and words – discourse – are not simply rhetoric but can acquire causal powers and effects. But I suggest that the authors' approach is not only irredeemably idealist, but also leads them to significant errors – again.

Thus, a passage analysing problems of recognition refers to 'self-develop-ment' (its denial includes exploitation and violence), 'self-determination' (in the context of democratic decision-making), and 'self-governance' (in the context of decolonisation).[68] These three terms seem to be used interchangeably. Yet it is 'self-determination' which has, as I have shown in Chapter 1, acquired a scandalous and revolutionary content through the Russian Revolution and the decolonisation battles. To use the term 'self-governance' in this context is not only an error, but is symptomatic of a failure to grasp the material revolutionary content of human rights.

This, I suggest, is the reason why for Douzinas and Gearey human rights are either a utopian fantasy or a component in a programme of individual self-development. Here again, the spirit of Heidegger lurks close by.

As I have already indicated, Douzinas' latest text, while purportedly devoted also to the topic of human rights, represents yet another dramatic turn in the orientation of this always unexpected scholar. This time, Douzinas is fascinated by what he describes, early in the book, as the 'dark ruminations of Carl Schmitt[69] and Giorgio Agamben,[70] his contemporary disciple'.[71] His reading of Schmitt and Agamben is mediated by the ultra-Schmittean book he was instrumental in publishing, William Rasch's *Sovereignty and Its Discontents*,[72] a work he describes as 'extremely interesting'. While Bloch is mentioned only a couple of times, and not discussed, Schmitt appears more often than even the Index, with 11 entries, would suggest. I counted at least five more substantive references. The tone of these references is instructive. Despite brutal attacks, Habermas is obliged to confess that Schmitt 'may have carried the day'.[73] Douzinas refers a page further on to Schmitt's 'prescience',[74] and a passage begins 'according to Carl Schmitt . . .'.[75]. Indeed, 'according to Schmitt' and similar formulations appear several times.[76] Douzinas refers at

68 Douzinas and Gearey (2005) pp. 188–189.
69 Schmitt (1985); Schmitt (1996); and Schmitt (2003).
70 Especially Agamben (1998); and Agamben (2005).   71 Douzinas (2007) p. 6.
72 Rasch (2005).   73 Douzinas (2007) p. 171.   74 Douzinas (2007) p. 172.
75 Douzinas (2007) pp. 172–173.   76 Douzinas (2007) pp. 161, 256.

one point to 'Carl Schmitt's influential theory . . .',[77] which is certainly accurate in his own case. However, 'dark ruminations' is mild criticism of a scholar of the extreme right, the 'crown jurist of the Third Reich'. I prefer the work of Jan-Werner Müller, who has brilliantly analysed Schmitt's malign influence in post World War II European thought, especially among authoritarian Catholic scholars.[78]

There is one critical passage, leading incidentally to an important formulation on human rights. A discussion of Jean-Luc Nancy leads Douzinas to 'understand the error of Carl Schmitt and his followers'.[79] For Douzinas, Schmitt's famous 'emphasis on the relationship between friend and enemy is extremely perceptive as regards the international stage'; but the price Schmitt pays is 'a largely incorrect picture of domestic politics', which 'underplays or even misunderstands the importance of internal social and political conflict'. Astonishingly for me, Douzinas continues: 'isn't this precisely the operation of human rights too?'

> Human rights claims and struggles bring to the surface the exclusion, domination and exploitation and the inescapable strife that permeates social and political life. But at the same time, they conceal the deep roots of conflict and domination by framing struggle and resistance in the terms of legal and individual remedies, which, if successful, lead to small individual improvements and a marginal rearrangement of the social edifice.[80]

The attentive reader will have noted that this formulation is the precise opposite of my own. In Douzinas' world, it is the critic who 'keeps the rift open', and discovers and fights 'for transcendence in immanence'. The masses don't come into it!

Similarly, Douzinas asserts that 'human rights are protected or violated locally',[81] and that 'despite the various international agreements and mechanisms, it must be emphasised that human rights are violated or protected at the local level'.[82] He even declares: 'Human rights can meaningfully survive only within the context of the nation-state.'[83]

Chapter 1 of this book, and all the succeeding arguments, place me in diametrical opposition to Douzinas.[84] I look forward to the continuing debate.

---

77 Douzinas (2007) p. 280.   78 Müller (2003).   79 Douzinas (2007) p. 109.
80 Douzinas (2007) pp. 109–110.   81 Douzinas (2007) p. 14.
82 Douzinas (2007) p. 26.   83 Douzinas (2007) p. 231.
84 I should also note that I appear, on pp. 177–178, note 3, as believing the precise opposite of what I in fact believe; and a similar fate befalls Robert Fine on p. 169.

Perrin

Compared to the text of Perrin's recent formative article, Douzinas' style is indeed that of a textbook – demanding, but written *en clair*. Perrin's work is sometimes obscure, but repays close attention, as a compelling critique from a quite different direction. The '. . . relativist or postmodern idea of difference' lies at the heart of his discussion.[85] His choice as primary reference of Maurice Blanchot, who died in 2003, is also at first glance surprising. Blanchot is best known for his 'constant engagement with the "question of literature", a simultaneous enactment and interrogation of the profoundly strange experience of writing'.[86] He was close to Georges Bataille and Emmanuel Levinas, and although, like Douzinas, he had a clear debt to Heidegger, his position is to be distinguished from Heidegger's account of seizing my own existence as my existence – 'I myself am in that I will die.'[87] As Lars Iyer explains it: '. . . what Blanchot asks us to consider is a relation to the death of the other that debars me from the possibility of taking over my own death and thereby assuming myself as myself. To be before the Other as that other dies is to be affected by that death in such a way that my own self-relation is transgressed.'[88] In this way, Perrin wishes, 'but only very indicatively' to '. . . situate at least the possibility of eliciting the alternative understanding of human rights that I am outlining here in the *Universal Declaration of Human Rights*'.[89]

Perrin proceeds economically. He engages with two texts: the UN's 1948 Universal Declaration of Human Rights, and the series of appeals run by Amnesty International in the UK broadsheet press during the 1990s, of which he selects two. These are, as Perrin points out, designed to '. . . confront "us" with images and descriptions of the pain, suffering and death of others'. He argues that the basis of the appeal does not lie in the 'assumption of the adequacy of language or indeed the adequacy of human rights'.[90] This brings Perrin to a consideration of the 'disaster', the Holocaust – '. . . thought, experience, language: all are inadequate to the disaster.'[91] Thus, he contends, 'It is exactly because language falls short of the disaster that, vitally, it always falls short of making one suffer what the other has suffered.'[92] This 'subversion' is the impossibility of communicating or sharing the suffering of another, which, however, must be communicated. But this involves the demand by Amnesty International to its readers to listen to its appeals. The paradox is that one must listen to that which cannot be communicated.

This is a real paradox, and is a central difficulty for the discourse of human rights. It is sensitively explicated by Perrin. His response is as follows:

---

85 Perrin (2004) p. 139.
86 See, for a rough introduction, http://www.spikemagazine.com/0602blanchot.php.
87 Heidegger (1985) p. 317.   88 Iyer (2001) pp. 66–67.   89 Perrin (2004) p. 143.
90 Perrin (2004) p. 138.   91 Perrin (2004) p. 139.   92 Perrin (2004) p. 141.

'Amnesty International's demand for language may be understood accordingly: not as a demand to represent the other's suffering but rather as a demand that one signify its unpresentability . . .'[93] and 'the demand for as little language as possible, as little as is necessary . . .'[94]. And, he concludes, '. . . the demand for language, for law, and so for human rights, remains insatiable' – with Amnesty International '. . . there has to be a "deluge of letters", "an infinite chain" of human rights'.[95]

I have no doubt as to the deep seriousness of Perrin's postmodern project. This is no exercise in playfulness or deconstruction for the sake of paradox. Rather, he responds with full humanity to the horrors disclosed by Amnesty International's appeals. It is for this reason above all that reflection on the paradox he so accurately locates at the heart of human rights discourse will benefit every aspiring human rights scholar or activist. It is also quite clear that for Perrin there can be no question of natural law or indeed any other philosophical foundations for human rights after the Holocaust. On this point he is more explicit than Douzinas. What I miss, however, is the 'alternative understanding of human rights' which Perrin promises, even if in a highly tentative manner. And, as always, the question remains – what is to be done? The final chapter of this book endeavours to explore at least one mode of active response – and its shortcomings.

Conclusion

I cannot conclude this chapter without reference to Slavoj Žižek's ironic pronouncement on 'postmodernism'. He refers to:

> . . . the resigned 'postmodern' acceptance of the fact that society is a complex network of 'subsystems', which is why a certain level of 'alienation' is constitutive of social life, so that a totally self-transparent society is a utopia with totalitarian potentials. (In this sense, it is Habermas who is 'postmodern', in contrast to Adorno who, in spite of all his political compromises, to the end remained attached to a radically utopian vision of revolutionary redemption.)'[96]

There is no reason to doubt the deep seriousness of Douzinas, Gearey or Perrin. All are seeking for a formulation of human rights which escapes from the unbearable boredom of official discourse. However, there is a world of difference between projects of self-improvement or identity construction, and the uncertainty and risk of political intervention capable of breaking the boundaries of the social world.

---

93 Perrin (2004) p. 142.   94 Perrin (2004) p. 147.   95 Perrin (2004) p. 145.
96 Žižek (2004a) p. 514.

It is a constant claim of postmodernism is that it is anti-foundational, that it militates against totalities, that it expresses the multiple voices of difference. I want now to make a counter-claim: that the postmodern is answered not by the modern, but by the *classical*.

For this purpose I want to point to a singular philosophical constellation – Spinoza, Negri, Deleuze, Balibar, Badiou. What unites them is their constant reference to Spinoza, who not only, in Deleuze's words, was the 'Christ of philosophy',[97] but also, as Negri asserted of Spinoza in his great monograph of 1981, 'His terrific metaphysical installation was quickly recognised as politics and presented itself immediately as revolutionary thought.'[98] Balibar in his own excellent small book on Spinoza explains that freedom, for the Spinozist, '. . . does not consist in the absence of causes for human action. It is neither a right that we acquire at birth nor an eschatological perspective that is indefinitely deferred.[99] For our *liberation has always already begun*. It is the *conatus* itself, the movement by which activity preponderates over passivity.'[100]

One of Deleuze's most powerful works in my opinion is *Expressionism in Philosophy: Spinoza*,[101] and, as already noted, Spinoza plays a central role in Deleuze's philosophy. What Badiou establishes through a close and sympathetic reading is that Deleuze subscribes without a trace of equivocation to Spinoza's univocity of Being. Deleuze said in *Difference and Repetition*: 'There has only ever been one ontological proposition: Being is univocal.' As Badiou notes, this is fully compatible with the existence of multiple *forms* of Being: '. . . this is true of Spinoza's Substance, which is immediately expressed by an infinity of attributes.'[102]

In his work on Deleuze, Badiou goes on to show that, far from repudiating the notion of ground, Deleuze has 'a sort of unwavering love for the world as it is, a love that, beyond optimism and pessimism alike, signifies that it is always futile, always falling short of thought to *judge* the world'.[103] For Badiou, his philosophy, like Deleuze's philosophy, is resolutely *classical*. He means by 'classical' any philosophy that does not submit to the critical injunctions of Kant, which considers that Kantian indictment of metaphysics as null and void, which upholds against neo-Kantianism that '. . . the rethinking of the univocity of ground is a necessary task for the world in which we are living today'.[104]

Indeed, Badiou has condemned 'postmodernist' philosophy, which in rebutting grand narratives leads to a 'kind of general equivalence of discourses, a rule of virtuosity and obliquity', and tries to 'compromise the very idea of truth in the fall of historic narratives'.[105] For Badiou, the discourse of postmodernism is 'nothing but modern sophistry'. I concur.

---

97 Badiou (2000) p. 101.   98 Negri (1991) p. 266, n. 1.   99 *Pace* Douzinas.
100 Balibar (1998).   101 Deleuze (1992).   102 Badiou (2000) pp. 23–24.
103 Badiou (2000) p. 43.   104 Badiou (2000) p. 45.   105 Badiou (1999) p. 117.

In this chapter I criticised two scholars who are theorists working in the UK, both of whom draw their inspiration from continental European philosophy. My next chapter does not withdraw from theory, but attempts to dig deeper. I explore a theoretical impasse at the heart of debates on international law or human rights: the stranglehold of methodological individualism.

Chapter 9

The challenge of methodological individualism

Introduction

This chapter analyses a key problem for international law and human rights, already sketched in the preceding chapters. This is the prevailing ideological foundation for human rights discourse namely liberalism, and especially methodological individualism. The emergent powers materialism to which I referred in my Introduction requires that groups, and group rights, be given appropriate recognition.

Indeed, Tony Carty argues that international law loses cogency and determinacy through neglecting ethnicity and nationhood.[1] While not following him into Husserlian phenomenology,[2] I agree this is particularly true of minority and group rights. These are areas in which the law has recently made the most sweeping territorial claims. There is now a burgeoning treaty-based law of minority rights,[3] and of the rights of indigenous peoples.[4] However, this law and its implementation mechanisms are often perceived as irrelevant by precisely the persons to whom it is addressed. The argument of this chapter is that there are theoretical reasons for this, and the beginnings of solutions are only to be found in another methodology.

A new approach must distinguish itself from the present dominant discourse. In a paper on the content of minority rights, John Packer asserts, as he has done consistently,[5] that there is 'Human Rights Philosophy'.[6] This is

---

1 Anthony Carty (1997).   2 Anthony Carty (1996) p. 22.

3 This includes: (1) the 1966 *International Covenant on Civil and Political Rights*, Article 27; (2) the *UN Declaration on the Rights of Minorities* adopted without a vote on 18 December 1992; (3) the 1994 Council of Europe's *Framework Convention for the Protection of National Minorities*, opened for signature on 1 February 1995; and (4) the inspiration for the Framework Convention, the Conference (now Organisation) for Security and Cooperation in Europe's 1990 *Document of the Copenhagen Meeting of the Conference on the Human Dimension*.

4 Notably Convention (No. 169) Concerning Indigenous and Tribal Peoples in Independent Countries, adopted by the General Conference of the ILO, Geneva, June 27, 1989. Entered into force 5 September 1991.

5 See Packer (1993) p. 23.   6 Packer (1996) p. 121.

the philosophy of liberalism, especially as formulated, in answer to communitarian critics, by the Argentine Kantian Carlos Nino.[7] Liberalism requires and entails individualism. There is considerable empirical evidence for Packer's claim. To date, all human rights instruments are resolutely individualist in content; all the relevant instruments since 1966 – and there were none before that date – refer to the persons who are members of minority groups. For Packer, no deviation is permitted. Even Kymlicka's attempt to extend the boundaries of liberalism so as to take account of a right to a 'societal culture'[8] is condemned by Packer as lending itself to 'cultural relativist arguments which can lead to nationalism' – itself a slippery slope to fascism.

Liberalism may be the dominant discourse, but it is not uncontested. That is not to say that the only alternative is one or another form of communitarianism – indeed, this chapter condemns a number of unnecessary and confusing binary oppositions. Instead, I would argue for a perspective and method drawing from Hegel; in short, a dialectical approach to the problem. Here I draw on the work of Michael Salter.

Using this approach, this chapter seeks to address a number of aspects of the problem of minority and group rights. First, I repeat an ontological argument made by me and by others elsewhere that there are social entities other than individuals; indeed, that it is not possible except trivially to recognise persons except in a context of collectivities. It is part of my argument that groups can and must not be hypostasised or treated as rigid and unchanging (or, as Packer puts it, 'fairly pure and virtually static social groups'). Social being is as dynamic if not more so than personal being. If this is the case, then the law should recognise and engage with such entities.

Second, even if it is accepted that the law should account for groups, a number of more practical (at first sight) problems arise. Which groups should be included in or excluded from those the law should recognise? What about homosexuals, blacks in the United States, immigrants in any country? Should the rights of these groups be recognised or adjudicated?

Third, the law has often successfully engaged with and adjudicated in respect of groups, and, I would argue, should do in this case. While there is a perfectly understandable aversion to group rights, especially in the Common Law tradition, because of the perversions of Nazism, the common law has been perfectly adept at dealing with groups of many kinds. Nevertheless, this has been in the context of freedom of choice, of a special kind of voluntarism. This finds its way through into the recent writings of a number of English authors.

Fourth, I argue that none of these problems is insoluble – on one condition. This is that the law learns new ways to recognise change and dynamism, and the extraordinary diversity of groups and minorities – I claim that this

---

7 Nino (1993).   8 Kymlicka (1995); and Kymlicka (1995).

can be done – but only by way of a qualitative break from previous theoretical practice.

The ontological status of groups

Peoples are the bearers of one of the most important rights to have become enshrined in international law in the second half of this century. Though necessarily composed of individuals, peoples thus have their own interests and claims independently of those who compose them, subject to questions of the dynamics and trajectory of the group itself. The rights of peoples are, of course, highly contested, not least as to whether these rights extend beyond political questions of decolonisation within existing boundaries, limited always by the *uti possidetis* doctrine.[9] There is a continuing problem of definition. James Crawford concludes that 'peoples' rights embodies a category, not a definition. What constitutes a people may be different for the purpose of different rights.'[10] For example, the right to existence in his view extends to a much greater range of groups than the right to self-determination.

At all other levels of international law-making, save for the comparatively new area of indigenous rights, groups do not appear save through their members, who only individually (though sometimes in common with members of their groups) are the bearers of rights. In this way, the law often proves inadequate in the face of gross violations of rights. For example, the European Convention on Human Rights contains no free-standing provision prohibiting discrimination against minorities, and no other minority rights provision. This means that for the large number of Turkish Kurds who brought cases to the Strasbourg organs complaining of grave violations of their cultural rights,[11] quite apart from the mass destruction of villages and property, with the way of life that goes with them,[12] there were no adequate or effective remedies.[13]

If this is the case for law, however, it is not so for political science, sociology, and philosophy. In each of these fields of enquiry, powerful arguments have been made for the independent existence of groups and collectivities; for their status as moral agents.

Will Kymlicka, for example, has had no difficulty, in the context of North American tribes, in saying, for example, that 'nations can choose not to exercise their legitimate rights'.[14] Nations are, here, moral agents. Indeed, the area

9 See Crawford (1988).   10 Crawford (1988) p. 170.
11 See Pierse (1997) p. 325. She concludes that: 'more recent developments in the international protection of minority rights would seem to suggest a new emerging international consensus that positive State action is necessary in order to fully ensure the rights of minorities to express their identity and enjoy their own culture.'
12 Reidy, Hampson and Boyle (1997) p. 161.   13 Bowring (1996) p. 23.
14 Kymlicka (1995) p. 256.

of greatest concern to him is the problem of what he terms 'intra-group relations', the right of a group against its own members, as distinguished from the rights of particular groups against the larger society.[15] He is in favour, in appropriate cases, of special status for groups, so as to maintain the individual's rights to a 'societal culture'. However, he distinguishes between the autonomy rights of long-established minorities, and the more limited 'poly-ethnic rights' possessed by immigrants. Perry Keller has criticised Kymlicka's very use of the concept 'societal culture', ultimately because this 'resurrects the outworn concept of bounded national cultures'.[16] In Keller's view, Kymlicka has failed to recognise 'widely recognised observations' about culture: first, that group identity is born out of social interaction, not essential, objectified group attributes; second, that groups have no one identity but a variety of possibilities; and third, that ethnicity is not per se more significant than any other aspect of group identity. He stresses that each point applies as much to individuals as to groups.[17] He is particularly critical of Kymlicka's 'potentially harmful' distinction between immigrant and indigenous minorities. This critique accurately identifies the tendency of Kymlicka's analysis to create rigid distinctions, reflecting Canadian multicultural practice. But it fails to locate Kymlicka's inadequacy in his individualism and his tendency to hypostasise.

A line of enquiry which is much closer to my own position is pursued by Victor Segesvary, who brings what he calls a socio-cultural analysis to bear.[18] He identifies a 'standard position' according to which the individual is held in a 'virtually sacralised position'.[19] Segesvary questions this position, insisting that the individual human being and his group or community are *ontologically* interdependent – that is the life and destiny of individual and group are inextricably intertwined. He adds: '. . . the community is not only the sum of the individuals who constitute it; it is more because its institutions, mental and symbolic orders and traditional values represent the accumulated experiences and cultural treasures of past generations.'[20] For him, group identity is located in culture and history. It takes the forms of shared symbolism, shared belief and value systems, and common historical consciousness. This is also the position, for example, of Anthony Smith, who speaks of the way in which the 'sense of self is viewed through the prism of symbols and mythologies of the community's heritage'.[21] But Segesvary goes no further than to record the increasing recognition given to minority groups in international instruments. It is these very instruments which are, in my opinion, the problem.

15 Kymlicka (1994) p. 19.   16 Keller (1996) p. 918.
17 Keller (1996) pp. 910–911.   18 Segesvary (1995).
19 This phrase is taken from Donnelly (1999) p. 57.   20 Segesvary (1995) p. 92.
21 Smith (1986) p. 14.

The sociologist Margaret Archer has pursued this line of enquiry significantly further. She seeks to develop a form of realist sociology – realist in a special sense, committed to the independent efficacy of both structure and agency.[22] She deploys Roy Bhaskar's 'ontological realism premised explicitly upon emergence',[23] which can be summarised in six points: (1) societies are irreducible to people; (2) social forms are a necessary condition for any intentional act; (3) their pre-existence establishes their autonomy as possible objects of investigation; (5) their causal power establishes their reality; and (6) the causal power of social forms is mediated through human agency.[24] For her, social realism accentuates the importance of emergent properties, but considers these as proper to the strata in question, and therefore *distinct* from each other and *irreducible* to one another.[25] Emergent properties are *relational*, arising out of combination, where the later reacts back upon the earlier, and has its own causal powers, which are causally irreducible to the powers of its components. This for her signals the *stratified nature of social reality*, where the different strata possess different emergent properties and powers.[26] She insists that:

> Instead of a one-dimensional reality coming to us through the 'hard-data' supplied by the senses, to speak of 'emergence' implies a *stratified* social world including non-observable entities, where talk of its ultimate constituents makes no sense, given that the relational properties pertaining to each stratum are all real, that it is nonsense to discuss whether something (like water) is more real than something else (like hydrogen and oxygen), and that regress as a means of determining 'ultimate constituents' is of no help in this respect and an unnecessary distraction in social or any other type of theorising.[27]

Much social theory, in Archer's view, has sought to confine itself to observables. This perceptual criterion, reducing enquiry to a series of observational statements about people, is, for empiricist individualists, the only guarantor of reality.[28] On the contrary, Archer argues, there are large categories of the social which are ontologically independent from the activities of people presently alive.[29] She stresses that:

> The circumstances confronted by each new generation were not of their making, but they do affect what these contemporary agents can make of them (structural and cultural elaboration) and how they reconstitute themselves in the process (agential elaboration). At any given time,

22 Archer (1995).   23 Archer (1995) p. 136. See also Archer (1996).
24 Archer (1995) p. 137.   25 Archer (1995) p. 14.   26 Archer (1995) p. 9.
27 Archer (1995) p. 50.   28 Archer (1995) p. 8.   29 Archer (1995) p. 145.

structures are the result of human interaction, including the results of the results of that interaction – any of which may be unintended, unwanted and unacknowledged.[30]

Archer is herself primarily concerned with interest groups rather than ethnic minorities, but her insistence that 'sociocultural complexity is an unintended consequence of interaction, which escapes its progenitors to constitute the unacknowledged conditions of action for future agents'[31] seems to me to provide the conceptual context without which adequate study of the problem of group rights is impossible.

For example, the entirely serious work of Marlies Galenkamp suffers, in my view, from the absence of such an approach. She has attempted to conceptualise and analyse collective rights – which she asserts are now *en vogue*.[32] In her review essay 'Much Ado About Nothing?' she recognised that collective rights have to go beyond the 'standard individualistic framework', and rejected the notion that they are simply aggregative, fictional or represent the social dimension of rights. They 'presuppose the presence of non-reducible collectivities, having collective interests'. The paradigmatic case is the collective right to preserve a cultural identity.

Later, she argued that collectivities may be viewed as moral agents, and thus as rights bearers. But she has concluded that collective rights have meaning only in the context of 'tradition', of the struggle of traditional (indigenous or ethnic minorities) to retain their identity. She has subsequently[33] published an extended study in which she counterposes liberal and communitarian conceptions, so as to show that each of them ends in crisis, not least because of the 'inevitability of an antithetical way of thinking'. She too follows Kymlicka in preferring 'constitutional provisions which are flexible enough to allow for legitimate claims of cultural membership, but are not so flexible as to allow systems of cultural oppression'.[34]

There are, then, powerful arguments in favour of recognising the independent efficacity and moral agency of groups. There is a prima facie case for their recognition by the law. But a number of objections are not only routinely made, but arise seemingly inevitably from the nature of minority rights.

Why the law has problems in recognising groups

These are, in essence, three questions. The first is a problem of definition: the question whether some or any groups should be excluded from the category of a group which can claim minority rights. The second is the problem of representation: which individuals or organisations speak or should speak for

---

30 Archer (1995) p. 196.   31 Archer (1995) p. 251.   32 Galenkamp (1992) p. 291.
33 Galenkamp (1993).   34 Galenkamp (1993) p. 185.

the group. The third is the problem of toleration by liberal polities of illiberal practices. For many scholars, these problems, taken separately or together, are prime reasons why the law should never accommodate group rights.

Nigel Rodley, for example, considers the following questions.[35] How can minority demands for special rights be reconciled with the principles of non-discrimination and equality before the law? How can special arrangements for minority groups be reconciled with individual rights? How can special arrangements be reconciled with the rights of minorities within the minority? This last question is crucial for him. When he considers the problem of 'double minorities', of members of a group that is a minority both within the sub-unit of another minority group and of the state as a whole, he argues that the notion of minority rights (apart from indigenous peoples) should be treated as a 'conceptual diversion'. For him the issues at stake are those of equality under the law, non-discrimination, and what he describes as 'substantive human rights' – that is, individual human rights.[36]

The first problem, that of definition, cannot be resolved within the dominant discourse. Rodley asserts: 'Even if international law were to require a recognition of group rights, it could neither identify the group nor lay down the appropriate institutions for any given society.'[37] Kymlicka does not attempt a definition, but, as I have already mentioned, poses a distinction between national minorities, rooted in history and culture, which they seek to defend, with the ultimate possibility of secession; and ethnic minorities, immigrants who have chosen to leave their native culture, and for whom there is no conceivable prospect of state-building. But there are larger and even more diffuse groups, for example, homosexuals. Is there any good reason to include indigenous peoples, but not gays? And what about oppressed majorities, such as in apartheid South Africa? Capotorti's well-known attempt at a definition[38] is expressly limited to Article 27 of the 1966 ICCPR, and excludes non-citizens – and Capotorti is in any event firmly opposed to the recognition by law of claims by groups rather than the persons belonging to them.[39]

Even in the context of indigenous peoples, the problem of definition has proved insoluble. This is precisely the problem which deterred the UN Working Group on Indigenous Populations. At its 14th session in 1996[40] its Chairperson-Rapporteur, Mrs Daes, insisted: '. . . no single definition could capture the diversity of indigenous people world-wide, and all past attempts to achieve both clarity and restrictiveness in the same definition had resulted in greater ambiguity.'

---

35 Rodley (1995) pp. 49–50.   36 Rodley (1995) p. 71.   37 Rodley (1995) p. 64.
38 Capotorti (1979).   39 Capotorti (1992) pp. 509–510.
40 'Discrimination Against Indigenous Peoples' *Report of the Working Group on Indigenous Populations, on its Fourteenth Session* (Geneva, 29 July – 2 August 1996), UN Doc. E/CN.4/Sub.2/1996/21.

Representation poses problems of a different order. How is the minority to appear before the state within whose territory it falls, or before an adjudicating instance, save through representatives? What rights does the state have to impose conditions, for example as to democratic election, or procedures for accountability? And what if there are competing would-be representatives, for example the ANC and PAC in apartheid South Africa? The answer that these are procedural questions – the approach adopted by the Working Group – begs a key question: who is to decide the procedure and its implementation? This is a problem which Rodley simply does not begin to engage with. He simply assumes that groups will have claims which they will assert. For the Human Rights Committee, whose case law he analyses closely, this is true. But, in any event, the Committee only considers claims by individual members of groups – so the problem does not arise for them either. Nonetheless, this is perhaps the crucial problem of relations between minority and host communities.

The third problem, of liberal tolerance, is the question now faced so acutely by the Russian Federation, a secular state with a modern constitution, which has long since ratified the main international instruments and has acceded to the Council of Europe. One of its constituent parts, the Republic of Chechnya, adopted Sharia Law during its brief period of de facto independence from 1997 to 1999, for example in its Criminal Code, and was executing convicted criminals in public. Military intervention from 1994 to 1997 had not been successful in suppressing the movement for Chechen independence. What of the future of the other constituent parts of the Federation?

Russia is not alone in facing such problems. Hanneman points out, in the context of the Baltic states and their ethnic Russian minorities, that 'problems like that of a double minority exist only if group rights do have independent value'.[41] She thinks they do; but her prescription is limited to a call for a 'balance of rights for each minority group . . . by establishing basic individual rights and bolstering these with special group protections only when necessary'.[42] Leslie Green has explored the question of the moral standing of such minorities,[43] and concludes that without respect for internal minorities, 'a liberal society risks becoming a mosaic of tyrannies, colourful perhaps, but hardly free'. Yet Green has to acknowledge that 'it may just be true of some groups that respect for the rights of their internal minorities would undermine them', and that conflict may thus arise.[44]

Each of these problems poses real difficulties for the law, and I do not seek to diminish them. However, they have been exacerbated by political considerations; are not different in kind from problems which have been successfully

---

41 Hanneman (1995) p. 525.   42 Hanneman (1995) p. 527.   43 Green (1994) p. 101.
44 Green (1994) pp. 113–114.

overcome in domestic law; and are perceived as barriers primarily for reasons of methodological individualism and the tendency to freeze living processes into fixed categories.

Politics, and the other side of the common law

As Segesvary and many other writers have pointed out, the 'standard view' of group rights had its origin after the Second World War, and the calamity caused by the failure, on the one hand, of League of Nations procedures to provide effective protection of minorities, and the perversion, on the other, of the bilateral treaty system by Nazi aggression. The perfectly proper moral distaste for recognition of group rights thus engendered has attached itself to later attempts to revive them. For example, Vernon van Dyke published a number of works during the 1970s and 1980s in which he argued strongly for the grant of special rights to ethnic minorities as collective entities.[45] In his view, those in the majority community could insist on individualism and non-discrimination, knowing that this would help to ensure their dominance. Marlies Galenkamp, in her essay asking whether the debate over collective rights was 'much ado about nothing', roundly condemned van Dyke for coming close to a defence of South Africa's apartheid policy.[46] Galenkamp was prepared to acknowledge the existence of collective rights, but was anxious that these should not be established 'empirically' but rather 'normatively', from theoretical first principles, as I have outlined above.

I hope it has been established above that there are powerful arguments for the real existence and moral standing of groups and collectivities. I suggest that the reluctance to recognise group rights has its roots both in the problems I have described, and in political and moral apprehension. For example, Ernest Barker wrote, in 1942, of 'the eruption of the group' in the context of fascism. He swore to defend the freedom of the individual to free association in groups to the end. Indeed, since World War II there has been the strongest resistance, in Anglo-American legal thought, to any notion of the group as possibly primordial, as constituting the ineluctable context of individuals' lives, rather than a club to be joined or left at will.

Yet despite the staunch individualism which permeates most English language writing on minority rights,[47] English law has not found too much difficulty, at least since the fifteenth century, in recognising and accommodating groups of many kinds. As explained by the so-called 'legal pluralists' at the

---

45 van Dyke (1995) p. 200. See also van Dyke (1977).
46 Galenkamp (1992) p. 293.
47 See, for example, Higgins (1994), especially p. 105: '. . . human rights are demands of particularly high intensity made by individuals *vis-a-vis* their governments'; or Rodley (1995) who considers that '. . . international law does not and cannot reasonably be expected to recognise minority group rights as such', p. 64.

turn of the last century, all sorts of unincorporated associations made themselves perfectly acceptable to the law by way of the institution of the trust, and the interposition of trustees. Thus, F. W. Maitland pointed in 1904 to such institutions as the Inns of Court, Lloyds, the London Stock Exchange, the London Library, and the Jockey Club – as well as the gentlemen's clubs of Pall Mall, and trade unions.[48] For him, groups were real persons, with wills of their own.

Here is another example. The same Ernest Barker, in 1915, noted that 'while law has not been tender to the State, it has been tender enough ... to all manner of groups. Here we touch on that peculiarly English thing, the Trust.' For him, the trust had 'sheltered group-life more fully than any legal recognition of the "real personality" of groups could have done'.[49] England, he added, is a place where groups and associations have always flourished, have always been budding and maturing.

Of course, the law of trusts does not exist primarily to benefit disadvantaged social groups, and is as full of complexity as any other area of English law. Furthermore, most of the groups referred to by Maitland had a somewhat privileged relation to power in society. The exception was the trade unions, and it is interesting that Maitland, in the work referred to, was writing shortly after the *Taff Vale* decision[50] in the House of Lords. He could not predict what the result of trade union agitation would be, but, for him, 'the one thing that it is safe to predict is that in England social policy will take precedence over jurisprudential consideration'.[51] This proved to be the case. It is well known that A. V. Dicey strongly disapproved of the Trade Disputes Act 1906, recognising trade unions and giving them certain legal immunities; his conception of the rule of law excluded special protections for specific groups in society.[52]

My point is that English law, and the common-law tradition in general, have generally had the flexibility and resourcefulness to adapt to new demands, and especially the appearance of new groups. Lack of internal democracy or procedurally fair representation has not prevented recognition – the Inns of Court and the gentlemen's clubs have not been notoriously democratic institutions. Problems of exclusion and representation have regularly been overcome. Difficulties for the law have had a more political than jurisprudential or procedural character. I suggest that it is now somewhat anomalous that ethnic or linguistic groups, national minorities or homosexuals, should be denied recognition as groups.

---

48 Maitland (1995) p. 14 *et seq.*   49 Barker (1995) p. 81.
50 *Taff Vale Railway Co v Amalgamated Society of Railway Servants* [1901] AC 426.
51 Maitland (1995) p. 23.   52 See McEldowney (1985) p. 52.

The complex dynamism of groups

I have argued above that groups exist, are efficacious, and are moral agents. For most of the groups with which the contemporary law of minority rights is concerned, individuals did not choose entry to the group, though they may choose exit from it. It is also always the case, if trivially, that groups do not exist apart from their members. That is, each person who belongs to a group is not only constituted to a greater or lesser extent by the group into which she is born, but also reproduces that group (including participating perhaps in its complete assimilation and disappearance) during her lifetime. Moreover, there have been few if any periods in time or places in space in which a group has lived in isolation from humankind. So, I would argue, a group identity is never constructed by the persons who compose the group. No significant minority has come into existence through an act of will or choice. Rather, group identity is reproduced, subject always to more or less evolutionary change.

Take Benedict Anderson, best known for his description of nations as 'imagined communities'. This does not mean that national communities are imaginary in the sense of illusory, since at the root of such imagination is language. Anderson points out that 'no-one can give the date for the birth of a language. Each looms up imperceptibly out of a horizonless past . . . languages thus appear rooted beyond almost anything else in contemporary societies.' Languages are thus inseparably linked to histories:

> If nationalness has about it an aura of fatality, it is nonetheless a fatality embedded in history . . . For it shows that from the start the nation was conceived in language, not in blood, and that one could be 'invited into' the imagined community. Thus, even today, the most insular nations accept the principle of naturalisation (wonderful word) no matter how difficult they make it in practice.[53]

That is, Anderson is here conveying both the contingent historical (and for the individual, inevitable though escapable) reality and the porosity of national belonging.

The same is true for culture. Abdullahi An-Na'im has commented on the fact that: '. . . one of the apparent paradoxes of culture is the way it combines stability with dynamic continuous change . . . induced by internal adjustments as well as external influences.'[54] He stresses that both kinds of change must be justified through culturally approved mechanisms and adapted to pre-existing norms and institutions. Otherwise the culture loses the coherence and stability that enable it to reproduce and survive.

---

53 Anderson (1983) pp. 144–145.   54 An-Na'im (1992) p. 27.

There are a number of ways in which groups (and their cultures) may change. First, there is the possibility of conquest, of deportation, of forced migration. The fact of diaspora may strengthen ethnic or national identity, but will inevitably expose the bearers to different cultures and beliefs. Second, and part of the first, there is the inevitability of intermarriage, of mixed parentage. The Crimean Tatars, who are the subject of research by this author, have a strong identity born of long history and recent terrible injustice. Nonetheless, their rate of intermarriage with the surrounding, primarily ethnic Russian, community in Crimea is, according to their own leaders, about 30 per cent. It is well know that the proportion of persons of mixed descent in former Yugoslavia is very high. Third, and permeating both the previous categories, is the ever-present fact of cultural, linguistic and religious interpenetration. Thomas Franck has succinctly described the 'definitional categories and the realities they obscure' – the fact that no nation state is a nation state.[55]

All these – and more – are the reasons why minorities, national or otherwise, are so hard to define or categorise, and the rights they claim are so variable. But they are none the less real and independently effective, and the consequences of failure to recognise them are no less dangerous and uncontrollable.

Dialectics and minority rights

Perhaps the common law has been able to adapt to all manner of (voluntary) groups. Whatever the normative status of the English common law, however, international human rights law should not be expected to achieve adequacy and legitimacy in the recognition of minority rights simply by a process of organic, haphazard and partial development over centuries. This is least of all the case where the passions of justice and identity are in play. Instead, theoretical resources must be found from which to develop forms of law and procedure which are adequate and legitimate.

It is my case that liberalism and analytical philosophy do not provide those resources. The only philosophical tradition expressly premised on change and dynamic development is dialectic, as practised from the Greeks through Hegel[56] to the present day. A renewed interest in the theory of recognition as a means of apprehending multiculturalism and minority rights is exemplified by the recent collection on the politics of recognition, which contains a debate between Charles Taylor and Jurgen Habermas.[57] Taylor argues for a *presumption* of equal worth as a logical extension of the politics of dignity – the presumption that traditional cultures have value.[58] Habermas' reply is

---

55 Franck (1996) p. 365.   56 See, for example, O'Neill (1996).
57 Taylor (1994), with Habermas' afterword 'Struggles for Recognition in the Democratic State', pp. 105–148.
58 Taylor (1994) p. 68.

very interesting: for him, the primary question that multiculturalism raises is the question of the ethical neutrality of law and politics.[59] This means that the democratic elaboration of a system of rights has to incorporate not only general political goals but also the collective goals that are articulated in struggles for recognition.[60] However, Habermas' proceduralism inclines him to doubt the utility of recognising collective rights: these, he argues, would 'overtax a theory of rights tailored to individual persons':

> Even if such group rights could be granted in the democratic consti-
> tutional state, they would not only be unnecessary but questionable from
> a normative point of view. For in the last analysis the protection of forms
> of life and traditions in which identities are formed is supposed to serve
> the recognition of their members; it does not represent a kind of preser-
> vation of species by administrative means.[61]

Habermas also insists that the universalism of legal principles is reflected in a procedural consensus, which must be embedded in the context of a historic-ally specific political culture through a kind of constitutional patriotism.[62]

Here Axel Honneth's account is superior to Habermas'. Habermas notes that the struggle over historically unredeemed claims is a struggle for legitim-ate rights in which collective actors are involved, 'combating a lack of respect for their dignity'. He cites Axel Honneth as showing that in this struggle for recognition, collective experiences of violated integrity are articulated.[63] Honneth, however, argues[64] that Habermas' conception of communicative action is excessively limited, and that it must admit collective as well as indi-vidual actors as the bearers of communicative action. He adds that: 'The social struggle over the legitimacy of valid norms unambiguously represents a form of interaction that is realised not only between particular subjects but also between social groups . . . it becomes clear that organised or unorganised groups are also able to relate to one another communicatively.'[65]

In a more recent work,[66] Honneth also criticises the way in which Hegel's turn to the philosophy of consciousness in the *Phenomenology of Spirit* allowed him to 'completely lose sight of the idea of an original intersubjec-tivity of human kind and blocks the way to a completely different solution that would have consisted in making the necessary distinctions between vari-ous degrees of personal autonomy within the framework of a theory of

---

59 Habermas (1994) p. 122.   60 Habermas (1994) p. 124.
61 Habermas (1994) p. 130. He adds: 'When a culture has become reflexive, the only traditions and forms of life that can sustain themselves are those that bind their members while at the same time subjecting themselves to critical examination and leaving later generations the option of learning from other traditions or converting and setting out for other shores.'
62 Habermas (1994) p. 135.   63 Habermas (1994) p. 108.   64 Honneth (1993).
65 Honneth (1993) p. 275.   66 Honneth (1996).

intersubjectivity'.[67] Honneth argues that had Hegel carried the logic of this 'ethical learning process' into the constitution of ethical community, 'that would have opened up the form of social interaction in which each person, in his or her individual particularity can reckon with a feeling of recognition based on solidarity'.[68] The goal for Honneth is that of defining 'an abstract horizon of ethical values that would be open to the widest variety of life-goals without losing the solidarity-generating force of collective identity-formation'.[69] He refers to this as a 'moral grammar of social conflicts'. There is the sense here of a more dynamic and materialist dialectic than that at work in Habermas, one more in tune with the turbulence and passion of minority struggles.

It is clear that there is a new interest in dialectic on the part of some legal theorists.[70] For example, Michael Salter, reviewing Habermas' *Between Facts and Norms* (1996), commends Habermas' use of 'critical theory's familiar dialectical categories, methods and modes of argumentation, for example, "reciprocal mediation", "immanent critique", "contradiction", the implicit "unity of apparent polar opposites", and "totality" '.[71] Salter does not fail to notice the idealism and conservatism of Habermas' limiting conviction that communication is the medium in which *all forms* of social life emerge and are then both co-ordinated and reproduced, nor the Kantian transcendental procedure whereby the work seeks to demonstrate the conditions of possibility of – the German (patriotic) constitutional state.

Salter himself has described a dialectical approach to comparative law.[72] He notes the way in which reductionism loses sight of cultural diversity, distinctiveness and complexity in comparative law. In its place he advocates a 'negative' dialectic method which has its roots in the German post-war school of critical theory, notably Adorno. For him, a dialectical approach will typic-ally proceed from an analysis of internal contradictions which result when-ever dualisms are allowed to structure a research programme around either/or choices. Such analysis requires cultural mediation, by which he means an empirical analysis of the various strata and relations of reciprocal cultural interaction. Analysing law dialectically means working up to richer concep-tions of the concrete through elucidation of its contextual mediations. Social constructivism has a particular meaning for Salter, simply that the 'reality' of law is always socially constructed (intergenerationally, of course), linguistic-ally sustained and interpretatively relative. Like Carty, he calls for phen-omenological exposition. This means to treat law as the object of lived experience, what it means for insiders to belong to a particular legal cul-ture. Analysis must also be imbued with methodological reflexivity, which

---

67 Honneth (1996) p. 30.   68 Honneth (1996) p. 62.   69 Honneth (1996) p. 179.
70 See also Norrie (1999).   71 Salter (1997) p. 292.
72 Puchalska-Tych and Salter (1996) p. 177.

recognises that the researcher's own understanding of legal culture is itself grounded in, mediated by, and a contributory part of culture's experiential manifestation to its own members. Finally, Salter subscribes to immanent critique; getting inside the law's own rhetorical claims, taking them seriously, and exploiting the space opened up between rhetoric and institutional practice. Salter explores these possibilities with regard to comparative law. But his remarks have considerable interest for the problems of group rights.

> The identification of the object of comparative studies as that of cultural dynamics introduces a constellation of problems relating to methodology that a dialectical analysis attuned to mutual determination is particularly well suited to respond to.[73]

Dialectics and law

In considering the role of law, there is merit in considering Theodor Adorno's *Negative Dialectic*, with its incisive account of dialectic methodology and unsparing critique of identity thinking with respect to law. Adorno wrote:

> In large measure, the law is the medium in which evil wins out on account of its objectivity and acquires the appearance of good ... Law is the primal phenomenon of irrational rationality. In law the formal principle of equivalence becomes the norm; everyone is treated alike. An equality in which differences perish secretly serves to promote inequality; it becomes the myth that survives amidst an only seemingly demythologised mankind. For the sake of an unbroken systematic, the legal norms cut short what is not covered, every specific experience that has not been shaped in advance; and then they raise the instrumental rationality to the rank of a second legality *sui generis*. The total legal realm is one of definitions.[74]

Conclusion

What does this all mean for the study of group and minority rights, and for law's engagement with real contemporary issues? First of all, it means the rejection of methodological individualism and reductionism, and recognition of the existence and efficacy of groups. Second, it means abandoning the two pairs of 'opposites' which bedevil the analysis of problems of group rights, notably liberalism/communitarianism, and universalism/cultural relativism – or at least putting these into their proper context as analytical tools. Third, it means an appreciation of the extraordinarily dynamic development not only

---

73 Puchalska-Tych and Salter (1996) p. 180.   74 Adorno (1990) p. 309.

between groups and the larger community, between each other, between themselves and their internal minorities, but also, and crucially, within the group itself.

There can be no hope of resolving the bitter complexities of double minorities unless the law adopts procedures which will look more like political negotiation than formal adjudication, and which take account of all aspects of internal and external group dynamics.

This would not mean abandoning the international community's commitment to fundamental human rights, but, as An-Na'im has urged, 'admitting that every cultural tradition has problems with some human rights'.[75] For all of this a dialectic of identity and recognition – of the group's understanding of itself in the symbolic order, and of the group's relation with the larger society – is in my view indispensable. At the very least, the law needs to be both larger, more encompassing, less rigid – but also very much more concrete in its field of application. This is a large research programme, and beyond the scope of this chapter, which does no more than lay some foundations.

---

75 An-Na'im (1992) p. 28.

Chapter 10

The scandal of social and economic rights

Introduction

In the previous chapter I provided a critique of liberalism and methodological individualism.

This chapter takes as its case study the very specific ideological problems of the United Kingdom with regard to human rights, especially the UK government's long-standing 'allergy' to social and economic rights. At the same time, I analyse some of the specificities of the 'second generation' of human rights, and articulate this in relation to my aim to illuminate the substantive content of human rights.

A starting point, a source of reference and engagement is provided by Michael Ignatieff's Tanner Lectures delivered in 2000 at the Princeton University Center for Human Values, and published under the title *Human Rights as Politics and Ideology*.[1] Ignatieff's discussion is rich and profound, but situated firmly in the Western, or rather the Atlantic, conception of rights. As aptly summarised by Amy Gutmann, who introduces the lectures, Ignatieff's position is that Human Rights should not be conceived as guarantors of social justice, or substitutes for comprehensive conceptions of a good life.[2] But he does note that: '. . . the Communist rights tradition – which put primacy on economic and social rights – kept the capitalist human rights tradition – emphasising political and civil rights – from overreaching itself. . . .'[3] This is a point to which I will return.

I want to go further than Ignatieff. I will explore the relationship between the two concepts. My intention in this chapter is to explore and illustrate three aspects of the relationship between human rights and social justice.

First, confrontation. This refers to the conflict between human rights (or at least, some liberal conceptions of human rights) on the one hand and social justice on the other, exemplified in the political history of the last century, as well as in the writings of some leading scholars, and certain reluctances of the UK government.

---

1 Ignatieff (2001).   2 Ignatieff (2001) p. x.   3 Ignatieff (2001) p. 19.

Second, mediation. This refers to the way in which, for Europeans and increasingly, perhaps for the UK, social justice provides a check on human rights. Or at least on the possessive individualism which characterises the liberal theories of human rights. This stands in contrast to the US practice, in which certain individual rights, notably freedom of expression, and rights to property, will always trump (social) policy considerations.

Third, mutual realisation through struggle. I argue that neither the concept of human rights nor that of social justice can have content, meaning and significance except through their constant reinvention and reintegration in the real activity of women and men in the always turbulent and dangerous world into which they are thrown.

This framework also has the advantage of conveying some of the dynamism and turbulence – one might say dialectic – associated with the two concepts. The reader may note the Hegelian flavour.

But first it is necessary to say a few words about these two concepts. The proviso on which I must insist, as does Adorno in his *Negative Dialectics*,[4] is that in this area above all, the concept is always and necessarily inadequate to its object.

What meaning do these concepts have?

Human rights and social justice are two phrases which have never before been so much in constant use, especially at the level of government. At times, they seem to be empty, of rhetorical significance only. What, indeed, are their referents? Take human rights first.

There is no dispute that the present 'dominant discourse' of human rights has its roots in Western traditions of natural law. But I agree with Alasdair MacIntyre, the present-day interpreter of Aristotle and fierce critic of liberalism in ethics and rights talk, that before the eighteenth century the concept had no referents or content at all – no one used it, and it would have had no meaning.[5] I also enjoy his comment that: 'In the United Nations declaration on human rights of 1949 what has since become the normal UN practice of not giving good reasons for any assertion whatsoever is followed with great rigour.'[6]

The first statements of natural rights, the 'first generation' of civil and political rights, are to be found in the revolutionary documents of the French and American Revolutions. What has characterised talk of natural or human rights then and to this day is their inherently problematic – indeed self-problematising – nature. This is what makes the subject a joy to teach.

What I mean is amply demonstrated in Jeremy Waldron's indispensable *Nonsense Upon Stilts*.[7] Here the validity, legitimacy and indeed coherence of

4 Adorno (1990).   5 MacIntyre (1990).   6 MacIntyre (1990) p. 69.
7 Waldron (1987).

human rights are challenged from the right – Edmund Burke, the Irish father of English conservatism – from the centre, Jeremy Bentham, the founder of utilitarianism and of much liberal thought, the English Lenin, at least in terms of his mummified remains preserved at University College London – and from the left – Karl Marx himself, attacking the egotism and atomism of the rights of man, separating himself from society, losing his 'species being'.

In the contemporary world, these challenges are to be found in three main areas. First, in the debates as to universalism and cultural relativism – are human rights really the property of all human beings everywhere and at all times, or are they historically determined and culturally specific? Second, in the odious notion of the 'clash of civilisations', between two cultures that share the same roots, and the ideas of cross-cultural approaches to human rights developed by courageous thinkers like Abdullahi An-Na'im.[8] Third, in the suggestion by Alston and others that the so-called 'third-generation' 'rights of peoples', the rights to self-determination, to development, to a clean environment, to peace – were an effusion of Seventies radicalism and have had their day.[9]

There is a more fundamental problem. There is scarcely a government now that does not proclaim its devotion to human rights, at the same time as many of them flagrantly violate them. Costas Douzinas, in *The End of Human Rights*,[10] points out that human rights are the 'new ideal that has triumphed on the world stage', yet 'if the twentieth century is the epoch of human rights, their triumph is, to say the least, something of a paradox. Our age has witnessed more violations of their principles than any of the previous and less "enlightened" epochs.'[11] He warns: 'As human rights start veering away from their initial revolutionary and dissident purposes, as their end becomes obscured in ever more declarations, treaties and diplomatic lunches, we may be entering the epoch of the end of human rights. . . .'[12]

This is rather an apt description of the problematic of the UK, the country where, on 17 July 1997, the late Robin Cook launched an 'ethical foreign policy', with his speech 'Human rights into a new century', and its promise of 12 policies to put into effect the new government's commitment to human rights.[13] The rhetoric of human rights is not nearly so apparent now, at least when it comes to ministerial pronouncements. And Ignatieff makes the adroit comment that: 'When values do not actually constrain interests, an "ethical foreign policy" – the self-proclaimed goal of Britain's Labour government – becomes a contradiction in terms.'[14]

Nevertheless, the UK enacted the Human Rights Act 1998 and brought it

---

8 See for example An-Na'im (1992).   9 Alston (2001).   10 Douzinas (2000).
11 Douzinas (2000) p. 2.   12 Douzinas (2000) p. 380.
13 'Human Rights into a New Century', speech delivered in the Locarno Suite, FCO, London, 17 July 1997.
14 Ignatieff (2001) p. 23.

into force in 2000, and in this way introduced the principles of the European Convention on Human Rights into UK law and practice. This was without doubt a significant achievement, but subject to some important provisos, as explained below.

Social justice

The concept of social justice, too, has deep roots. Most notably, these are to be found in the teachings of the Catholic Church. Many of the websites which a search on the words 'social justice' throws up are church sites. This subversive aspect of Catholic teaching finds its expression in liberation theology and a focus on workers' rights – the Catholic trade unions of the European continent. Social justice plays a central role in Islam also. Whether it is the influence of the Pope or of the imams is hard to say, but the objective of social justice, too, is, in the UK, a central part of government rhetoric.

It is only possible with a strong sense of irony and regret to recall the launch in 1994 of the Report of the Commission on Social Justice, *Social Justice. Strategies for National Renewal.*[15] Tony Blair presided. He had just become leader of the Labour Party, following the sudden death of John Smith. The Commission was John Smith's brainchild. Blair said (as reported on the book's cover) that it was 'essential reading for everyone who wants a new way forward for our country'. The Report suggested that social justice could be defined in terms of a hierarchy of four ideas. It is worth repeating them, just for the record.

> First, the belief that the foundation of a free society is the equal worth of all citizens, expressed most basically in political and civil liberties, equal rights before the law, and so on. Second, the argument that everyone is entitled, as a right of citizenship, to be able to meet their basic needs for income, shelter and other necessities. Basic needs can be met by providing resources or services, or helping people acquire them: either way, the ability to meet basic needs is the foundation of a substantive commitment to the equal worth of all citizens. Third, self-respect and equal citizenship demand more than a meeting of basic needs: they demand opportunities and life chances. That is why we are concerned with the primary distribution of opportunity, as well as its redistribution. Finally, to achieve the first three conditions of social justice, we must recognise that although not all inequalities are unjust, unjust inequalities should be reduced and where possible eliminated.

It is plain that the Blair government sacrificed every one of these four principles

15 Commission for Social Justice (1994).

on the altar of the market economy and the war on terror. It is highly debatable whether the Brown government will be any more beholden to Blair's two imperatives. The UK is the Western European state with the greatest social stratification, the gap between rich and poor widening inexorably, and the worst record on commitment to human rights and civil liberties.

The UK is of course not completely homogeneous. Scotland (and Wales) have a rather different record to England's in the seriousness with which they engage with issues of social justice. After devolution, Scotland followed India's good example, and had, in the McLeish government of 2000–2001, a Minister, Jackie Baillie, and a Ministry for Social Justice, tasked with helping Scotland to meet clearly defined objectives in line with the four principles outlined above. Iain Gray, followed by Margaret Curran, became Minister for Social Justice in the government of Jack McConnell from 2001–2003. The Ministry disappeared following the elections of 1 May 2003. Margaret Curran became Minister for Communities. In October 2004 Malcolm Chisholm became Minister for Communities.[16] More importantly, perhaps, on 1 July 2002 McConnell launched the Scottish Centre for Research on Social Justice.[17]

But later in this chapter I will return to recent developments in the UK's discourse of social justice and human rights, in relation to the vexed topic of globalisation.

Russia – a test case

First, however, I will illustrate the problems associated with human rights and social justice in relation to Russia. My own work in Russia for the UK government was as contracted Adviser to the Department for International Development (DfID) from 1997 to 2004. I assisted in concretising one of the five outputs of the 'Country Strategy for Russia 2001–2005'. This was based on the UK government's commitment to work for the elimination of poverty – the UK's new 'Five Year Plan'. This output was entitled 'More responsive and transparent political systems, wider access to justice and adherence to human rights', and sought to support the legal and judicial reform process in Russia.

At that time there was indeed, contrary to the view of some pessimists, a reform process, much of which was situated in a human rights framework. Thus, Russia joined the Council of Europe in 1996, and ratified the European Convention on Human Rights in 1998. I refer in much greater detail in other chapters to these processes and their contradictions.

---

16 http://www.scotland.gov.uk/About/Ministers/communities (accessed on 1 January 2006).
17 http://www.scrsj.ac.uk/GlasgowLaunch/index.html.

This was part of what the DfID strategy described as the 'transition process'. However, in 2001, three highly significant books were published in the USA. Each was written by way of an act of penitence for US aid intervention in Russia since 1989, albeit not shared as yet by the US government. Their titles tell the story. First, there is the historian Stephen Cohen's *Failed Crusade: America and the Tragedy of Post-Communist Russia*.[18] Next, political scientist Janine Wedel's *Collision and Collusion: The Strange Case of Western Aid to Eastern Europe*.[19] Finally, there is a massive volume, with perhaps the most resonant title: *The Tragedy of Russia's Reforms: Market Bolshevism Against Democracy* by political scientists Peter Reddaway and Dmitri Glinski.[20] Each of these books describes and analyses, with a wealth of evidence, from a variety of perspectives and academic disciplines, a common phenomenon.

In Stephen Cohen's words:

> Since 1991, Russia's realities have included the worst peacetime industrial depression of the twentieth century; the degradation of agriculture and livestock herds even worse in some respects than occurred during Stalin's catastrophic collectivisation of the peasantry in the early 1930s; unprecedented dependence on imported goods (foremost food and medicine); the promotion of one or two Potemkin cities amid the impoverishment or near-impoverishment of some 75% or more of the nation; more new orphans than resulted from Russia's almost 30 million casualties in world war II; and the transformation of a superpower into a beggar state existing on foreign loans and plagued, according to the local press, by 'hunger, cold and poverty' and whose remote regions 'await the approaching winter with horror'.[21]

As Cohen points out with understandable irony: 'All this, scholars and journalists have called reform, remarkable progress, and a success story.'

Wedel explores the remarkably influential partnership between Harvard academics (now being prosecuted in the USA for their activities in Russia) and Russian government figures like Anatolii Chubais – in 1989 a humble lecturer, now one of the richest men in the world – which determined so much of Russian social and economic policy during the 1990s, and to this day.

Reddaway and Glinski identify the fundamental problem firmly in the realm of social justice.

> The failure to redistribute power and wealth in the period of 'reforms' in a way that would be legitimate by the standards and norms of Russian

18 Cohen (2001).   19 Wedel (2001).   20 Reddaway and Glinski (2001).
21 Cohen (2001) p. 32.

culture is the most fundamental reason that the present system possesses little legitimacy. This lack of legitimacy corrupts the very foundations of the state . . . the basic reason for this pervasive illegitimacy is that under Yeltsin the state abrogated its unspoken social contract with the population – a contract that was deeply rooted in the nation's history and culture, at least as an ideal.[22]

Russia is supposed to have gained democracy, and from this human rights will follow. However, Tony Evans argues[23] that we should treat the relationship between democracy and human rights with caution. His own conclusion – not too startling to many of us – is that democracy promotion has more to do with global economic interests than with delivering human rights to the poor and excluded in less developed countries. Thus, he argues that: 'By adopting a definition of democracy that places emphasis on the creation of formal institutions, which promises limited changes to civil and political rights but has little to say about social and economic reform, "repressive abuses of human rights continue, usually against the familiar targets of labour, students, the left and human rights activists".'[24]

This is a good point at which to turn to the first of my three aspects of the relationship between human rights and social justice.

Confrontation

There is a strong tradition within liberal thought according to which social justice is a dangerous threat to freedom. This was perhaps epitomised by Friedrich Hayek. Volume II of his *Law, Legislation and Liberty* was entitled *The Mirage of Social Justice*.[25] For him, social justice 'is a mirage . . .'. The expression described 'the aspirations which were at the heart of socialism'; indeed 'the prevailing belief in "social justice" was at present probably the gravest threat to most other values of a free civilisation'.[26] 'So long as the belief in "social justice" governs political action, this process must progressively approach nearer and nearer to a totalitarian system.'

He added that: 'The phrase embodies a quasi-religious belief, almost the new religion of our time, but has no content at all, serves merely to insinuate that we ought to consent to a demand of some particular group.'

As Steven Lukes points out, this perception is perhaps the key to Hayek's entire political philosophy: justice not as fairness, as it is for the classic liberal, John Rawls, but as the elimination of arbitrary coercion.[27] Thus, the version of utilitarianism which Hayek espoused was that which maximised average expectations: 'the good Society is one in which the chances of anyone selected

---

22 Reddaway and Glinski (2001) p. 630.   23 Evans (2001).   24 Evans (2001) p. 630.
25 Hayek (1976).   26 Hayek (1976) pp. 66–67.   27 Lukes (1997) p. 77.

at random are likely to be as great as possible.'[28] As Lukes points out, this was the principle Rawls considered to be one of the main rivals to his own.[29]

Taken with one other factor, this perception – or prejudice – is at the heart of British problems with social justice, indeed with the notion of social and economic rights.

The other factor is the legacy of the Cold War. It should not be forgotten that the Council of Europe was founded in 1949 as the ideological counterpart of NATO. Its purpose was to demonstrate in the clearest way that the Western side of the Iron Curtain was really serious about the Council's 'three pillars'. These are pluralistic democracy, the rule of law (defined as the absence of arbitrary rule), and the protection of human rights. Thus, the promulgation of the European Convention on Human Rights in 1950 was truly revolutionary, in a way which made the United Kingdom deeply uneasy. For the first time in history, an international court was created with the power to interfere in the internal affairs of member states, and to render obligatory, binding judgments. But note that the rights protected were, with the exception perhaps of rights not to be deprived of education, and a circumscribed right to private property, the 'first generation' civil and political rights of the French and American revolutions. As time has gone by, the Convention has looked increasingly 'long in the tooth'.

If the role of the Council of Europe was to demonstrate that the West's rights were serious and capable of being enforced by individuals against their governments, the Soviet Union and its allies had their own ideological counterpart. It is often forgotten that the Soviet Constitutions – the Stalin Constitution of 1936, the Brezhnev Constitutions of 1977–1978 – were endowed with fully articulated human rights chapters. The difference was that these chapters started with social and economic rights. The Soviets did not invent social and economic rights. As binding legal documents these made their first appearance in the West in 1919, in response to the Russian Revolution, in the International Labour Organisation, now an organ of the United Nations. But the USSR and its allies put them into practice. Thus, in the Soviet Constitutions, we find, in pride of place, the right to work, followed by the right to social security and protection, the rights to health care and free education, the right to leisure and to culture. And, indeed, the Soviet state redeemed these constitutional promises to a greater or lesser extent – the social contract to which Reddaway and Glinski refer. Of course, the Soviet citizen was probably in a job she did not want – it was a crime not to work, and female employment was very high in the USSR – and her living accommodation was likely to be shared. But health care, education, and cultural provision were second to none, while freedoms of expression and association, to respect for

---

28 Hayek (1976) p. 132.   29 Lukes (1997) p. 79.

private life and belief and conscience, did not exist. These were indeed protected, but only if exercised in the interests of the working class.

This polar opposition, which lasted from 1949 until 1989, is (along with Hayek's influence) one of the root causes of UK suspicion of social and economic rights. It is notable that the Human Rights Act 1998 does not protect the full range of rights contained in the United Nations 1948 Universal Declaration on Human Rights – since the Soviets participated in its drafting, it is no surprise that it does enshrine both civil and political and social, economic and cultural rights, as well as solidarity rights.

In her popular book *Values for a godless age. The story of the United Kingdom's new bill of rights*,[30] Francesca Klug describes the omission of social and economic rights, save education and property rights, from the Human Rights Act, as an aspect of its outdatedness.[31] She is unhappy with the notion of 'generations of rights', and locates what she calls the 'second wave' of rights not in 1919 and the aftershock of the Russian Revolution, but in the post World War II reckoning. In this way, I contend, she misses the political content of the very real dichotomy between civil and political rights on the one hand, and social and economic rights on the other. Her 'third wave', in which she situates the Human Rights Act, is connected to globalisation, a theme to which I will turn shortly. But she does acknowledge that: '. . . the inclusion of social and economic rights is crucial if the relevance of the human rights approach to current political debate is to become clear.'[32]

Her argument is that the '. . . combined values that have driven human rights thinking since the Second World War – liberty, justice, dignity, equality, community and now mutuality – inevitably lead to a concern with social and economic rights, whatever means of enforcement is adopted'. This leads '. . . straight back to the terrain of those seeking a new progressive politics, distinct from the Left and Right of old'.[33]

The problem, in my view, is that not only does this not explain the omission of social and economic rights from the Human Rights Act, it does not give any reason for three further phenomena. These are, first, Britain's adamant refusal to accede, at Maastricht, to the European Union's Social Charter. Britain's emphasis to this day is on private provision and labour deregulation. Second, is the prolonged rearguard action which the UK fought to exclude solidarity – mainly labour – rights from the EU's Charter of Fundamental Rights, and its insistence that these rights should never become justiciable.[34]

Third, and for me the most shameful, is the UK's deep reluctance to ratify the Council of Europe's Revised Social Charter of 1996, which the UK signed in 1997. This is the revised, updated version of the Council's 1961 Social Charter, intended as the social and economic counterpart to the European

30 Klug (2000).   31 Klug (2000) p. 165.   32 Klug (2000) p. 204.
33 Klug (2000) p. 205.   34 See Federal Trust (1999).

Convention on Human Rights, but never until now giving a right of redress to a judicial organ. The new Revised Social Charter not only protects a wide range of rights to and at work, to housing, to social security, etc, but for the first time gives a right of collective complaint, by trade unions and non-governmental organisations, to the European Committee for Social Rights.[35]

Despite signature in 1997, the UK is no closer to ratification. On 13 January 2005 the then Minister, Bill Rammell, gave a written parliamentary answer that the UK had signed but not yet completed the ratification process of several Council of Europe Conventions since 1997, including the Revised Social Charter.[36] He gave no reason, but in 2003 he had answered that: 'The Department for Work and Pensions is keeping under review how the Revised Charter will operate and, with other interested departments and the Devolved Administrations, will consider the provisions of the original Charter in the context of future decisions about ratification of the Revised Charter.'[37] It is not known when the UK will ratify. Russia signed in 1999, and is quite likely to ratify before the UK.

It is clear that for the United Kingdom – as for the United States, which has to date not even ratified the United Nations' Covenant on Civil, Political and Cultural Rights of 1966 – the key argument is that only civil and political rights are justiciable. Since, according to the classic common-law principle, there cannot be a right if there is no judicial remedy, it follows that social and economic rights are not human rights. In fact, I contend, it is the second generation of rights, social and economic, which alone can underpin social justice. As Churchill and Khaliq show, this argument no longer has any credibility. They note that the argument goes as follows. Economic and social rights are often progressive in nature, and many such rights are '. . . couched in language that is too imprecise to be judicially enforceable'.[38] However, they remind us that the Indian Supreme Court and South African Constitutional Court already have a substantial jurisprudence as to the obligations imposed by the constitutions of India and South Africa, 'many of which are couched in terms similar to those found in treaties protecting economic and social rights, in which they have not only defined the obligation but also the remedy'.[39] Thus, it is clear that there is nothing inherent in social and economic rights that prevents judicial determination of their content.

It is also important to note the inclusion in the Revised Social Charter of the right of collective complaint. Another aspect of the confrontation between liberal human rights is the deep antipathy in the West, and in the United

35 See Churchill and Khaliq (2004).
36 http://www.publications.parliament.uk/pa/cm200405/cmhansrd/cm050113/text/
    50113w17.htm.
37 http://www.publications.parliament.uk/pa/cm200203/cmhansrd/vo030514/text/
    30514w13.htm.
38 Churchill and Khaliq (2004) p. 419.   39 Churchill and Khaliq (2004) p. 420.

Kingdom in particular, to collective or group rights, a theme which I deal with elsewhere in this book. For John Packer, for example – and he was Adviser to the OSCE's High Commissioner on Human Rights and one of the most serious theorists and practitioners of minority rights – human rights philosophy is necessarily liberal and individualist, so that any tendency to communitarianism leads to nationalism, which itself is 'inherently conflict-creating'.[40] The UK has ratified the Council of Europe's 1994 Framework Convention for the Protection of Rights of National Minorities, but on the basis that UK law does not recognise the existence of national minorities, simply a right of individuals to non-discrimination.

But it is readily apparent that social justice will never be exclusively a matter of individual rights. Groups, collectivities, minorities will always be the largest part of its subject matter. Ignatieff notes, taking the Kurds as an example, that: 'For too long human rights has been seen as a form of apolitical humanitarian rescue for oppressed individuals.'[41] But Ignatieff sticks resolutely to individualism. In his way of thinking, '. . . human rights is only a systematic agenda of "negative liberty", a tool kit against oppression, a tool kit that individual agents must be free to use as they see fit within the broader frame of cultural and religious beliefs that they live by.'

However, there is an aspect of the relationship between human rights which the UK has not escaped.

Mediation

Despite what I have said above, the European approach to human rights was not simply a Cold War artefact. That is one reason why the UK was, despite its distinctive common law heritage, able by stages, reluctantly, to embrace the European Convention. And, as the government is from time to time obliged to realise, the institutions of the welfare state and a strong collectivism are deeply rooted in the UK. As Professor David Feldman, Legal Adviser to the Joint Select Committee on Human Rights from 2000 to 2004, has noted: '. . . the Convention's approach is far more closely in tune with the essentially collectivist cultural heritage which forms part of the bedrock on which the constitution of the United Kingdom developed and must build. . . .'[42]

What this means is that protection of many of the first generation, civil and political rights protected by the Convention, is coupled with and balanced by the right of the government to interfere, providing this interference is carried out for a legitimate purpose in the interests of society, according to law, and is proportionate to its aim. This does not apply to the rights to life and to freedom from torture. But it most certainly applies to rights to personal liberty and fair trial, to respect for family and private life, and to freedoms of

40 Packer (1993) p. 23.   41 Ignatieff (2001) p. 26.   42 Feldman (1999) p. 178.

conscience, expression, and association. Particularly with regard to freedom of expression, this approach could not differ more sharply from American traditions of 'rights as trumps', in Ronald Dworkin's phrase, especially freedom of expression. In Europe, at least, human rights are always the product of the balance between the interests of the individual and of society. Ignatieff, too, criticises the '. . . larger illusion that human rights is above politics, a set of moral trump cards whose function is to bring political disputes to closure and conclusion'.[43]

Nowhere is this brought out more clearly than in the case of *James v United Kingdom*,[44] one of the strangest cases – at least for my ex-Soviet students – which the European Court of Human Rights has considered. James was none other than the Duke of Westminster's surveyor, with the Duke himself as second applicant. The Duke complained that his Convention right to private property had been violated by the then Labour Government's Leasehold Reform Act 1967, enabling his Belgravia tenants to purchase their homes. The relevant provision of the Convention asserts that no one shall be deprived of his possessions 'except in the public interest'. The Court was obliged to decide the meaning of the words 'public interest' in the case of the Duke and the Labour Government. In doing so it used the phrase 'social justice' no less than four times.

Here are the most significant passages. Note the reference to 'social justice'.

> Neither can it be read into the English expression 'in the public interest' that the transferred property should be put into use for the general public or that the community generally, or even a substantial proportion of it, should directly benefit from the taking. The taking of property in pursuance of a policy calculated to enhance social justice within the community can properly be described as being 'in the public interest'. In particular, the fairness of a system of law governing the contractual or property rights of private parties is a matter of public concern and therefore legislative measures intended to bring about such fairness are capable of being 'in the public interest', even if they involve the compulsory transfer of property from one individual to another.

The same applied to compensation, which could be less than the full market value. The Court stated that the Convention:

> . . . does not, however, guarantee a right to full compensation in all circumstances. Legitimate objectives of 'public interest', such as pursued in measures of economic reform or measures designed to achieve greater social justice, may call for less than reimbursement of the full market

---

43 Ignatieff (2001) p. 21.   44 Judgment of 21 February 1986.

value. Furthermore, the Court's power of review is limited to ascertaining whether the choice of compensation terms falls outside the State's wide margin of appreciation in this domain.

In my view the significance of this decision, and the language used by the Court, have received insufficient attention in the New Labour UK, except perhaps in Clare Short's DfID (as opposed to Hilary Benn). That is, that human rights as now entrenched by legislation are not so much constrained and balanced by individual responsibility, as the communitarians in the Cabinet insist, at any rate where the responsibility is that of single parents and welfare recipients. On the contrary, the true responsibility is that of individuals and corporations which wield true economic power, and whose rights to unfettered enjoyment of their property have been significantly enhanced.

I now turn to this aspect of the relationship between human rights and social justice.

Mutual realisation through struggle

One reason I especially enjoy the teaching and study of human rights is that the topic can only be approached through a number of disciplines. Lawyers will always tend to reduce human rights to just another set of positive instruments. To understand the roots of the concept, philosophers and anthropologists are needed. It is impossible to understand the practical application and content of human rights in the absence of collaboration with political scientists and sociologists.

Social justice does not yet exist as a separate discipline, though an impressive International Social Justice Project, with sociologists from Germany, the USA, and Eastern Europe and the former USSR, has studied the relationship between political culture and the post-communist transition from a social justice point of view.[45]

But it can be seen that social justice concerns inform not only social policy, but other substantive disciplines. Here is a selection of very recent journal articles. Take, for example, health policy: Fabienne Peter explores health equity '. . . on the premise that social inequalities in health are wrong not simply because actual health outcomes deviate from some pattern of health outcomes that is considered ideal, but rather because, and insofar as, they are the expression and product of unjust economic, social and political institutions. It thus embeds the pursuit of health equity in the pursuit of social justice in general.'[46]

In the field of urban and regional research, my former colleague Michael Harloe reflects on the fact that the concern with competitiveness which is

45 Wegener (2000).   46 Peter (2001) p. 160.

central to New Labour breaks away from social democratic ideology, 'with an attack on "welfare dependency" as well as a strong emphasis on individual and community self-reliance and on a conservative conception of community and core values'.[47]

Closer to the discipline of law, Jonathan Stein argues that the new Community Legal Service, designed to improve access to justice, needs a social justice mission.[48] He argues that the CLS has, by seeking cost efficiency in individual legal aid cases, missed the opportunity to promote social justice. Education policy is another area in which social justice considerations play a central role.

It will be seen that the content of all of this critical research is not simply the exploration of an academic discipline. It concerns the real lives of women and men. In particular, it touches on the centre of government policy, here and abroad. Marcel Wissenburg has in my view put his finger on the nature of the problem.[49] He argues that New Labour's 'third way' practice contradicts both John Rawls' ideas about redistributive justice, and social justice in a wider sense. He observes: 'Rather than obliterating the worst of socialism and replacing it with the best of liberalism, it seems that as far as social justice is concerned, the "third way" has replaced the best part of socialism, distributive justice, by the worst part of liberalism, the survival of the fittest.'[50]

Why do I use the word 'struggle'? I would argue that questions of social justice always and inevitably concern the lives and hopes of groups, collectivities of people. That is why individualist liberalism is so hostile to the concept.

I have argued elsewhere for an application of a critical realism, finding its roots in the insights of Karl Marx. As Norman Geras explains:

> Marx's apparent statements of moral relativism expressed, in fact, a moral realism, specifying the material conditions necessary for achieving 'higher' standards of fairness, rather than denying that such historically transcendent ethical judgments could be made. Categorising principles of justice as juridical is too narrow; they can be envisaged also, independently of any instruments of coercion, as simply ethical principles for evaluating and determining the allocation of social benefits and burdens. 'To each according to their needs' is such a principle, a norm of distributive justice, its aim an equal right to self-realisation; even though viewed by Marx as to be achieved with the disappearance of coercive state apparatuses.[51]

In his early work, the philosopher Roy Bhaskar showed how these insights rather than the currently fashionable social constructivism could underpin

---

47 Harloe (2001) p. 890.   48 Stein (2001).   49 Wissenburg (2001).
50 Wissenburg (2001) p. 235.   51 Geras (1991) pp. 276–277.

the possibility of a genuine social science.[52] One of the most powerful insights of this mode of thinking, for me, is insistence on the scientific reality of social structures. The sociologist Margaret Archer explains that 'the church-goer or language user finds their beliefs or language ready made at birth', so 'people do not create society. For it always pre-exists them . . . Social structure . . . is always already made.'[53]

If the concept of social justice acquires a content through the injustices suffered by people, individually and in groups, human rights come to life through struggle. The black American legal scholar Patricia Williams has described how the language of human rights, which for the most part is the discourse of the powerful and privileged, is transformed into a material force, capable of bringing about social change, through the 'alchemy' of their capture by the poor and dispossessed.[54]

The spectre of globalisation

Finally, I would like to return to UK government policy. It is interesting to note how social justice has acquired a new partner, globalisation, in the discourse of government. It is beyond the scope of this book to unravel the complexities of this apparently illicit relationship. I simply propose that it could be the subject matter of more than one research project.

Gordon Brown, following in the footsteps of John Smith, has been the most fervent advocate of social justice, to judge by his public pronouncements. He elaborated on this theme not only in speeches to Oxfam (the Gilbert Murray lecture on 11 January 2000), and the Child Poverty Action Group on 15 May 2000, but also in his 16 November 2001 speech to the Federal Reserve Bank in New York. He mentioned social justice no less than four times in the speech. His theme was breathtaking – that the alliance forged against terrorism since September 11 'confirms a profound and pervasive truth . . . that this generation has it in its power – if it so chooses – to abolish all forms of human poverty'. Thus, according to Brown, 'well-managed, globalisation . . . is the road to rising prosperity and social justice'. His answer to anti-globalisation campaigners was 'we shall not retreat from globalisation. Instead, we will advance social justice on a global scale . . .'

Of course, there are many who question the content or utility of the word globalisation, or its very existence. But, according to my colleague Peter Gowan, 'most of the notions of what globalisation is about focus on the growing mobility of capital across the globe, and upon the impact of this mobility on national economies'.[55] He says that '. . . global capital markets' are 'about trading in royalties on future production in different parts of the

52 Bhaskar (1991) pp. 458–460.   53 Archer (1995).   54 Williams (1991).
55 Gowan (1999) p. 8.

world, or about businesses engaging in various kinds of insurance against risks'.[56] His argument, based on detailed analysis, is that: '. . . the central features of what has been called globalisation have their origins in deliberate decisions of the Nixon administration taken in order to secure the continued international dominance of American capitalism.'[57]

That is, of course, not the UK government's conception.

The Department for International Development has publicly espoused globalisation. Its policy underwent an interesting development while Clare Short was Minister. The first White Paper of November 1997, 'Eliminating World Poverty: A Challenge for the 21st Century',[58] was followed by a research report of April 1999, entitled 'Global Social Policy Principles: Human Rights and Social Justice'.[59] This argued for the development of a global social policy on the basis of the human rights agreements and minimum standards. Its author, Clare Ferguson, stated that: 'One of the biggest challenges to the achievement of social justice, in the context of globalisation, is finding ways to ensure that these organisations – transnational corporations and non state providers of public services as well as governments – accept their responsibilities to respect minimum standards in all their activities.' But the December 2000 White Paper had a new message. Its title once more starts 'Eliminating World Poverty', but this time no challenge. Instead, 'Making Globalisation Work for the Poor'.[60] This title has the ring of the kind of contradiction in terms sometimes inflicted as an examination question. Discuss!

In her speech to the TUC Congress on 16 September 1999, Clare Short spoke of the trade union movement and Labour Party's 'struggle for social justice', 'managing' industrialisation. The new challenge was to 'manage the globalisation process equitably and sustainably'. Yet in her speech to the United Nations on 1 February 2001, 'Making globalisation work for the poor: A role for the United Nations', Clare Short made no mention of social justice (mentioned once in the second White Paper), or of human rights (frequent references). Instead, she spoke of the '. . . struggle to ensure that the benefits of globalisation reach the poor . . . to ensure that the wealth and abundance being generated by globalisation brings real benefit to the poor of the world'.

It is not my intention to criticise DfID unduly, not because I have worked for it in promoting human rights and access to justice for the poor of Russia, but because I admire its uniquely consistent attempt to put a pro-poor policy into practice. But the notion of 'the benefits of globalisation' cries out to be problematised.

---

56 Gowan (1999) p. 12.   57 Gowan (1999) p. 126.
58 Cm 3789, http://www.dfid.gov.uk/pubs/files/whitepaper1997.pdf.
59 Ferguson (1999).   60 http://www.dfid.gov.uk/pubs/files/whitepaper2000.pdf.

Conclusion

How are human rights and social justice to be brought together? For my sins, I am a lawyer, and one answer is to seek to bring about change at the constitutional level. This is what Professor Keith Ewing does, in relation to the Canadian experience, but with direct relevance to the UK. He says:

> It may well be true that the 'struggle for social justice is much larger than constitutional rights' and that it is waged through political parties and movements, demonstrations, protests, boycotts, strikes, civil disobedience, grassroots activism, political commentary and art.
>
> But if so, political action must be undertaken for a purpose, and that purpose presumably is to effect political change, which one way or another will be reflected in law if it is to be sustained. That being so, the highest form of expression which Western legal systems typically acknowledge is constitutional law, and it is there that we should aim to entrench social gains made in the political process, without denying that 'rights discourse' is a 'blunt tool' for 'redressing social injustice'.[61]

A good start for the United Kingdom would be ratification of the Revised European Social Charter, and its entrenchment in domestic legislation in the same way that the Human Rights Act entrenches the European Convention on Human Rights.

If this chapter has engaged with the problems of the UK, the next chapter turns to a polity which shares with the UK the experience of empire. Russia, however, has been (and perhaps still is) a continental empire, spreading inexorably in every direction across Eurasia. This raises many specific problems with regard to human rights, and, returning to themes already broached in previous chapters, the rights of minorities.

---

61 Ewing (1999).

Chapter 11

The problem of 'legal transplantation' and human rights

Introduction

This chapter asks whether the discourse and practice of human rights can be transplanted from one part of the world to another – indeed from one culture to another.

Russia is a relatively recent addition to the European Convention system for the protection of human rights. Its membership of the Council of Europe since 1996 represents a supreme irony of history, given the origins of the Council in the Cold War, and the question of its admission was highly controversial, both in Russia and Strasbourg. There are those who continue to warn that the world's most successful human rights protection mechanism could be undermined.[1]

This chapter seeks to understand one aspect of what has happened through an exploration of issues concerning 'legal transplants'. The chapter first analyses ambiguities of the notions of sovereignty and transplantation, followed by a consideration of the theory of legal comparativism. What was the Western construction of 'socialist' law? The notion of legal transplantation is considered specifically in the context of human rights. Russia and other former Soviet states have now ratified most of the international and regional human rights instruments, and subjected themselves to interference by treaty bodies. Since 1 November 1998, the date of ratification of the Convention, the whole jurisprudence of the European Court of Human Rights has become part of Russian law. Is this the insertion of a healthy heart into a moribund body politic, or the writing of a fully modern human rights based legislation on an empty canvas? The paper therefore briefly considers the dynamic relationship between Western European and Russian law and legality from the eighteenth century. This is the necessary condition for evaluating the impact of international, especially European, instruments, standards and mechanisms – and waves of Western 'experts' and 'good governance' specialists – into post-Soviet states.

1 See Bowring (1995); Bowring (1997); Bowring (2000).

But I start with a description of the latest phases of Russia's plunge into a bracing new legal environment.

Russia and the European Convention

The Russian Federation joined the Council of Europe in 1996. On 1 November 1998 the Council of Europe's 1950 European Convention on Human Rights and Fundamental Freedoms (ECHR) entered into force for the Russian Federation, giving persons whose rights have been violated by Russia the right to petition the European Court of Human Rights.[2]

Russia has now begun to answer to the European Court of Human Rights in respect of issues that affect the foundations, indeed the good faith, of the Russian legal order. Three defeats for the Russian Federation throw this predicament into sharp focus. In *Gusinskiy v Russia*[3] the Court held that 'the restriction of the applicant's liberty permitted under Article 5 § 1 (c) was applied not only for the purpose of bringing him before the competent legal authority on reasonable suspicion of having committed an offence, but also for alien reasons', namely to intimidate him in commercial transactions. Thus, Russia had violated not only Article 5, but also Article 18.[4] In the other decision the Court involved itself in Russia's external policy and extraterritorial reach. In *Ilascu and Others v Moldova and Russia*[5] the majority of the Grand Chamber of the Court found that Russia rendered extensive political, military, financial and economic support to Transdniestria amounting to 'effective control' over the region and therefore exercised *de facto* 'jurisdiction' that came within the meaning of Article 1 of the Convention.

Finally, on 24 February 2005 the first six Chechen applicants against Russia won their applications to Strasbourg. They were represented at an oral hearing before the Court in October 2004 by the author of this book, with colleagues from his University's European Human Rights Advocacy Centre. The applicants made allegations of grave human rights violations committed during the early months of the present Chechen conflict. These cases were submitted in April 2000 by the Moscow-based 'Memorial' Human Rights Centre and arose from the events in Chechnya in October 1999 to February 2000. These were the cases of *M. Ch. Isayeva, Yusupova and Bazayeva v Russia*,[6] complaining of the aerial bombardment by Russian forces on 29 October 1999 of a refugee column seeking to leave Grozny, in which

---

2 For more on this, see Bowring (2000).

3 Application no. 70276/01, judgment of 19 May 2004.

4 Which provides: 'The restrictions permitted under this Convention to the said rights and freedoms shall not be applied for any purpose other than those for which they have been prescribed.'

5 Application no. 48787/99, judgment of 8 July 2004.

6 Application nos. 57947/00, 57948/00 and 57949/00.

Isayeva's children were killed, Isayeva and Yusupova were wounded, and Bazayeva's property was destroyed; *Z. A. Isayeva v Russia,*[7] complaining of the aerial bombardment on 4 February 2000 in which her son died; and *Khashiev and Akayeva v Russia,*[8] complaining of the killing of their relatives by federal forces on 20 January 2000. The cases were all declared admissible in December 2002. This is the Court's 'fast track'. On 1 July 2005 the Committee of the Grand Chamber rejected Russia's application for an appeal, and the process of enforcing the judgment and its consequences has now begun in the Committee of Ministers.

The author of this book also represented, in July 2004, the applicants in the first environmental case against Russia, *Fadeyeva v Russia,*[9] which dealt with issues of severe environmental pollution and the right of the applicants to be relocated from the area, around the Severstal plant in Cherepovets, where they live, especially since they obtained a court order for their rehousing from the local court. On 9 June 2005 the applicants won their case. Russia is seeking to appeal this decision too.

This case, as much as the Chechen cases, touches not only Russia's sovereignty, but also the most sensitive and potentially embarrassing issues of state policy.

Russia is now one of the best customers of the Court, with a flood of applications. An excellent recent summary is given in the latest (June 2005) Report by the Parliamentary Assembly of the Council of Europe on Russia's honouring of its commitments.[10] The Co-Rapporteurs noted that:

> As of mid-April 2005 a total of 44 judgments have been delivered, of which 42 were findings of violations. Only during January–April 2005 the Court has delivered 22 judgments in Russian cases. By October 2004 the Court had received slightly over 19,000 complaints against Russia. More than 250 complaints were communicated to the Russian Government and the Court has found over 60 complaints admissible. Since January 2002, Russia has been the second country (after Poland) in terms of newly lodged complaints. Geographically, the complaints are coming from all over Russia, not only from big cities.

With the two noisy exceptions of *Gusinskiy* and *Ilascu*, both of which have led to demands from nationalist politicians that Russia should leave the

---

7 Application no. 57950/00.   8 Application nos. 57942/00 and 57945/00.
9 Application no. 55723/00.
10 Parliamentary Assembly Doc. 10568 (3 June 2005) *Honouring of obligations and commitments by the Russian Federation Report Committee on the Honouring of Obligations and Commitments by Member States of the Council of Europe* (Monitoring Committee) Co-rapporteurs: Mr David Atkinson, United Kingdom, European Democrat Group and Mr Rudolf Bindig, Germany, Socialist Group.

Council of Europe forthwith, it will be seen that most of these cases do not concern the most controversial events in Russia. Rather, most of them go directly to the problem addressed by this paper: the systematic failure of the Russian legal and judicial system to provide effective remedies for violation of Convention rights.[11]

Antinomies of sovereignty and the law

A transplant is inconceivable without the existence of two sufficiently separated and independent bodies. No analysis of the concept of the legal transplant can begin without a dissection of the complexities of the relations between one polity and another.

In the first antinomy, we find two aspects of sovereignty which are indissolubly linked, especially when sovereignty is contested, or is under threat. The first is external, what is not, other than, whatever it is we define as ourselves. Sovereignty is defined against an other, can only be realised in opposition to the alien. For the most part this is the realm of fantasy, of paranoia, of projection of what is unacceptable in one's own self, or the obscenity which cannot consciously be enjoyed, but is always constructed as a theft of what is precious to us. As Slavoj Žižek puts it, 'The late Yugoslavia offers a case study of such a paradox, in which we witness a detailed network of "decantations" and "thefts" of enjoyment. Every nationality has built its own mythology narrating how other nations deprive it of the vital part of enjoyment the possession of which would allow it to live fully.'[12] This means, in particular, the gross violations of human rights which 'we' would never contemplate, but which 'they' perpetrate, or at least secretly desire to carry out.

The second antinomy is internal, the organic, the substance of nationhood – so often in English jurisprudence the true seed-bed for legal development, the almost primordial soil, developing by accretion through the case law.[13]

---

11 See, for the technical considerations, Kirill Koroteev 'Exhaustion of remedies as a criterion for admissibility of an application to the European Court of Human Rights: The Russian legal system' (EHRAC Case Bulletin No. 2, December 2004); and *Mezhdunarodnaia zaschita prav cheloveka s ispol'zovaniyem nekotorykh mezdunarodno-pravovykh mekhanizmov* (International human rights protection through international legal mechanisms), 2nd edition, edited by K. A. Moskalenko. M., 2001, p. 20 (the author of the relevant chapter is M. R. Voskobitova); V. G. Bessarabov, *Evropeyskiy Sud po pravam cheloveka* (The European Court of Human Rights), M., 2003, p. 74; V. A. Tumanov, *Evropeyskiy Sud po pravam cheloveka. Ocherk organizatsii i deyatel'nosti* (European Court of Human Rights. An essay on organisation and activity), M., 2002, p. 55.

12 Žižek (1993) p. 204.

13 See Allan (1993): 'In the absence of a higher "constitutional law", proclaimed in a written Constitution and venerated as a source of unique legal authority, the rule of law serves in Britain as a form of constitution. It is in this fundamental sense that Britain has a *common law constitution*: the ideas and values of which the rule of law consists are reflected and embedded in the ordinary common law . . .' (p. 4).

It should be no surprise that talk of 'legal culture' is contagious, and has all the ambiguity of any use of the Pandora's box which is the word 'culture'. We of course have the 'culture of human rights' without which there can be no rights or remedies: and the legal culture of the Others is not really legal at all, however they may excel in art, literature or music.

This second antinomy of sovereignty also binds the internal and the external. For England, parliamentary sovereignty was the bastion of national character, for many on the left the guarantee of a future for democratic socialism. It is to be defended at all costs against foreign innovation, especially in the form of positive rights, ever since 1789. At the same time, it has always meant domination, especially the supremacy of Westminster over Edinburgh or Cardiff – for A. V. Dicey, the implacable opponent of Home Rule and defender of Union between Britain and Ireland, over Dublin.[14]

Indeed, the language of sovereignty frequently employs anthropomorphic, often biological, metaphors. We speak of the 'body politic', of the body of law. That is why the concept of 'legal transplant' has proved so resonant, even if other terms such as 'transposition' or 'irritant' may be more accurate in particular contexts.[15]

It is at this point that law itself is ambiguous. It is what forms us, as English or American; it is what, if not primordial, is already there. Its inherent conservatism is augmented by the practice of judges and lawyers. At the same time, it is continually transformed through practice, not least because ours is not the only law. The others also have law as history and as practice, and it has never in recorded history been possible to avoid contamination.

Antinomies of the 'transplant'

I wish to distinguish two senses of transplant. The first is voluntary reception into 'our' law, often almost imperceptible, perhaps passive, or even, in some cases, a function of resistance to a greater foreign threat to sovereignty. The former is represented by the gradual, almost reluctant, reception into English law of the German administrative law concept of proportionality, or, more painfully, of the principles and standards of interpretation of the European Convention on Human Rights, and the latter, resistance, the role played by Roman Law in Scotland as a (defence) against the incursions of the English common law.

The second is more traumatic, more threatening. An obvious example is that of the reception into UK law of the European Convention on Human Rights, where the anguished debates within government have now been well

---

14 Dicey (1973); Dicey (1914).
15 Professor Esin Örücü prefers the language of 'transposition, tuning and fitting' – see Örücü (2002) p. 205.

documented. Lord Chancellor Jowett and others were quite clear that what was at stake was the vision of the seamless and organic development of the common law. It is ironical that the strongest opposition has come from both the ideologists of the specifically English legal culture, and from defenders of democratic socialism like Keith Ewing. Hence his qualified support for the Human Rights Act.[16]

This second sense of transplant is even more clearly exemplified by Russia, where the implant of Council of Europe principles and submission to the discipline of Strasbourg and other mechanisms have been met by a statist and nationalist discourse of appropriation. Ironically, Russia's accession to the Council of Europe and ratification of the European Convention on Human Rights were supported by a majority of nationalists and communists, for reasons of naked national interest.[17]

The problems of legal comparison

In their profound and sensitive study[18] of problems of mainstream comparative law, Bogumila Puchalska-Tych and Michael Salter observe that '. . . only by understanding the "socialist" past of contemporary Eastern European societies can we properly grasp the current processes of systemic transformation that these societies are now undergoing . . .'.[19] More importantly for the purpose of this chapter, they argue that:

> . . . both the socialist doctrine, and the systemic apparatus subservient to it, did not transform the Eastern European societies into homogeneous, socialist ones. If anything, the legacy of distinctive cultural traditions had been continuously interacting with the ordering of these societies in a much more complex manner than the crudely undifferentiated terms 'socialist' or 'totalitarian' can ever hope to reflect.[20]

The dialectical analysis for which they call would '. . . be the process of reflexive and sensitive constitution of the "other culture" in its specific context via one's own cultural and cognitive structures, and relating it to the theoretical framework of comparative legal studies'.[21] Thus, they commend John Bell's repeated call for reciprocal mediation and contextualisation,[22] and suggest that '[a]n agenda of mediation promises a valuable insight into the meaning, operation and place of law within diverse social, political and cultural contexts'.[23] They strongly criticise the '. . . static and abstract, i.e.,

---

16 Ewing (1999).   17 Bowring (1997).   18 Puchalska-Tych and Salter (1996).
19 Puchalska-Tych and Salter (1996) p. 163.
20 Puchalska-Tych and Salter (1996) pp. 166–167.
21 Puchalska-Tych and Salter (1996) p. 180.   22 Bell (1994).
23 Puchalska-Tych and Salter (1996) p. 181.

decontextualised, depiction [which can] ... only fail to grasp – let alone account for – the socio-political and legal dynamism which drives the various political and social upheavals involved in the systemic transformation still taking place in Eastern Europe'.[24]

It is part of the argument of this chapter that the complex relations between Russia and international human rights standards and mechanisms can only be understood through an appreciation of the history – the dialectic – of the intellectual history of Russia, always inseparably linked to Western Europe, for more than two centuries.

Absences in the theory of transplantation

The theory of legal transplantation is a crucial domain within the theory of legal comparativism. The debate concerning 'legal transplants' can be said to have begun in earnest in an exchange between Alan Watson and Otto Kahn-Freund in the 1970s, to which I will return.[25] There is now an extensive and growing scholarly literature on legal transplants, especially as concerns the former Soviet Union and Eastern Europe. Most of it – with a few exceptions – concerns commercial law. Thus, Frédérique Dahan writes:[26]

> What is indisputable is that for the legal systems of Central and Eastern Europe, *transplantation is a reality*. Because transition economies cannot afford and do not wish to go through the same process of slow and tentative development as the developed economies did in the past in order to achieve their modern legal and regulatory structures, they must, to a large extent, import them.

But importing a legal doctrine, mechanism or even a statute is not the same as importing an automobile; and even the automobile may need adapting for left-hand driving. Scott Newton, commenting on Dahan's remark, points out that:

> ... the very term 'transplantation', biased towards the technical, masks the political realities, for 'legal transplantation' is always necessarily a species of the genus legislation. That is, even supposing a jurisdiction decides to import a foreign law lock, stock and barrel, it nonetheless must *enact* it, with all the sovereign political implications any enactment brings ... in transplantation as in transition, the emphasis on product over process works to privilege legality over legitimacy.[27]

---

24 Puchalska-Tych and Salter (1996) p. 183.
25 Watson (1993); Kahn-Freund (1974); see Watson's reply (1976).
26 Dahan (2000) p. 372.   27 Newton (2001) SOAS Working Paper, pp. 3, 7.

That is why the antinomies of sovereignty are vital to any consideration of the transplant. And one has the strong sense that legality which is illegitimate ought to be a contradiction in terms.[28] Newton's own work is a profound reflection on two substantial items of commercial legislation, an Insolvency Law and a Pension Law, on which he worked on behalf of the US aid agency in Kazakhstan.

Most writers on transplantation, for the most part transplants in the commercial arena, do not share Newton's sensitivity to the issues. Some allow themselves to be carried away by the obvious physicality of the metaphor, in addition to losing sight of the real underlying issues. An example is the – informative at the level of description – work of Christopher Osakwa, who performed a 'biopsy' of the 1994 Civil Codes of Russia and Kazakkstan,[29] and employed a colourful biological metaphor. For him, these two Codes:

> . . . are ideological siblings – they share a common genealogy, have the same genetic traits . . . suffer from the same genetic disease . . . are both test tube babies that were conceived by in vitro fertilisation in a textbook-perfect feat of genetic engineering, both function like potted plants in their respective societies . . .[30]

The reader must pause to recover from the shock of comparing test-tube babies and potted plants.

Nevertheless, Osakwa acknowledges that the 'true heroes' of the Code were the Russian 'civilists', who 'with the benevolent assistance of their Dutch masters and American consultants' drafted a code which, he believes, will go down in history as one of the great codes of the twentieth century. But he fails to recognise that there was more than a little tension between the two sides: the Dutch lawyers from Leiden, who from the outset wanted to work supportively and respectfully with established Russian experts, albeit those from the older, Soviet-educated generation, and Americans who wanted to impose an Anglo-Saxon import. He notes that 'right from the inception . . . the Russian drafters fell under the spell of Dutch consultants'[31] . . . but this is not the real story. This error is compounded by his view that the Soviet Civil Codes of 1922 and 1964 were founded on Marxist-Leninist philosophy. Far from it. These codes, the first the product of the New Economic Policy, were firmly based on Swiss and German models, and reflect Russia's orientation to the 'continental civil law tradition', which is not, as he believes, a post-1991 innovation. This is perhaps as misguided as his view that 'the purpose of USAID funding was entirely altruistic'![32]

28 See Habermas (1997).   29 Osakwa (1998).   30 Osakwa (1998) p. 1413.
31 Osakwa (1998) p. 1417.   32 Osakwa (1998) p. 1440.

Osakwa's is not the only methodology. Steven J. Hein's article[33] on his proposal for Russia's adoption of an entirely new (for it) law on servitudes (easements), is more thoughtful. His approach is, however, unusual in that no such law is yet proposed. His method is to compare and contrast the efficacy for such a transplant of the competing theories of Alan Watson[34] and Otto Kahn-Freund.[35] Their differences are presented by Hein as beginning with Watson's 'proposition that there is no inherent relationship between a State's laws and its society', whereas Kahn-Freund stands with Montesquieu in what Ewald[36] has described as a 'mirror theory' – Montesquieu's claim that:

> laws should be so appropriate to the people for whom they are made that it is very unlikely that the laws of one nation can suit another . . .

Thus, Kahn-Freund argued that 'we cannot take for granted that rules or institutions are transplantable'.[37] He proposed a two-stage process. First, determine the relationship between the legal rule to be transplanted and the sociopolitical structure of the state from which it is taken – its macro-political structure (democracy or dictatorship), the distribution of power, and the role played by organised interests. Second, compare the sociopolitical environments. The closer the first relationship, the greater must be the similarity between environments for the transplant to succeed.

Watson, similarly, can be said to recommend two steps. First, the logic of the foreign law must be analysed. If the foreign law is not inimical to the political, social or economic circumstances of the receiving state, it can be successfully transplanted. Second, the sociopolitical environment of the receiving state must be examined to see if conditions are ripe for legal change by transplantation.[38] He identified nine factors which determine whether a transplant will succeed.[39] The *Pressure Force* (1) is the persons or groups who believe that benefit would result from a change. The *Opposition Force* (2) is the converse: those who believe that change will harm them. The *State's Transplant Bias* (3) is its receptivity to a particular foreign law – the general attitude to legal borrowing. The *Discretion Factor* (4) asks whether the transplanted rule can be evaded by choice, or whether its application is inescapable. The more choices an individual has to avoid undesired aspects of a law, the more likely it is that the law will be accepted. The *Generality Factor* (5) is the scope of the legal rule, or its effects. The greater it is, the more likely there is to be an Opposition Force. *Social Inertia* (6) is the desire for stability, since elites especially have a desire for no change. The society's *Felt-Needs* (7) indicate whether a society feels itself in need of the particular change. The

33 Hein (1996).   34 Watson (1993); Watson (2001); Watson (1966); Watson (1981).
35 Kahn-Freund (1974).   36 Ewald (1995).   37 Kahn-Freund (1974) p. 27.
38 Hein (1996) p. 195.   39 Watson (1993) p. 322.

Source of Law (8) indicates whether the new law will enter as a statute, case law, custom, or through scholarly writing. *Law-Shaping Lawyers* (9) are prime actors in bringing about change.

In the contest proposed by Hein, where the criterion for judgment is adequacy in relation to the (imaginary) proposed transplant, Watson wins on points. But, it is suggested, the argument is sterile. The assumption seems to be that the new law on servitudes will come from the USA. But Hein nowhere indicates why Russia could not develop its own law if it so desired, drawing as has so often been the case on a variety of foreign resources. And, unlike Alford (and Trubek before him) there is no sense that there might be a dynamic reciprocal effect. What is most surprising is that the historical context of development is entirely absent. This reflects a one-sided appropriation of Watson, most of whose work is based on rich historical empirical research.

Much the same territory is explored in a fascinating article[40] by Gunther Teubner, the authorised representative of Niklas Luhmann's 'autopoesis theory' in English legal academe.[41] His starting point is not a hypothetical law, but the real imposition on English law of the continental European principle of *bona fides* through the mechanism of an EU Directive. He too compares Watson and Kahn-Freund. He ascribes to Watson three main arguments. First, comparative law should no longer simply study foreign laws but study the interrelations between different legal systems. Second, transplants are the main source of legal change. Third, legal evolution takes place rather insulated from social changes, tending to use the technique of 'legal borrowing', and can be explained without reference to social, political or economic factors. These arguments are criticised for their incompleteness, and are compared with two sets of key distinctions introduced by Kahn-Freund. First, 'mechanic' (relatively easy transfer) as against 'organic' (transfer dependent on interlocking with the specific power structure of the society concerned). Second, 'comprehensive' (the social embeddedness of law) as against 'selective' (where the primary interdependency is concentrated on politics). On this basis, Teubner proposes four theses:[42]

1   Law's contemporary ties to society are no longer comprehensive, but are highly selective and vary from loose coupling to tight interwovenness.
2   They are no longer connected to the totality of the social, but to diverse fragments of society.
3   Where, formerly, law was tied to society by its identity with it, ties are now established via difference.
4   They no longer evolve in a joint historical development but in the conflictual interrelation of two or more independent evolutionary trajectories.

---

40 Teubner (1998) p. 17.   41 See Teubner (1993).   42 Teubner (1998) p. 18.

A compelling examination of the utterly different German and English legal mind-sets, the former based on a high degree of conceptual systematisation and abstract dogmatisation, the latter on a distinction and elaboration of different factual situations, as well as the contrasting 'production regimes' of the two countries, leads Teubner to his conclusion:

> This shows how improbable it is that a legal rule will be successfully transplanted in a binding arrangement of a different legal context. If it is not rejected outright, either it destroys the binding arrangement or it will result in a dynamics of mutual irritations that alter its identity fundamentally.[43]

But because for Teubner legal systems are only 'operationally closed social discourses', the historical factor, so important for Russia, cannot perform its exceptionally important mediating role. Nor can Teubner account for the dialectical reflexivity of legal comparativism in theory and practice.

Jonathan Wiener has perhaps come closer to a historicised account of legal transplants, writing in the context of environmental law.[44] He rightly points out that nations frequently borrow doctrines from each other, often across vast distances of time and place, and much of American law was received from England and from France and Spain. Thus, while there is much literature on the question of borrowing from one country to another, there had been none on transplants into international treaty law. He approves[45] Watson's remark that:

> . . . the time of reception [of a legal idea] is often a time when the provision is looked at more closely, hence a time when law can be reformed or made more sophisticated.[46]

He concludes that:

> . . . the metaphor of 'legal transplants' is apt: we are selecting a bit of regulatory DNA from national law, inserting it into an international law embryo, and hoping that this new legal hybrid will grow to be a hardy offspring.[47]

It is noteworthy in the survey above that none of the scholars cited have explored the notion of legal transplants in the context of human rights, although Wiener's metaphor of DNA comes closer to what is needed in order to account for this phenomenon.

---

43 Teubner (1998) p. 28.   44 Wiener (2001).   45 Wiener (2001) p. 1369.
46 Watson (1993) p. 99.   47 Wiener (2001) p. 1371.

Transplants and human rights

Only Julie Mertus, well known for her writings on women's rights, and on international interventions in Kosovo, has (to my knowledge) so far made the link.[48] Her starting point is an exploration of the meaning of globalisation for ideas of democracy and good governance and problems with 'international civil society'. This leads her to a consideration of the role of NGOs at work on 'legal transplant' projects – projects mostly grouped under the rubric 'rule of law' – an area in which she has considerable experience. These she describes as attempts 'to transplant laws and, in some cases, entire legal systems from one place to another, usually from a country perceived as "working properly" to one deemed in great need'.[49] She sees two waves. The first was after World War II, when the victors rewrote the constitutions of the vanquished to conform to their own ideology. The second came in the 1960s, the UN's 'Decade of Development', when '. . . departing colonial powers hastily impose carbon copies of their own documents and laws which evolved from different cultural and historical backgrounds'.[50] This coincided with the 'law and development' movement, which sent so many US lawyers to Latin America and Africa to train problem-solving legal engineers, and 'promote a modern vision of law as an instrument of development policy along capitalist and democratic lines'.[51] Mertus cites Gardner, to say that 'the history of the law and development movement is rather sad'[52] – 'It is a history of an attempt to transfer the American legal models that were themselves flawed.'[53] As Mertus notes, one of the movement's shortcomings was its failure to understand that local people are actors, and not mere subjects, and generally turn to American legal assistance for their own ends.[54]

These lessons were not heeded when the collapse of the USSR and the end of 'communism' ushered in 'a new wave of legal transplants that duplicates wholesale the techniques of earlier times: sending in American lawyers in an attempt to reconstruct the local legal system in a manner more compatible with United States interests'.[55] The American Bar Association's CEELI (Central and Eastern European Law Initiative), funded by USAID, has often sought not only to transplant American methods of legal education (the 'Socratic' method), but to encourage the wholesale replacement or rewriting of local law.[56]

Unfortunately, although her criticisms of US policies are acute, Mertus accepts without question the project of 'transformative democratic goals',

---

48　Mertus (1999).　　49　Mertus (1999) p. 1378.

50　See Lis Wiehl 'Constitution, Anyone? A New Cottage Industry' *New York Times*, 2 February 1990.

51　See Gardner (1980).　　52　Gardner (1980) p. 22.　　53　Mertus (1999) p. 1380.

54　For further critiques, see Faundez (1997).　　55　Ajani (1995); Mertus (1999) p. 1380.

56　It should be noted that ABA/CEELI's current programmes, especially in Russia, are primarily focused on issues such as violence against women and juvenile justice.

namely the 'right to democratic governance' for which Thomas Franck has argued so persuasively.[57] It is hard to escape the conclusion that such a project is an unproblematised and unreflective product of a specific, American, form of political liberalism. This has two consequences. On the one hand, Mertus rightly identifies a need to make transnational civil society democratic[58] – it does not live up to its own ideals. She points out that many non-governmental organisations, especially those with the most influence in the human rights discursive community, are not democratic at all – Amnesty International, Human Rights Watch, Lawyers Committee for Human Rights. Moreover, they are much more powerful than NGOs outside the US and Western Europe. As Mertus puts it:

> Quite simply, well-financed western NGOs are likely to have more power than their poorer and non-Western counterparts, and the lack of transparency and accountability in transnational civil society is likely to keep this power unchecked.[59]

On the other hand, she fundamentally mistakes – in the view of this chapter – the reasons why 'many legal transplants do not take root in Eastern Europe'. She puts this down to low salaries of judges, inadequate classrooms, courtrooms and record keeping, 'dead wood' – legal officers who simply refuse to change, and so on.

The answer is, I suggest, elsewhere. Writing about US experience at a different time on the other side of the world – the US transplant of an Antimonopoly Law to Japan in 1947, and its rejection by the host legal system – Robert Stack gets much closer to the roots of the problem.[60] Not only did the Americans give Japan a law without explaining why,[61] they never understood that during the Meiji era, 1868–1912 (also the period of Russian reforms), the Japanese governments had carefully, thoroughly, and with great sophistication, carried out reforms drawing primarily from European civil law models. The reception of human rights standards into Japanese law has, as in Russia, been for this reason, quite different, despite 'Japan's reluctance to engage in human rights discourse generally'.[62] There is perhaps a paradox, since, as Alston notes, the 1946 Japanese Constitution, albeit a 'classic case of a foreign transplant',[63] has been a success story, never amended. But as

---

57 Franck (1992); (1990); (1995).
58 Mertus (1999) p. 1384. See also An-Na'im (1994) p. 122; Otto (1997) p. 3.
59 Mertus (1999) p. 1385.   60 Stack (2000).   61 Stack (2000) p. 408.
62 Alston (1999) p. 627, and see Iwasawa (1998).
63 Alston notes that 'Popular sovereignty was asserted, equality rights for women were recognised, US-style separation of church and state was mandated, respect for a full range of individual civil and political rights was mandated, and a comprehensive American-style system of judicial review was mandated.' (p. 629).

Alston points out, following Inoue,[64] sexual equality and individual dignity were subsumed within the traditional Japanese notion of aristocratic honour in society, within a hierarchical ordering of social relations, while religious freedom and separation of church and state were consistent with the particular nature of Shintoism.[65]

Thus, no one can question the transformation of the Russian legal system since the mid-1980s – and especially since 1991, with accession to the Council of Europe in 1996, and ratification of the European Convention on Human Rights in 1998. But it should be obvious that, especially in the spheres of constitutional and human rights, Russia has not been importing US models. Instead, it has, through its own choice, drawn closer once more to the Western European mainstream. This is not a process that is unique to Russia. As David Feldman has pointed out in connection with the UK's belated, slow, reluctant and partial incorporation of European human rights principles,[66] '. . . the Convention's approach is far more closely in tune with the essentially collectivist cultural heritage which forms part of the bedrock on which the constitution of the United Kingdom developed and must build . . .'.[67] This collectivist tradition contrasts strikingly with US 'fundamentalist' liberalism, and must contribute to reassuring sceptical Russians.

The question is: what was there before? Was there a 'legal culture' simply anathema to human rights, as Osakwa suggests? Was Russia simply the home of backwardness and despotism? Is it really the case that the Russians are condemned to catching up with the enlightened West from a position of legal barbarism? To answer these questions, the historical perspective is essential.

I suggest just two anecdotal examples. Serfdom, *krepostnoye pravo*, was abolished in Russia in 1861. Slavery was finally abolished in the USA in 1866 – the American Anti-Slavery Society was founded in 1833.[68] Jury trial has for some years been available in nine of Russia's 89 regions, and is about to be extended to the rest. This is not an innovation forced on Russia after defeat in the Cold War. It is the restoration of an effective system of jury trial for all serious criminal cases, presided over by independent judges, which existed in Russia from 1864 to 1917. Jury trial was introduced in a number of Western European countries at about the same time as in Russia, though it had been strongly advocated by leading law reformers from the late eighteenth century.

The Russian history of reform and innovation

What is frequently neglected is any recognition of Russia's own pre-revolutionary traditions, especially the reforms of Alexander II (1855–1881).

---

64 Inoue (1991).   65 Alston (1999) p. 630.
66 See Lester (1984) p. 46; Marston (1993); Lester (1998).   67 Feldman (1999) p. 178.
68 See the African American Mosaic on the struggle of abolition and slavery – http://lcweb.loc.gov/exhibits/african/afam007.html.

Starting with the revolutionary Law on Emancipation of the Serfs in 1861, these reforms culminated in the Laws of 20 November 1864.[69] The new Laws introduced a truly adversarial criminal justice procedure, and made trial by jury obligatory in criminal proceedings. Judges were given the opportunity to establish real independence, in part by freeing them of the duty to gather evidence, and enabling them to act as a free umpire between the parties. The Prokuracy lost its powers of 'general review of legality', and became a state prosecutor on the Western model. The institution of Justices of the Peace was introduced. It is ironical that the Bolsheviks reinstated the pre-reform model of the Prokuracy.

Indeed, as Samuel Kucherov wrote in 1953: 'Between 1864 and 1906, Russia offered the example of a state unique in political history, where the judicial power was based on democratic principles, whereas the legislature and executive powers remained completely autocratic.'[70] A collection on jury trial in Russia contains an extensive memoir by one of the most distinguished judges of the period, A. F. Koni.[71] Moreover, it also reproduces the advocates' speeches and judicial summings-up in some of the most famous trials, for example the trial in 1878 of Vera Zasulich, charged with the attempted murder of the governor of St Petersburg, Trepov, whom she had shot in broad daylight and before witnesses. Koni, who was presiding judge, refused to be pressured by the authorities, and Zasulich was acquitted, a verdict which was respected by the authorities.

It is noteworthy that in the major speeches made to legal audiences at the start of his presidency, Putin referred to just these issues. His speech of 24 January 2000[72] was delivered in his then capacity of Acting President to a colloquium of leaders of Republic, Krai, and Oblast Courts. His main theme was the independence of the judiciary. He quoted Judge Koni, and referred to the necessity for correspondence with generally recognised norms of international law. Most important, he made explicit reference to the ratification by Russia of the European Convention on Human Rights and Fundamental Freedoms, which had therefore become a constituent part of the Russian legal system. Above all, he said, the jurisdiction of the European Court of Human Rights had been recognised. Therefore special attention must be given to those problems of the Russian judicial system that were likely to call forth a reaction from the European Court. Furthermore, on 27 November 2000,[73] at the Fifth All-Russian Congress of Judges, while he made no mention of the dictatorship of law, or of international obligations, he stressed that judicial decisions should be 'rapid, correct and just', and noted that these simple but precise principles had already been formulated in Russia in 1864,

69 See Chistyakov and Novitskaya (1998).   70 Kucherov (1953) p. 215.
71 Kazantsev (1991).   72 At http://president.kremlin.ru/events/2.html.
73 At http://president.kremlin.ru/events/107.html.

at the time of the judicial reforms which had so closely followed the abolition of serfdom.

Putin's references to history and to the present obligations voluntarily accepted by Russia were no accident.

Russia's democratic legal traditions

In order to understand these processes, we should look deeper still into Russian history and traditions. Gross errors by US and other Western legal experts and commentators would be avoided by the realisation that judicial independence, adversarial court proceedings and trial by jury are not recent imports from the liberal West to the uncultured East, but the reinstatement of a rich and specifically Russian experience.

This history begins at a climactic time for the UK and for Western Europe, and with a surprise for Western scholars. A recent textbook, based on a course of lectures at Moscow State University,[74] points out that the first Russian professor of law, S. E. Desnitskii (1740–1789), was a product not so much of the French Enlightenment, that is of Diderot and Rousseau, but of the Scottish Enlightenment.

Desnitskii studied in Scotland, under Adam Smith and others, from 1761 to 1767, when he received a Doctorate of Civil and Church Law from the University of Glasgow. He was much influenced by the ideas of the Scottish Enlightenment, especially by the philosophy of David Hume, and especially by the Scottish emphasis on Roman Law traditions and principles – the focus of Alan Watson's pathbreaking work on legal transplants.[75] On the basis of his lengthy researches in Scotland, in 1768 Desnitskii sent the Empress Catherine II his 'Remarks on the institutions of legislative, judicial and penitentiary powers in the Russian Empire' – however, his suggestions were entirely unacceptable, and the work was sent to the archives. Among other radical proposals, Desnitskii urged the abolition of serfdom. He survived Catherine's rejection of these ideas, and became a full professor of law in 1777, shortly after the Pugachev uprising. He published books introducing Russians to the ideas of Adam Smith and John Millar. At Catherine's own instruction, he translated into Russian volume 1 of Blackstone's *Commentaries*, and this was published in Moscow in 1780–1783. His courses included the history of Russian law, Justinian's *Pandects*, and comparisons of Roman and Russian law.[76] He died in the year of the French Revolution, and the Declaration of the Rights of Man and of the Citizen.

It should be noted that Desnitskii did not undertake a simple transmission of some already existing Western liberalism to Russia. The period of his work

74 Azarkin (1999).   75 See Watson (1993).
76 Butler (1999) pp. 24–25 and pp. 52–53. See also Brown (1977).

was as much the period of the revolt of reason against autocracy in England as in Russia. Desnitskii was born only a few years after Thomas Paine.[77] The much better known Radishchev thus stood on the shoulders both of Desnitskii and Paine when in 1790 he published his scandalous *Puteshestvii iz Peterburga v Moskvu* (*Journey from Petersburg to Moscow*), which was a powerful manifesto for the abolition of serfdom. He was promptly arrested for this by Catherine II. She commuted his death sentence to exile for 10 years. Pavel I allowed him back in 1796, and Alexander I even sought to attract him to legislative work. But it was clear his liberal ideas were as unacceptable to his autocratic audience as were those of Thomas Paine to the English monarchy, and in 1802 he committed suicide.

There is no question, however, that political reaction was even deeper in Russia than in Britain, and the defeat of the Decembrist uprising in 1825 drove enlightenment and liberal thinking about rights deep underground. V. S. Solovyev (1853–1900) was the next Russian to think deeply about issues of rights. He, like Radishchev, was not a lawyer, and his approach, while committed to enlightenment values, had a specifically religious focus to it. This spiritual, idealistic dimension to Russian rights discourse is characteristic and a specific and unique contribution. B. N. Chicherin (1828–1904) was the first lawyer to work through issues of liberalism in connection with law and rights. He argued for a constitutional monarchy and strong state, and strongly opposed Aleksandr Gertsen (Hertzen to us) – a writer who spent much of his life in exile in England. He did, however, draw on both Russian and European experience and traditions. Another lawyer, P. I. Novgorodtsev (1866–1924), was the chief exponent of a natural law, Kantian approach to questions of the relationship between the individual and law. He too was strongly influenced by the Russian spiritual heritage. One of the latest proponents of this trend was N. A. Berdyaev (1874–1948), a member of the *Vekh* group, whose manifesto collection of articles appeared in 1909, attracting the strongest criticism from Marxists and liberals alike. It is a little odd that Berdyaev, a spiritual philosopher, appears in the textbook on human rights; for Berdyaev, inalienable human rights were the form of expression and existence on earth (Caesar's kingdom) of personal freedom, that is of the transcendental (and godlike) phenomena of the kingdom of Spirit. In his book *Gosudarstvo. Vlast i pravo. Iz istorii russkoi pravovoi mysli* (*The State. Power and law. From the history of Russian legal thought*), Berdyaev wrote 'The declaration of the rights of God and the declaration of human rights are one and the same declaration.'

---

77 Paine left England for the American colonies in 1774, and began writing his extraordinarily influential *Common Sense* in 1775. Its publication in 1776 was a sensation, selling at least 100,000 copies in that year alone. Its content was entirely unacceptable to the English ruling elite. His *Rights of Man* appeared in 1791, and he was forced to leave England, remaining in France for 10 years – he was imprisoned in 1793 after war broke out between England and France.

The point I wish to make by way of this brief survey is that there is a distinctively Russian approach to and thought about human rights which repays careful study by Western scholars. These are thinkers of the first rank. Moreover, the account above is sufficient to show that while it is possible to speak of Russian culture, and even of Russian legal culture, it would be a grave mistake to ignore the complex and dynamic interplay of Russian and Western European – especially Scottish! – histories and traditions.

Evidence of the interplay of restoration and transplant

I wish to point to three respects in which a dynamic of change can bring into close interrelation the elements of restoration and transplant already noted above.

The first concerns the work of the Constitutional Court. The whole jurisprudence of the European Court is now part of Russian law, and increasingly cited in Russian courts. There are many cases on individual human rights in which the Russian Constitutional Court has relied on international standards. In one of the most striking examples, the Court achieved a significant breakthrough in the implementation of international jurisprudence. This was the case of *Maslov*, decided on 27 June 2000.[78] The case concerned the constitutionality of Articles 47 and 51 of the Criminal Procedural Code, and the issue at stake was the right to defence counsel following detention. According to the Code, a person in detention as a 'suspected person' or an 'accused', was entitled as of right to the presence of a defender. But this was not the case for a person brought to a police station to be interrogated as a 'witness', even though attendance was compulsory, and might well lead to transformation into a suspect or accused.

The Court not only referred to Article 14 of the ICCPR and Articles 5 and 6 of the ECHR, but for the first time cited the jurisprudence of the European Court of Human Rights. The cases – six in all – to which they referred were *Quaranta v Switzerland*,[79] *Imbrioscia v Switzerland*,[80] *John Murray v United Kingdom*,[81] *Deweer v Belgium*,[82] *Eckle v Federal Republic of Germany*,[83] and *Foti v Italy*.[84] The legal reasoning in *Maslov* demonstrates that not only the ICCPR and ECHR, but the jurisprudence of the European Court of Human Rights, are now integral parts of the Russian legal system. This is further demonstrated not only by the constant reference to the Convention in the latest commentaries and textbooks, but also by the fact that every judge in

---

78 Case P-10 of 2000, at ks.rfnet.ru/pos/p11_00.html.   79 Series A No. 205 (1991).
80 Series A No. 275 (1993).   81 8 February 1996, Reports 1996-1, Vol 1.
82 Series A No. 35 (1980).   83 15 July 1982 (no. 51), 5 EHRR 12.
84 Series A No. 56 (1982).

Russia has received the two-volume collection of the 100 leading cases decided by the European Court of Human Rights, published in the year 2000, together with a comprehensive CD-ROM.[85] The first two volumes of cases of the Russian Constitutional Court (edited by Judge Morshchakova) appeared. The first, containing the jurisprudence of the years 1992 to 1996, was published in 1997; and the second, containing the jurisprudence of the Court from 1997–1998, reached the bookshops in April 2000.

It is to be noted with regret, however, that even though the Russian Constitutional Court is in many ways modelled on the Karlsruhe Constitutional Court of Germany (the Russian justices have all spent time in Germany besides visiting many other sister courts), the Russian Court has not to date begun to refer to the jurisprudence of the Karlsruhe Court, or indeed the other new constitutional courts of Hungary, Poland and other former Soviet and Eastern European states. Nevertheless, the Russian Court is itself increasingly developing a precedent-based jurisprudence for the purpose of Russian domestic law, in which European Court cases are an important source of binding precedents.

Another example is the result of Council of Europe pressure, but has been universally applauded. The penitentiary system was transferred from the Ministry of the Interior to the Ministry of Justice in 1998 as required by the Council of Europe, and the three years since have seen a remarkable opening up of the system, and a genuine reform process.

The Council of Europe was also anxious to see the restoration of trial by jury. This was no transplant, as noted above, but was the restoration of a system which worked surprisingly well in late Tsarist Russia. It was restored on 16 July 1993 by the enactment of a new Part X to the Criminal Procedural Code, and enshrined in the December 1993 Constitution. To date it has been introduced in only nine of 89 regions of Russia. This had a surprising consequence for another bone of contention, the death penalty, in abeyance by virtue of a Presidential moratorium, also a requirement of the Council of Europe until Russia ratifies the Sixth Protocol to the Convention. In February 1999 the Federal Constitutional Court held[86] that in order for the death penalty to be applied at all, the accused must be given a trial by jury, as provided in Article 20.2. The Court stated expressly that the death penalty could not be imposed anywhere until trial by jury is available everywhere. This decision means that the death penalty cannot, pending full introduction of jury trial, lawfully be imposed anywhere in the Federation. The Court also

---

85 *European Court of Human Rights. Collected Decisions in Two Volumes* (NORMA Publishers, the Institute of Europe at the Institute of International Relations of the Russian Foreign Ministry, COLPI Institute (Soros), the Council of Europe, and Interights (London), Moscow, 2000).

86 Decision of 2 February 1999, No. 3-P, *Rossiskaya Gazeta*, 10 February 1999, English summary in Venice Commission, *Bulletin on Constitutional Case-Law*, Edition 1999-1, pp. 96–98.

noted that it was over five years since the Constitution was adopted, which was a sufficient length of time for the necessary amendments to legislation. What was intended as a transitional provision had in fact become a permanent restriction, and therefore conflicted with Articles 19 (equality before the law), 20.2 (right to life) and 46.1 (legal protection of rights) of the Constitution.

President Putin has, in line with his manifesto noted above, pushed through even more dramatic reforms. Most provisions of the new Criminal Procedural Code, enacted on 19 December 2001, came into force on 1 July 2002. Jury trial was available in every region of Russia except Chechnya from 1 January 2003. The President was adamant that this would not permit the restoration of the death penalty.

Strikingly, the new Code finally enabled the 1993 Constitution to come fully into force. The reason is that the Constitution provides in Article 22 that arrest and detention are only permitted by judicial decision, and that a person may be held in custody for no more than 48 hours before being brought before a court. But this right could not be made effective until the former Code was replaced. The new Code also enabled Russia to withdraw the – highly embarrassing – Reservation it entered on ratifying the European Convention, in view of its inability to comply with Article 5.3 of the Convention. As a result of a startling decision of the Constitutional Court on 14 March 2002,[87] this part of the new Code came into force with the bulk of the Code, on 1 July 2002, and not in January 2004 as originally intended. The Court laid special emphasis on compliance with the Convention.

Finally, I should mention a transplant, or borrowing, of a more surprising nature – a borrowing from a much earlier period. On 8 March 2000, Russia submitted its first Report[88] on the Implementation of Provisions of the Council of Europe's Framework Convention (FCNM) for the Protection of National Minorities. Russia signed this Convention on 28 February 1996 on joining the Council of Europe. But a Law on National Minorities, as recommended by the Council of Europe, has not been enacted. Instead, in a process starting in 1988 and culminating in Yeltsin's conversion in 1994, Russia has undertaken the surprising innovation of resurrecting Austro-Marxist theory – that of Otto Bauer,[89] Rudolf Hilferding,[90] and Karl Renner,[91] anathema to the Bolsheviks and their successors, as the basis for the new Russian legislation,

---

87 Decision P6-02 of 14 March 2002, complaints of S. S. Malenkin, R. N. Martynov and S. V. Pustovalov, to be found at http://ks.rfnet.ru/pos/p6-02.htm.
88 To be found at www.riga.lv/minelres/reports/russia/russia.htm.
89 Born 5 September 1881, died 4 July 1938.
90 Born 10 August 1877, died 11 February 1941.
91 Born 14 December 1870, died 31 December 1950.

in particular the 1996 Federal Law 'On National-Cultural Autonomies'.[92] By 1999, about 126 NCAs had been created. Among them, the Ukrainian, Polish and German autonomies were the largest and had the most advanced programmes for their development. The process of forming an NCA for the more than one million Roma of Russia started in November 1999, and it was legally registered in the Ministry of Justice in March 2000. On 20 April the Roma were granted formal representation on the Ministry of Federation and Nationality Affairs. This ongoing experiment exemplifies the fact that borrowing is often a matter of conscious choice – selection, often surprising, from a set of alternatives.[93]

Can any good come of transplants?

Watson is right to argue that the history of law and legal systems displays so many examples of transplants – or at least of wholesale reception of the law of another country or period – that transplantation is a normal feature of the law of any country.[94] As he puts it: '. . . transplanting is, in fact, the most fertile source of development. Most changes in most systems are the result of borrowing.'[95] But, I argue, it must equally be true that comparative law can never be simply the comparison of two separate and unconnected entities, frozen in the present. If the laws of the countries in question are studied in their historical development, then in many cases, where there have been diplomatic, trade and cultural contacts, it will be found that there has been a rich and dynamic dialectic. At the very least, another valuable dimension will have been added to the domestic debate, providing authority to the arguments of those seeking change. That is, strengthening the case of those who wish their case to be strengthened – not necessarily those that 'we' would regard as radicals or reformers. This may happen even where the transplant appears to have been imposed by pressure or inducements, as with Russia. The process is most rich where there is a constant feedback – where those implementing the transplant, even if there is no reciprocal implantation, are obliged to reflect on their own law and legal traditions.

As indicated above, reception of one set of law may indeed serve resistance to – immunisation against – a set of laws and traditions unwelcome for political reasons. Thus, the continued importance of Roman Law in Scotland as resistance to England, or of the Netherlands Civil Code in Russia in preference to the blandishments of the Americans. To take the former, Watson cites T. B. Smith, Professor of Scots Law and later Scottish Law Commissioner, lamenting, in 1958, the acceptance of rules of English law:

---

92 Federal Law of the Russian Federation 'On National-Cultural Autonomies', of 17 June 1996, No. 74-FZ.
93 See Bowring (2002), (2005a).   94 Watson (1996).   95 Watson (1993) p. 95.

'But, alas . . . we in Scotland have gone a-whoring after some very strange gods.'[96]

One consequence of the analysis presented above is a respectful disagreement with Professor Örücü's assumption that '. . . systems in transition look to the pool of competing models available in Western Europe and America with the purpose of re-designing and modernising their legal, economic and social systems . . .'.[97] On close examination, the recent lived experience is much more interesting and dynamic. The decision to adopt the National Cultural Autonomy model referred to above did not choose from any model available in the West, but looked back instead to a model which was never implemented in its own time – a historical curiosity, perhaps.

And it should never be forgotten that Russia's apparent importation of Western human rights is in many important respects a restoration of Russia's own reform traditions.

Conclusion – and the importance of the existence of the Strasbourg mechanism

We have already seen, in Chapter 4, how Russia's own engagement with human rights is largely a history of gross and systematic violation of the very rights it undertook to protect in 1996 and 1998. My own conclusion is that for the Chechen applicants – and they are not victims, but survivors – taking a case to the Strasbourg Court was not at all the futile exercise described by Douzinas in the passage cited in Chapter 8. They took enormous risks in going to the Court; in another case, *Bitiyeva v Russia*,[98] Zura Bitiyeva brought a case in 2000 relating to the ill-treatment in detention of herself and her family, and was herself killed by the Russian forces in 2003. They derive some protection from the fact that they are well known to international institutions.

But they most certainly do not take their cases in order to obtain money from the perpetrator state. Instead, what is most important for them and for their communities is that the truth has, albeit several years later, at last been told, authoritatively and at the highest level, as to the tragedies which befell them and their families, and the responsibility of the state. This is not simply a question of competing narratives. Instead, on my arguments in this book, such applications are the means by which the rights declared in the darkest hour of the French Revolution are re-invested with revolutionary content. It is not that the Chechens' struggle is legitimised by virtue of the rhetoric or the

---

96 Watson (2001), p. 102, citing Smith (1958) p. 72.
97 Örücü (2002) p. 220.
98 Application nos. 57953/00 and 37392/03, judgment of 21 June 2007; the Court found violations of Articles 3 (ill-treatment), 5 (unlawful detention), 38(1)(a) (obstruction of the Court), 2 (killing by the State), and 13 (no effective remedy) – EHRAC represented the applicants.

meagre individual remedies on offer in Strasbourg.[99] On the contrary, the daring use made by the Chechen applicants is the means by which the dead rhetoric of government pronouncements or of worthy NGOs is transformed – transmuted – into words and ideas which have material force. It is possible to say that as a result of winning these cases, the relation of forces in Russia as a whole has been realigned, towards the survivors.

99 For an impassioned critique of recent Strasbourg case law on the right to political participation, see Bowring (2007).

Conclusion – what have I sought to do in this book?

The reader who has followed me in this book will long ago have realised that I do not attempt a systematic or methodical exposition of my views. Perhaps that will come later. Instead, the book should be read as a series of engagements, an attempt to achieve a unity of theory and practice. Thus, there are chapters, especially Chapters 2, 3, 4, 10 and 11 which explore fields of practice with which I am familiar, as a practitioner and as a political activist. Other chapters are the product of my deep conviction that engagement in 'embodied social practice' drives the thinking human being of necessity to seek to achieve as far as possible an adequate theoretical understanding of the grounds and purpose of the work undertaken. And, of course, theoretical work is none the less work. That is why several chapters contain a vigorous critique of a number of contemporary scholars – Habermas, Badiou, Žižek, Douzinas, Perrin, among others – who have sought in a variety of stylistic registers and philosophical traditions, to understand the extraordinary efflorescence of human rights discourse and practice since World War II. For me, it is only through such encounters that original thought can begin to appear.

It should also be apparent that the philosophical orientation of this book is towards Aristotle, Spinoza, Hegel, Marx (who not only drew deeply from what is critical in Hegel, but who early in his intellectual career copied out substantial parts of Spinoza's works), Lenin and Badiou. Although neither Marx nor Lenin would recognise as 'Marxist' much of the content of my book, I place myself firmly in their tradition. At this point, I do not entirely agree with Anthony Carty, who, in his new book says the following:

> Postmodernism is the exhausted moral spirit of the old Europeans and the ghosts of Marxist interpretations of imperialism offer us the most convincing explanations as to why the violence of the United States increases by the year.[1]

---

1 Carty (2007) p. 163.

For Carty, Marxism is 'a vision, an analysis of a condition, essentially pessimistic in its tracing of an increasing intensification of exploitation'.[2]

My account has sought not to be pessimistic, but instead to share in the 'heaven-storming' commitment of Marx and Lenin to the grandeur of the human spirit in resisting and sometimes overcoming exploitation. In the end, therefore, the argument of this book has been that the principles of contemporary international law and human rights, emerging as they have from revolutionary struggles before and especially after World War II, are not simply rhetoric, nor utopian and impossible prophecies, but real, material weapons of offence and defence in the human fight for emancipation.

That is the meaning I give to the phrase 'revolutionary conservatism'. I mean the vital importance for any serious theoretical and practical politics of 'defending the honour' of the great revolutions – French, Russian, and the extraordinary post World War II history of anti-colonial struggles. It is no accident that each of these historical events is linked to extraordinary and lasting developments in the actuality of human rights. That is the sense in which human rights are not mere rhetoric, a form of words hypocritically deployed by the powerful, and undermining the struggles of the oppressed. International law contains within its principles and concepts the content of world-shaking movements, a content that is capable, sometimes unpredictably, of reappearing with a terrible vengeance for injustice.

2 Carty (2007) p. 163.

References

Abresch, William (2005) 'A Human Rights Law of Internal Armed Conflict: The European Court of Human Rights in Chechnya' 16:4 *European Journal of International Law* pp. 741–767

Adiprasetya, Joas 'Whose Aristotle? Alasdair MacIntyre's Communitarian Virtues and Martha C. Nussbaum's Non-Relative Virtues', Boston University School of Philosophy, December 2003, at people.bu.edu/joas/papers/ts961-virtues.pdf

Adorno, Theodor (1978) *Minima Moralia* trans E. F. N. Jephcott (London: Verso)

Adorno, Theodor (1996) *Negative Dialectics* (London: Routledge)

Agamben, Giorgio (1998) *Homo Sacer: Sovereign Power and Bare Life* (Stanford: Stanford University Press)

Agamben, Giorgio (2005) *State of Exception* (Chicago: University of Chicago Press)

Ajani, Gianmaria (1995) 'By Chance and By Prestige: Legal Transplants in Russia and Eastern Europe' 43 *American Journal of Comparative Law* p. 93

Allan, T. (1993) *Law, Liberty and Justice. The Legal Foundations of British Constitutionalism* (Oxford: Clarendon Press)

Alston, Philip (1999) 'Review Essay: Transplanting Foreign Norms: Human Rights and Other International Legal Norms in Japan' 10:3 *European Journal of International Law* pp. 625–632

Alston, Philip (ed.) (2001) *Peoples Rights* (Oxford: Oxford University Press)

Anderson, B. (1983) *Imagined Communities* (London: Verso)

Anghie, Antony (2007) *Imperialism, Sovereignty and the Making of International Law* (Cambridge Studies in International & Comparative Law) (Cambridge: Cambridge University Press)

An-Na'im, Abdullahi and Deng, Francis M. (eds) (1990) *Human Rights in Africa: Cross-Cultural Perspectives* (Washington: Brookings)

An-Na'im, Abdullahi (ed.) (1992) *Human Rights in Cross-cultural Perspectives: A Quest for Consensus* (Philadelphia: University of Pennsylvania Press)

An-Na'im, Abdullahi (1992) 'Towards a Cross-Cultural Approach to Defining International Standards of Human Rights' in An-Na'im (ed.) *Human Rights in Cross-cultural Perspectives. A Quest for Consensus* (Philadelphia: University of Pennsylvania Press), pp. 19–43

An-Na'im, Abdullahi (1994) 'What Do We Mean by Universal?' Sept./October *Index on Censorship* pp. 120–128

An-Na'im, Abdullahi (2000) 'Human Rights and Islamic Identity in France and

Uzbekistan: Mediation of the Local and Global' 22:4 *Human Rights Quarterly* pp. 906–941

Archer, Margaret (1995) *Realist Social Theory: The Morphogenetic Approach* (Cambridge: Cambridge University Press)

Archer, Margaret (1996) *Culture and agency. The place of dualism in social theory* (Revised Edition) (Cambridge: Cambridge University Press)

Arendt, Hannah (2004) *The Origins of Totalitarianism* (New York: Schocken Books)

Arthur, Christopher J (1983) 'Introduction' to Y. Pashukanis *Law and Marxism: A General Theory. Towards a Critique of the Fundamental Concepts* (London: Pluto Press)

Arthur, Christopher J (2004) *The New Dialectic and Marx's* Capital (Leiden: Brill Academic Publishers)

Azarkin, N. M. (1999) Istoriya yuridicheskoi mysli Rossii: kurs lektsii (History of legal thought in Russia: a course of lectures) (Moscow)

Badiou, Alain (1999) *Manifesto for Philosophy* (New York: State University of New York Press)

Badiou, Alain (2001) *Ethics: An Essay on the Understanding of Evil* (London: Verso)

Badiou, Alain (2003a) *Saint Paul: The Foundation of Universalism* (Palo Alto: Stanford University Press)

Badiou, Alain (2003, reprinting) *Infinite Thought: Truth and the Return to Philosophy* (London: Continuum)

Badiou, Alain (2005) *Being and Event* (London: Continuum)

Badiou, Alain (2006) *L'Être et L'Événement T.2; Logiques Des Mondes* (Paris: Editions Seuil)

Badiou, Alain (2007) 'One Divides Itself into Two', Chapter 1, p. 17 in Sébastian Budgen, Stathis Kouvelakis and Slavoj Žižek (eds) (2007) *Lenin Reloaded: Toward a Politics of Truth* Sic 7 (Durham NC: Duke University Press)

Baker, Judith (ed.) (1994) *Group Rights* (Toronto: University of Toronto Press)

Balibar, Etienne (1998) *Spinoza and Politics* (London: Verso)

Balibar, Etienne (2004) 'Is a Philosophy of Human Civic Rights Possible? New Reflections on Equaliberty' 103:2–3 *South Atlantic Quarterly* pp. 311–322

Balzer, M. M. and Vinokurova, U. A. (1996). Nationalism, Interethnic Relations and Federalism: The Case of the Sakha Republic (Yakutia) *Europe-Asia Studies* 48: 101–120

Bankowski, Zenon and Mungham, Geoff (1976) *Images of Law* (London: Routledge)

Baratashvili, D. I. (1967) *Natsionalno-osvoboditelnoye dvizheniye i razvitiye mezhdunarodnovo prava* (The national liberation movement and the development of international law) No. 9 *Sovetskoye gosudarstvo i pravo* (Soviet state and law) pp. 69–75

Barker, E. (1995) 'The Discredited State: Thoughts on Politics before the War', in Julia Stapleton (ed.) *Group Rights: Perspectives Since 1900* (London: Thoemmes Press)

Barker, Jason (2002) *Alain Badiou. A Critical Introduction* (London: Pluto Press)

Baxi, Upendra (2002) *The Future of Human Rights* (Oxford: Oxford University Press)

Baylis, John and Smith, Steve (2004) *The Globalization of World Politics: An Introduction to International Relations* (Oxford: Oxford University Press)

Bell, J. (1994) 'Comparative Law and Legal Theory' in W. Krawietz, N. MacCormick and G. Wright (eds) *Prescriptive Formality and Normative Rationality in Modern Legal Systems* (Berlin: Duncker & Humboldt)

Bennoune, Karima (2002) ' "Sovereignty vs. Suffering"? Re-examining Sovereignty and Human Rights through the Lens of Iraq' in 'Symposium: The Impact on International Law of a Decade of Measures against Iraq' 13:1 *European Journal of International Law* pp. 243–262

Bennoune, Karima (2004) 'Toward a Human Rights Approach to Armed Conflict: Iraq 2003' 11 *University of California, Davis Journal of International Law and Policy* pp. 171–228

Benvenisti, Eyal (2004) 'The US and the Use of Force: Double-edged Hegemony and the Management of Global Emergencies' 15:4 *European Journal of International Law* pp. 677–700

Benvenuti, Paolo (2001) 'The ICTY Prosecutor and the Review of the NATO Bombing Campaign against the Federal Republic of Yugoslavia' 12 *European Journal of International Law* pp. 504–505

Bernstein, Jay (1991) 'Right, Revolution and Community: Marx's "On the Jewish Question" ' in Osborne, P. (ed.) *Socialism and the Limits of Liberalism* (London: Verso)

Bhaskar, Roy (1991) 'Realism', p. 458 in Tom Bottomore *A Dictionary of Marxist Thought* (2nd edn, Oxford: Blackwell Reference)

Bhaskar, Roy (1993) *Dialectic: The Pulse of Freedom* (London: Verso)

Bhuta, Nehal (2005) 'The Antinomies of Transformative Occupation' 16:4 *European Journal of International Law* pp. 721–740

Biddle, Stephen (2002) 'The New Way of War? Debating the Kosovo Model' May–June 2002 *Foreign Affairs* pp. 138–144

Blishchenko, Igor P. (1968) *Antisovyetism i mezhdunarodnoye pravo* (Antisovietism and international law) (Moscow)

Blishchenko, Igor P. (1991) *Nekotoriye problemy sovetskoi nauki mezhdunarodnovo prava* (Some problems of the Soviet science of international law) No. 3 *Sovetskoye gosudarstvo i pravo* (Soviet state and law) pp. 134–175

Blishchenko, Igor P. (1998) *Soderzhaniye prava narodov na samoopredeleniye* (The content of the right of peoples to self-determination), in Aleksandr Ossipov (1998) *Pravo Narodov na Samoopredeleniye: Ideya i Voploshcheniye (Right of Peoples to Self-Determination: Idea and Realisation)* (Moscow: Zvenya) pp. 41–52

Bothe, Michael (2003) 'Terrorism and the Legality of Pre-emptive Force' 14:2 *European Journal of International Law* pp. 227–240

Bowring, Bill (1995) 'The "droit et devoir d'ingérence": A Timely New Remedy for Africa?' 7 *African Journal of International and Comparative Law* pp. 493–510

Bowring, Bill (1995) 'Human Rights in Russia: A Discourse of Emancipation or Just Another Mirage?' in Istvan Pogany (ed.) *Human Rights in Eastern Europe* (Aldershot: Edward Elgar) pp. 87–110

Bowring, Bill (1996) 'The Kurds in Turkey: Defending the Rights of a Minority' in Kirsten Schulze, Martin Stokes and Colm Campbell (eds) *Nationalism, Minorities and Diasporas: Identity and Rights in the Middle East* (London: I. B. Tauris) p. 23

Bowring, Bill (1997) 'Russia's accession to the Council of Europe and human rights: compliance or cross-purposes?' Issue 6 1997 *European Human Rights Law Review* pp. 628–643

Bowring, Bill (2000) 'Russia's accession to the Council of Europe and human rights: four years on' Issue 4 2000 *European Human Rights Law Review* p. 362

Bowring, Bill (2001) 'Review of Costas Douzinas *The End of Human Rights*' 12 *Kings College Law Journal* pp. 252–259

Bowring, Bill (2002) 'The Degradation of International Law?' in John Strawson (ed.) *Law After Ground Zero* (London: Glasshouse) pp. 3–19

Bowring, Bill (2005) 'Chechnya Justice' *Counsel* December 2005 pp. 65–67

Bowring, Bill (2005a) 'Burial and Resurrection: Karl Renner's controversial influence on the "National Question" in Russia' in E. Nimni (ed.) *National-Cultural Autonomy and its Contemporary Critics* (London: Routledge)

Bowring, Bill (2005b) 'Russia in a Common European Legal Space. Developing effective remedies for the violations of rights by public bodies: compliance with the European Convention on Human Rights' in Kaj Hober (ed.) *The Uppsala Yearbook of East European Law* 2004 (London: Wildy, Simmonds and Hill, 2005) pp. 89–116

Bowring, Bill (2007) 'Negating pluralist democracy: the Strasbourg Court forgets the rights of the electors' 11 *KHRP Legal Review* pp. 67–96

Brown, A. (1977) 'The Father of Russian Jurisprudence: The Legal Thought of S. E. Desnitskii' in W. Butler (ed.) *Russian Law: Historical and Political Perspectives* (Oxford: Oxford University Press) pp. 117–42

Brownlie, Ian and Goodwin-Gill, Guy (2006) *Basic Documents on Human Rights* (5th edn, Oxford: Oxford University Press)

Brubaker, R. (1996). *Nationalism Reframed. Nationhood and the national question in the New Europe* (Cambridge: Cambridge University Press)

Brunnée, Jutta and Toope, Stephen J. (2004) 'The Use of Force: International Law After Iraq' Vol. 53 October *International and Comparative Law Quarterly* pp. 785–806

Budgen, Sébastian, Kouvelakis, Stathis and Žižek, Slavoj (eds) (2007) *Lenin Reloaded: Toward a Politics of Truth* Sic 7 (Durham NC: Duke University Press)

Burke, Edmund (1987) 'Reflections on the Revolution in France' in Jeremy Waldron *Nonsense Upon Stilts: Bentham, Burke and Marx on the Rights of Man* (London: Methuen)

Burns, Tony (2000) 'Aquinas's Two Doctrines of Natural Law' 48 *Political Studies* pp. 929–946

Butler, William (1974) 'Introduction' to G. I. Tunkin *Theory of International Law* (London: George Allen & Unwin)

Butler, William (1999) *Russian Law* (Oxford: Oxford University Press)

Butler, William (2002) 'The Learned Writings of Professor G. I. Tunkin' 4:2 *Journal of the History of International Law* pp. 394–423

Byers, Michael (1999) *Custom, Power and the Power of Rules: International Relations and Customary International Law* (Cambridge: Cambridge University Press)

Byers, Michael (ed.) (2001) *The Role of Law in International Politics: Essays in International Relations and International Law* (Cambridge: Cambridge University Press)

Byers, Michael (2002) 'The Shifting Foundations of International Law: A Decade of Forceful Measures against Iraq' in Symposium: The Impact on International Law of a Decade of Measures against Iraq, 13:1 *European Journal of International Law* pp. 21–41

Byers, Michael (2002a) 'Terrorism, the Use of Force and International Law After September 11' 51 *International and Comparative Law Quarterly* pp. 401–414

Byers, Michael (2005) *War Law* (London: Atlantic Books)

Byers, Michael and Chesterman, Simon (1999) 'Has US power destroyed the UN?' 21:9 *London Review of Books*

Byers, Michael and Nolte, George (2003) *United States Hegemony and the Foundations of International Law: The Effects of US Predominance on the Foundations of International Law* (Cambridge: Cambridge University Press)

Capotorti, F. (1979) 'Study on the Rights of Persons Belonging to Ethnic, Religious and Linguistic Minorities', UN Doc. E/CN.4/Sub.2/384/Rev.1 (Special Rapporteur to the UN Sub-Commission on the Prevention of Discrimination and Protection of Minorities), pursuant to Sub-Commission Resolution 9(XX)

Capotorti, Francesco (1992) 'Are Minorities Entitled to Collective International Rights' in Y. Dinstein and M. Tabory (eds) *The Protection of Minorities and Human Rights* (Leiden: Brill Academic Publishers) pp. 505–511, pp. 509–510

Caron, David D. (1991) 'Iraq and the Force of Law: Why Give a Shield of Immunity?' in 'Agora: The Gulf Crisis in International and Foreign Relations Law' 85 *American Journal of International Law* pp. 89–92

Carty, Anthony (1986) *The Decay of International Law: A Reappraisal of the Limits of Legal Imagination in International Affairs* (Manchester: Manchester University Press)

Carty, Anthony (1996) *The Failed State and the Tradition of International Law – Towards a Renewal of Legal Humanism*, Inaugural Lecture 6 December 1996, p. 22 (copy in possession of author)

Carty, Anthony (1997) 'Myths of International Legal Order: Past and Present' X Winter/Spring *Cambridge Review of International Affairs* 3

Carty, Anthony (2004) 'Marxism and International Law: Perspectives for the American (Twenty-First) Century?' 17 *Leiden Journal of International Law* pp. 247–270

Carty, Anthony (2005) 'The Iraq Invasion as a Recent United Kingdom "Contribution to International Law"' 16:1 *European Journal of International Law* pp. 143–151

Carty, Anthony (2007) *Philosophy of International Law* (Edinburgh: Edinburgh University Press)

Cassese, Antonio (ed.) (1979) *The New Humanitarian Law of Armed Conflict* Volume I (Oxford: Oceana, 1981)

Cassese, Antonio (1981) 'The Status of Rebels under the 1977 Geneva Protocol on Non-International Armed Conflict' 30 *International and Comparative Law Quarterly* 415

Cassese, Antonio (1995) *Self-Determination of Peoples: A Legal Reappraisal* (Cambridge: Cambridge University Press)

Cassese, Antonio (1999a) '*Ex iniuria ius oritur*: Are We Moving towards International Legitimation of Forcible Countermeasures in the World Community?' 10:1 *European Journal of International Law* pp. 23–31

Cassese, Antonio (1999b) 'A Follow-up: Forcible Humanitarian Countermeasures and *Opinio Necessitatis*' 10:4 *European Journal of International Law* pp. 791–801

Cassese, Antonio (2001) 'Terrorism is Also Disrupting Some Crucial Legal Categories of International Law' 12:5 *European Journal of International Law* pp. 993–1001, p. 1001

Cassese, Antonio (2005) *International Law* (2nd edn, Oxford: Oxford University Press) – the first edition was 2001

Chandler, David (2002) *From Kosovo to Kabul. Human Rights and Humanitarian Intervention* (London: Pluto)

Chandler, David (2006) *From Kosovo to Kabul and Beyond. Human Rights and International Intervention* (London: Pluto)

Charlesworth, Hilary (2002) 'International Law: A Discipline of Crisis' 65 *Modern Law Review* pp. 377–392

Charney, Jonathan A. (2001) 'The Use of Force Against Terrorism and International Law' in Editorial Comments, 95 *American Journal of International Law* pp. 835–839

Chimni, B. S. (1993) *International Law and World Order: A Critique of Contemporary Approaches* (New Delhi: Sage)

Chimni, B. S. (2004) 'An Outline of a Marxist Course on Public International Law' (2004) 17 *Leiden Journal of International Law* pp. 1–30

Chinkin, Christine M. (1999) 'Kosovo: A "Good" or "Bad" War?' 93 *American Journal of International Law* pp. 841–847

Chistyakov O. I. and Novitskaya T. E. (eds) (1998) *Reformi Aleksandr II (Reforms of Aleksandr II)* (Moscow, *Iuridicheskaya Literatura*)

Churchill, Robin R. and Khaliq, Urfan (2004) 'The Collective Complaints System of the European Social Charter: An Effective Mechanism for Ensuring Compliance with Economic and Social Rights?' 15:3 *European Journal of International Law* pp. 417–456

Cohen, Stephen (2001) *Failed Crusade: America and the Tragedy of Post-Communist Russia* (New York: Norton)

Commission for Social Justice (1994) *Social Justice. Strategies for National Renewal: The Report of the Commission for Social Justice* (London: Vintage Books)

Cook, Robin 'British Foreign Policy', Locarno Suite, Foreign and Commonwealth Office, London 12 May 1997

Cooper, Robert (2004) *The Breaking of Nations: Order and Chaos in the Twenty-first Century* (Atlantic Books)

Council of Europe *Collected edition of the 'Travaux préparatoires' of the European Convention on Human Rights* in eight volumes (1975–1985) (Dordrecht: Martinus Nijhoff)

Cox, Christoph and Whalen, Molly 'On Evil: An Interview with Alain Badiou' *Cabinet magazine online*, Issue 5 Winter 2001/2, at http://www.cabinetmagazine.org/issues/5/alainbadiou.php (accessed 1 January 2006)

Crawford, James (ed.) (1988) *The Rights of Peoples* (Oxford: Clarendon Press)

Crawford, James (1988) 'Some Conclusions' in James Crawford (ed.) *The Rights of Peoples* (Oxford: Clarendon Press)

Dahan, F. (2000) 'Law Reform in Central and Eastern Europe: The "Transplantation" of Secured Transactions Laws' 2:3 *European Journal of Law Reform*, pp. 369–384

Damrosch, Lori Fisler (1991) 'Constitutional Control of Military Actions: A Comparative Dimension', in 'Agora: The Gulf Crisis in International and Foreign Relations Law' 85 *American Journal of International Law* pp. 92–104

Damrosch, L. F. and Müllerson, R. (1995) 'The Role of International Law in the Contemporary World' in L. F. Damrosch, G.M. Danilenko and R. Müllerson (eds) *Beyond Confrontation: International Law for the Post-Cold War Era* (Boulder, Colorado: Westview Press) p. 1

Dean, Jodi (2006) *Žižek's Politics* (London: Routledge)

Delcourt, B. (2002) 'De quelques paradoxes liés à l'invocation de l'Etat et du droit', in K. Bannelier and others *Le droit internationale face au terrorisme* (Paris: Pedone)

Deleuze, Gilles (1992) *Expression in Philosophy: Spinoza* (London: Zone Books)

Deleuze, Gilles and Guattari, Felix (2004) *A Thousand Plateaus* (London: Continuum)

Dembour, Marie-Bénédicte (2006) *Who Believes in Human Rights? Reflections on the European Convention* (Cambridge)

Derrida, Jacques (1994) *Specters of Marx: State of the Debt, the Work of Mourning and the New International* (London: Routledge)

Derrida, Jacques (2004) 'The Last of the Rogue States: The "Democracy to Come", Opening in Two Turns' in 103:2/3 *South Atlantic Quarterly* pp. 323–341

Dicey, A. (1914) *Lectures on the relation between law and public opinion in England during the Nineteenth Century* (2nd edn, London: Macmillan)

Dicey, A. (1973) *England's case against home rule* (Richmond, Surrey: Richmond Publishing, 1973 – English political history series)

Donnelly, J. (1999) 'The social construction of international human rights' in T. Dunne and N. Wheeler (eds) *Human Rights in Global Politics* (Cambridge: Cambridge University Press)

Donnelly, Jack (2002) 'Genocide and humanitarian intervention' 1:1 *Journal of Human Rights* pp. 93–109

Doswald-Beck, Louise and Vité, Sylvain (1993) 'International Humanitarian Law and Human Rights Law' 293 *International Review of the Red Cross* pp. 94–119

Douzinas, Costas (1991) *Postmodern Jurisprudence: the Law of the Text in the Texts of the Law* (London: Routledge)

Douzinas, Costas (1996) *Justice Miscarried: Ethics, Aesthetics and the Law* (Edinburgh: Edinburgh University Press)

Douzinas, Costas (2000) *The End of Human Rights* (Oxford: Hart Publishing)

Douzinas, Costas (2007) *Human Rights and Empire: The political philosophy of cosmopolitanism* (London: Routledge Cavendish)

Douzinas, Costas and Gearey, Adam (2005) *Critical Jurisprudence: The Political Philosophy of Justice* (Oxford: Hart Publishing)

Dupuy R. J. and Leonetti T. (1979) 'La notion de conflit armé à caractère non international' in Antonio Cassese (ed.) *The New Humanitarian Law of Armed Conflict* Volume I p. 272.

Eagleton, Terry (2003) *After Theory* (London: Allen Lane)

Eagleton, Terry 'Living in a material world' *The Guardian Review* 20 September 2003

Easter, G. (1997) 'Redefining Centre-Regional Relations in the Russian Federation: Sverdlovsk *Oblast*' 49 *Europe-Asia Studies* pp. 617–635

Evans, Malcolm (2003) (ed.) *International Law* (Oxford: Oxford University Press)

Evans, Tony (2001) 'If democracy, then human rights?' 22 *Third World Quarterly* pp. 623–642

Ewald, W. (1995) 'Comparative Jurisprudence (II): The Logic of Legal Transplants' 43 *American Journal of Comparative Law* pp. 489–510

Ewing, Keith (1999) 'Just Words and Social Justice' 15 *Review of Constitutional Studies* pp. 53–75

Ewing, Keith (1999) 'The Human Rights Act and Parliamentary Democracy' 62:1 *Modern Law Review* pp. 79–99

Faundez, Julio (1989) 'International Law and Wars of National Liberation: Use of

Force and Intervention' 1 *African Journal of International and Comparative Law* pp. 85–98

Faundez, Julio (ed.) (1997) *Good Governance and Law: Legal and Institutional Reform in Developing Countries* (London: Macmillan)

Federal Trust (ed.) (1999) *The European Charter of Fundamental Rights* (London: Federal Trust)

Feldman, David (1999) 'The Human Rights Act 1998 and Constitutional Principles' 19:2 *Legal Studies* pp. 165–206

Ferguson, Clare (1999) 'Global Social Policy Principles: Human Rights and Social Justice', DFID, April 1999, at www.dfid.gov.uk/pubs/files/sdd-gsp.pdf (accessed on 16 October 2007)

Filippov, V. (1998) 'Natsionalno-Kulturnaya Avtonomiya: klassicheskaya kontseptsiya i yeyo sovremennaya interpretatsiya' (National-Cultural Autonomy: the classical conception and its contemporary interpretation), pp. 63–84 in Ye. Filippova (ed.) *Natsionalno-Kulturnaya Avtonomiya: problemy i suzhdeniya* (*National-Cultural Autonomies: problems and evaluation*) (Moscow: Etnosfera 1998) – Materials from the Round Table organised by the 'Etnosfera' Centre

Fine, Robert (1993) ' "The Rose in the Cross of the Present": Closure and Critique of Hegel's Philosophy of Rights' pp. 45–60, in Alan Norrie (ed.) *Closure or Critique: New Directions in Legal Theory* (Edinburgh: Edinburgh University Press)

Fine, Bob (2002) *Democracy and the Rule of Law. Marx's Critique of the Legal Form* (Caldwell, New Jersey: Blackburn Press)

Forsythe, David (2000) *Human Rights in International Relations* (Cambridge: Cambridge University Press)

Fox, Gregory and Roth, Brad (2000) *Democratic Governance and International Law* (Cambridge: Cambridge University Press)

Franck, Thomas (1990) *The Power of Legitimacy Among Nations* (New York: Oxford University Press)

Franck, Thomas M. (1992) 'The Emerging Right to Democratic Governance' 86 *American Journal of International Law* p. 46

Franck, Thomas M. (1995) *Fairness in International Law and Institutions* (Oxford: Oxford University Press)

Franck, Thomas M. (1996) 'Clan and Superclan: Loyalty, Identity and Community in Law and Practice' 90 *American Journal of International Law* p. 359

Franck, Thomas M. (1999) 'Lessons of Kosovo' in 'Editorial Comments: NATO's Kosovo Intervention' 93 *American Journal of International Law* pp. 857–860

Franck, Thomas M. (2001) 'Terrorism and the Right of Self-Defense' in 'Editorial Comments' 95 *American Journal of International Law* pp. 839–843

Franck, Thomas M. and Faiza Patel (1991) 'UN Police Action in Lieu of War: "The Old Order Changeth" ' pp. 63–74

Freeman, Alwyn M. (1968) 'Some Aspects of Soviet Influence on International Law' 62:3 *American Journal of International Law* pp. 710–722

Freeman, Michael (1994) 'The Philosophical Foundations of Human Rights' 16 *Human Rights Quarterly* pp. 491–514

Freeman, Michael (1997) 'Conference on Gross Human Rights Violations: Prevention, Intervention and Punishment' 31 *The Journal of Value Inquiry* pp. 557–567

Freeman, Michael (2001) 'Is a Political Science of Human Rights Possible?' 19:2 *Netherlands Human Rights Quarterly* pp. 123–139

Freeman, Michael (2002) *Human Rights: An interdisciplinary approach* (London: Polity)

Gaeta, Paola (1996) 'The Armed Conflict in Chechnya before the Russian Constitutional Court' 7:4 *European Journal of International Law* pp. 563–570

Gaete, Rolando (1993) *Human Rights and the Limits of Critical Reason* (London: Dartmouth)

Galenkamp, Marlies (1992) 'Collective Rights: Much Ado About Nothing? A Review Essay' 3 *Netherlands Quarterly of Human Rights* p. 291

Galenkamp, Marlies (1993) *Individualism versus Collectivism: The Concept of Collective Rights* (RFS Rotterdam)

Gardner, James A. (1980) *Legal Imperialism: American Lawyers and Foreign Aid in Latin America* (Madison: University of Wisconsin)

Garlan, Edwin (1954) 'Soviet Legal Philosophy' (review of Hazard, John (intr) *Soviet Legal Philosophy* (Cambridge, Mass.: Harvard University Press, 1951) 51:10 *The Journal of Philosophy* pp. 300–307

Gearey, Adam (2005) *Globalization and Law: Trade, Rights, War* (Lanham: Rowman & Littlefield)

Gearty, Conor (2006) *Can Human Rights Survive?* (Cambridge: Cambridge University Press)

Gellner, E. (1983) *Nations and Nationalism* (Oxford: Oxford University Press)

Geras, Norman (1991) 'Justice' in Tom Bottomore et al. (eds) *A Dictionary of Marxist Thought* (Blackwell, 2nd edn), pp. 276–277

Ginsburgs, George (1980) 'Review of Pashukanis *Selected Writings on Marxism and Law*' 28:4 *American Journal of Comparative Law* pp. 687–689

Glennon, Michael J. (1991) 'The Constitution and Chapter VII of the United Nations Charter' 85:1 *American Journal of International Law* pp. 74–88

Golan, Galia (1988) *The Soviet Union and National Liberation Movements in the Third World* (Boston: Unwin Hyman)

Goldsmith, Jack and Posner, Eric (2005) *The Limits of International Law* (Oxford: OUP)

Gorenburg, D. (1999) 'Regional Separatism in Russia: Ethnic Mobilisation or Power Grab?' 51 *Europe-Asia Studies* pp. 245–274

Gowan, Peter (1999) *The Global Gamble. Washington's Faustian Bid for World Domination* (London: Verso)

Gray, Christine (2002) 'From Unity to Polarisation: International Law and the Use of Force Against Iraq' in 'Symposium: The Impact on International Law of a Decade of Measures against Iraq' 3:1 *European Journal of International Law* pp. 1–19

Green, Leslie (1994) 'Internal Minorities and Their Rights' in Judith Baker (ed.) *Group Rights* (Toronto: University of Toronto Press) p. 101

Greenwood, Christopher (2002) 'International law and the "war against terrorism" ' 78:2 *International Affairs* pp. 301–317

Greenwood, Christopher (2003) 'International Law and the Pre-emptive Use of Force: Afghanistan, Al-Qaida, and Iraq' 4:7 *San Diego International Law Journal* pp. 7–37

Griffin, James (2000) 'Discrepancies between the best philosophical account of human rights and the international law of human rights' (September 2000) 101:1 *Proceedings of the Aristotelian Society*, pp. 1–28

Griffin, James (2001) 'First Steps in an Account of Human Rights' 9:3 *European Journal of Philosophy* pp. 306–327

Grushkin, Dmitrii (1997) 'Pravo Narodov na Samoopredeleniye: Istoriya Razvitiya i Voploshcheniye Ideyi' (Right of Peoples to Self-Determination: History of the Development and Realisation of the Idea) in Aleksandr Ossipov *Pravo Narodov na Samoopredeleniye: Ideya i Voploshcheniye (Right of Peoples to Self-Determination: Idea and Realisation)* (Moscow: Memorial)

Gubayeva, T. V. and Malkov, V. P. (1999) 'Gosudarstvenniy Yazyk i yevo Pravovoi Status' (The State Language and its Legal Status) 7 *Gosudarstvo i Pravo* (7 State and Law) pp. 5–13

Gumilev, L. (1990). *Geografika etnosa i istoricheskii period (The geography of the Ethnos in the Historical Period)* (Leningrad: Nauka)

Gupta, Bhabani Sen (1974) 'The Soviet Union in South Asia' in Roger Kanet (ed.) *The Soviet Union and the Developing Nations* (Baltimore: Johns Hopkins UP) pp. 119–152

Habermas, J. (1987) *Knowledge and Human Interests* (Cambridge: Polity Press)

Habermas, J. (1992) *The Philosophical Discourse of Modernity: Twelve Lectures* (Cambridge: Polity)

Habermas J. (1994) 'Struggles for Recognition in the Democratic State' in Charles Taylor (ed. Amy Gutmann) *Multiculturalism. Examining the Politics of Recognition* (Princeton: Princeton University Press), pp. 105–148

Habermas, J. (1995) 'Citizenship and National Identity: Some Reflections on the Future of Europe' in R. Beiner (ed.) *Theorising Citizenship* (New York: SUNY Press)

Habermas, J. (1997) *Between Facts and Norms: Contributions to a Discourse Theory of Law and Democracy* (Cambridge: Polity Press)

Habermas, J. (2001) 'Constitutional Democracy: A Paradoxical Union of Contradictory Principles?' 29:6 *Political Theory* pp. 766–781

Habermas, J. (2001) *The Postnational Constellation. Political Essays* (Cambridge: Polity Press)

Hall, J. (ed.) (1998) *The State of the Nation: Ernest Gellner and the Theory of Nationalism* (Cambridge: Cambridge University Press)

Hallward, Peter (2003) *Badiou: a subject to truth* (Minneapolis: University of Minneapolis Press)

Hampson, Françoise (2002) 'Study on Human Rights Protection During Situations of Armed Conflict, Internal Disturbances and Tensions' *Council of Europe, Steering Committee for Human Rights (CDDH), Committee of Experts for the Development of Human Rights (DH-DEV)*, DH-DEV(2002)001

Hampson, Françoise and Salama, Ibrahim (2005) 'Working paper on the relationship between human rights law and humanitarian law' *Commission on Human Rights, Sub-Commission on the Promotion and Protection of Human Rights, 53rd session,* Doc. E/CN.4/Sub.2/2005/14, 21 June 2005

Hanneman, Andrea J. (1995) 'Independence and Group Rights in the Baltics: A Double Minority Problem' 35 *Virginia Journal of International Law* p. 485

Hardt, Michael and Negri, Antonio (2000) *Empire* (Cambridge, Mass.: Harvard University Press)

Hardt, Michael and Negri, Antonio (2005) *Multitude: War and Democracy in the Age of Empire* (London: Hamish Hamilton)

Harloe, Michael (2001) 'Social Justice and the City: The New "Liberal Formulation" ' 25:4 *International Journal of Urban and Regional Research* pp. 889–897

Hayek, Friedrich (1976) *The Mirage of Social Justice* (Chicago: University of Chicago Press)

Hazard, John (1938) 'Cleansing Soviet International Law of Anti-Marxist Theories' 32:2 *American Journal of International Law* pp. 244–252

Hazard, John (1957) 'Pashukanis is No Traitor' 51:2 *American Journal of International Law* pp. 385–388

Hazard, John (1971) 'Renewed Emphasis Upon a Socialist International Law' 65:1 *American Journal of International Law* pp. 142–148

Hazard, John (1979) 'Memories of Pashukanis', Foreword to Evgeny Pashukanis, *Selected Writings on Marxism and Law* (eds. P. Beirne & R. Sharlet) (London & New York 1980) pp. 273–301 at http://www.marxists.org/archive/pashukanis/biog/memoir.htm

Head, Michael (2001) 'The Passionate Legal Debates of the Early Years of the Russian Revolution' vol. XIV no. 1 *Canadian Journal of Law and Jurisprudence* pp. 3–27

Head, Michael (2004) 'The Rise and Fall of a Soviet Jurist: Evgeny Pashukanis and Stalinism' (July 2004) vol. XVII no. 2 *Canadian Journal of Law and Jurisprudence* pp. 269–293

Hegel, G. W. F. (1967) *The Philosophy of Right* trans T. M. Knox (Oxford: Oxford University Press)

Heidegger, Martin (1985) *History of the Concept of Time* trans Theodore Kisiel (Bloomington: Indiana University Press)

Hein, S. (1996) 'Predicting Legal Transplants: the case of servitudes in the Russian Federation' 6 *Transnational Law and Contemporary Problems* pp. 187–223

Heintze, Hans-Joachim (2004) 'On the relationship between human rights law protection and international humanitarian law' 86:856 *International Review of the Red Cross* pp. 789–814

Heinze, Eric (2004) 'Humanitarian Intervention: Morality and International Law on Intolerable Violations of Human Rights' 8:4 *International Journal of Human Rights* pp. 471–490

Henkin, Louis (1999) 'Kosovo and the law of "humanitarian intervention" ' 93:4 *American Journal of International Law* pp. 824–828

Herring, Eric (2002) 'Between Iraq and a hard place: a critique of the British government's case for UN economic sanctions' (January) 28:1 *Review of International Studies* pp 39–56

Higgins, Rosalind (1994) *Problems and Process: International Law and How We Use It* (Oxford: Clarendon Press)

Honneth, Axel (1993) *The Critique of Power. Reflective Stages in a Critical Social Theory* (Cambridge, Mass.: MIT Press)

Honneth, Axel (1996) *The Struggle for Recognition. The Moral Grammar of Social Conflicts* (Cambridge: Polity Press)

Horton, John and Mendus, Susan (1994) (eds) *After MacIntyre: Critical Perspectives on the Work of Alasdair MacIntyre* (Cambridge: Polity)

Human Rights Watch (March 2005) *Worse than a War: 'Disappearances' in Chechnya – A Crime Against Humanity*, Human Rights Watch Briefing Paper, 21 March 2005, at http://hrw.org/backgrounder/eca/chechnya0305/

Huntingdon, Samuel P. (1993) 'The Clash of Civilisations' 72:3 *Foreign Affairs* pp. 22–28

Hutchinson, John (2001) 'Nations and Culture' in Montserrat Guibernau and John Hutchinson (eds) *Understanding Nationalism* (Cambridge: Polity), pp. 74–96

Ignatieff, Michael (2001) *Human Rights as Politics and Ideology* (Princeton: Princeton University Press)

Independent Commission on Kosovo (2000) *The Kosovo Report: Conflict, International Response, Lessons Learned* (New York: Oxford University Press)

Ingram, James (2005) 'Can Universalism Still Be Radical? Alain Badiou's Politics of Truth' 12:4 *Constellations* pp. 561–573

Inoue, K. (1991) *MacArthur's Japanese Constitution: A Linguistic and Cultural Study of its Making* (Chicago: University of Chicago Press)

Iwasawa, Y. (1998) *International Law, Human Rights Law and Japanese Law: The Impact of International Law on Japanese Law* (Oxford: Clarendon Press)

Iyer, Lars (2001) 'Our Responsibility: Blanchot's Communism' *Contretemps* 2 pp. 59–73

Johnstone, Ian (2003) 'Security Council Deliberations: The Power of the Better Argument' 14 *European Journal of International Law* 437

Johnstone, Ian (2004) 'US–UN Relations after Iraq: The End of the World (Order) As We Know It?' 15:4 *European Journal of International Law* pp. 813–838

Kaldor, Mary (2002) 'A response', in 'A Symposium on Kosovo' 1:1 *Human Rights Journal* pp. 129–132

Kahn-Freund, O. (1974) 'On Uses and Misuses of Comparative Law' 37 *Modern Law Review* p. 1

Kamminga, Menno (1994) 'Is the European Convention on Human Rights Sufficiently Equipped to Cope with Gross and Systematic Violations?' 12:2 *Netherlands Quarterly of Human Rights* pp. 153–164

Kanet, Roger (1974) 'The Soviet Union and the Colonial Question 1917–1953' in Roger Kanet (ed.) *The Soviet Union and the Developing Nations* (Baltimore: Johns Hopkins UP) pp. 1–26

Kautsky, Karl (1903) *Neue Zeit* No. 2

Kazantsev, S. (1991) *Sud Prisyazhnikh v Rossii: Gromkiye Ugolovniye Protsessi* (Trial by Jury in Russia: Great Criminal Trials) (St Petersburg: Leniizdat)

Keller, Perry (1996) 'Justice and Ethnicity' 59 *Modern Law Review* p. 903

Kitson, Frank (1971) *Low intensity operations: subversion, insurgency, peacekeeping* (Harrisburg PA: Stackpole Books)

Klug, Francesca (2000) *Values for a godless age. The story of the United Kingdom's new bill of rights* (London: Penguin)

Knight, Kelvin (2007) *Aristotelian Philosophy: Ethics and Politics from Aristotle to MacIntyre* (Cambridge: Polity)

Knop, Karen (2002) *Diversity and Self-determination in International Law* (Cambridge Studies in International & Comparative Law) (Cambridge: Cambridge University Press)

Korovin, E. A. (1923) *Mezhdunarodnoye pravo perekhodnovo vremeni (International law of the transitional period)* (Moscow: Izd. Kommunisticheskoi akademii), Chapter IV, part 2, pp. 26–35

Korovin, E. A. (1928) 'Soviet Treaties and International Law' 22 *American Journal of International Law* 753, at p. 763 (emphasis added)

Koskenniemi, Martti (1996) ' "Intolerant Democracies": A Reaction' 37 *Harvard International Law Journal* pp. 234–235

Koskenniemi, Martti (2003) Fragmentation of International Law: Topic (a): The function and scope of the lex specialis rule and the question of 'self-contained regimes': An outline for the International Law Commission Study Group on Fragmentation http://untreaty.un.org/ilc/sessions/55/fragmentation_outline.pdf

Koskenniemi, Martti (2004) 'What Should International Lawyers Learn from Karl Marx?' 17 *Leiden Journal of International Law* pp. 229–246

Koskenniemi, Martti (2007) *Fragmentation of International Law: Difficulties Arising from the Diversification and Expansion of International Law* Report of the Study Group of the International Law Commission (Helsinki: The Erik Castrén Institute Research Reports 21/2007)

Kranz, J. (1998) (ed.) *Law and Practice of Central European Countries in the Field of National Minorities Protection After 1989* (Warsaw: Center for International Relations)

Krisch, Nico (2005) 'International Law in Times of Hegemony: Unequal Power and the Shaping of the International Legal Order' 16:3 *European Journal of International Law* pp. 369–408

Kristesky, A. (1981) *Pravo narodov na samoopredeleniye: istoricheskoye i sovremennoye razvitiye* (Right of peoples to self-determination: historical and contemporary development (New York: UN ECOSOC)

Kritsiotis, Dino (2004) 'Arguments of Mass Confusion' 15:2 *European Journal of International Law* pp. 233–278

Kucherov, S. (1953) *Courts, Lawyers and Trials under the Last Three Tsars* (New York)

Kymlicka, W. (1994) 'Individual and Community Rights' in Judith Baker (ed.) *Group Rights* (Toronto: University of Toronto Press) p. 17

Kymlicka, W. (1995) *Mulicultural Citizenhip* (Oxford: Clarendon Press)

Kymlicka, W. (ed.) (1995) *The Rights of Minority Cultures* (Oxford: Oxford University Press)

Lankina, T. (1999) 'Local self-government or local political control in Russia? The case of Bashkortostan' *EWI Rossisskii Regionalni Bulleten (Russian Regional Bulletin): Local Government* 26 July

Leach, Philip (2005) 'Beyond the Bug River – A New Dawn for Redress Before the European Court of Human Rights?' Issue 2 2005 *European Human Rights Law Review* pp. 148–164

Leach, Philip (2005a) 'The British Military in Iraq – The Applicability of the *Espace Juridique* Doctrine under the European Convention on Human Rights' Autumn *Public Law* pp. 448–458

Lefort, Claude (1986) 'Politics and Human Rights' in John B. Thompson (ed.) *The Political Forms of Modern Society: Bureaucracy, Democracy, Totalitarianism* (Cambridge: Polity), at http://www.geocities.com/~johngray/impl13.htm

Lenin, V. I. (1913) 'The Cadets and The Right of Nations to Self-Determination', *Proletarskaya Pravda* No. 4, 11 December 1913, *Collected Works* (1977) Vol. 19, pp. 525–527, at http://www.marxists.org/archive/lenin/works/1913/dec/11.htm

Lenin, V. I. (1913a) 'National-Liberalism and the Right of Nations to Self-Determination' *Proletarskaya Pravda* No. 12, 20 December 1913, *Collected Works* (1972) Vol. 20, pp. 56–58 at http://www.marxists.org/archive/lenin/works/1913/dec/20.htm

Lenin, V. I. (1914) 'The Right of Nations to Self-Determination' *Prosveshcheniye*

Nos. 4, 5 and 6, *Collected Works* (1972) Vol. 20, pp. 393–454, at http://www.marxists.org/archive/lenin/works/1914/self-det/index.htm

Lenin, V. I. (1915) 'The Revolutionary Proletariat and the Right of Nations to Self-Determination' *Collected Works* (Moscow: Progress, 1974) Vol. 21, pp. 407–414, at http://www.marxists.org/archive/lenin/works/1915/oct/16.htm

Lenin, V. I. (1916) 'The Discussion on Self-Determination Summed Up' *Sbornik Sotsial-Demokrata* No. 1, October 1916, *Collected Works* (Moscow: Progress, 1974) Vol. 22, pp. 320–360, at http://www.marxists.org/archive/lenin/works/1916/jul/x01.htm

Lenin, V. I. (1968a) *Complete Collected Works* (2nd edn) (Moscow: Progress) Vol. 7, p. 92, first published in *Iskra* 22 October 1903, no. 51

Lenin, V. I. (1968b) *Complete Collected Works* (2nd edn) (Moscow, Progress) Vol. 19, p. 117, first published in *Za Pravda* 28 November 1913, no. 46

Lenin, V. I. (1968c) *Complete Collected Works* (2nd edn) (Moscow: Progress) Vol. 20

Lenin, V. I. (1968d) *Complete Collected Works* (2nd edn) (Moscow: Progress) Vol. 21

Lester, A. (1984) 'Fundamental Rights: The United Kingdom Isolated?' *Public Law* pp. 46–72

Lester, A. (1998) 'UK acceptance of the Strasbourg Jurisdiction: What really went on in Whitehall in 1965' (Summer) *Public Law* pp. 237–253

Levin, David B. (1958) *Osnovniye problemy sovremennovo mezhdunarodnovo prava* (Fundamental problems of contemporary international law) (Moscow)

Lewin, Moshe (2005) *Lenin's Last Struggle* (Ann Arbor: University of Michigan Press)

Lippens, Ronnie (2005) 'Tracing the Legal Boundary between Empire and Multitude: Wavering with Hardt and Negri (2000–2005)' 18 *Leiden Journal of International Law* pp. 389–402

Loucaides, Loukis (2006) 'Determining the Extra-territorial Effect of the European Convention: Facts, Jurisprudence and the Bankovic Case' 4 *European Human Rights Law Review* pp. 391–407

Loughlin, Martin (2001) 'Rights, Democracy, and Law' in T. Campbell, K. D. Ewing, A. Tomkins (eds) *Sceptical Essays on Human Rights* (Oxford: Oxford University Press) pp. 41–60

Loughlin, Martin (2004) *The Idea of Public Law* (Oxford: OUP)

Love, Nancy S. (1995) 'What's left of Marx?' Chapter 3 in Stephen K. White (ed.) *The Cambridge Companion to Habermas* (Cambridge: Cambridge University Press)

Lowe, Vaughan (2003) 'The Iraq Crisis: What Now?' October, 52 *International and Comparative Law Quarterly* pp. 859–871

Lubell, Noam (2005) 'Challenges in applying human rights law to armed conflict' 87:860 *International Review of the Red Cross* pp. 737–754

Lukacs, Georg (1975) *The Young Hegel: Studies in the Relations Between Dialectics and Economics* (London: Merlin Press)

Lukes, Steven (1981) 'Can a Marxist Believe in Human Rights?' 4 *Praxis International* pp. 334–345

Lukes, Steven (1997) 'Social Justice: The Hayekian Challenge' 11 *Critical Review* pp. 65–80

MacIntyre, Alasdair (1967) *A Short History of Ethics. A History of Moral Philosophy from the Homeric Age to the Twentieth Century* (London: Routledge, 1999 (1967))

MacIntyre, Alasdair (1983) 'Are there any natural rights?' The Charles F. Adams

Lecture, Bowdoin College, Brunswick, Maine, 28 February 1983 (published by the President and Trustees, Bowdoin College, Brunswick, Maine), on file with the author

MacIntyre, Alasdair (1985) *After Virtue: A Study in Moral Theory* (2nd edn, London: Duckworth, 1990 (1985))

MacIntyre, Alasdair (1988) *Whose Justice? Which Rationality?* (London: Duckworth)

MacIntyre, Alasdair (1990) 'The Privatisation of Good: An Inaugural Lecture' 52:3 *Review of Politics* pp. 344–361

MacIntyre, Alasdair (1991) 'Community, Law and the Idiom and Rhetoric of Rights' 26 *Listening: Journal of Religion and Culture* pp. 96–110

MacIntyre, Alasdair (1994) 'A Partial response to my Critics' in John Horton and Susan Mendus (eds) *After MacIntyre: Critical Perspectives on the Work of Alasdair MacIntyre* (Cambridge: Polity)

MacIntyre, Alasdair (1999) *Dependent Rational Animals: Why Human Beings Need the Virtues* (Chicago: Open Court)

MacIntyre, Alasdair (2006) 'Epistemological crises, dramatic narrative, and the philosophy of science', Chapter 1, pp. 3–23 in *The Tasks of Philosophy: Selected Essays, Volume 1* (Cambridge: Cambridge University Press)

MacIntyre, Alasdair (2006a) 'Three perspectives on Marxism: 1953, 1968, 1995' (first published in 1995) Chapter 8, pp. 145–158, in *Ethics and Politics: Selected Essays, Volume 2* (Cambridge: Cambridge University Press)

Macpherson, C. B. (1964) *The Political Theory of Possessive Individualism: Hobbes to Locke* (Oxford: Oxford Paperbacks)

Maitland, F. W. (1995) 'Trust and Corporation', in Julia Stapleton (ed.) *Group Rights: Perspectives Since 1900* (London: Thoemmes Press)

Malanczuk, Peter (1991) 'The Kurdish Crisis and Allied Intervention' 2 *European Journal of International Law* 114

Mansell, Wade and Haslam, Emily (2005) 'John Bolton and the United States' Retreat from International Law' 14(4) *Social and Legal Studies* pp. 459–485

Marks, Susan (2000) 'International law, democracy and the end of history', Chapter 14, pp. 532–566 in Gregory Fox and Brad Roth *Democratic Governance and International Law* (Cambridge: Cambridge University Press)

Marks, Susan (2000a) *The Riddle of All Constitutions* (Oxford: Oxford University Press)

Marks, Susan (2001) 'Big Brother is Bleeping Us – With the Message that Ideology Doesn't Matter' 12:1 *European Journal of International Law* pp. 109–123, at p. 112

Marston, G. (1993) 'The United Kingdom's Part in the Preparation of the European Convention on Human Rights, 1950' Vol. 42, Part 4 *International and Comparative Law Quarterly* pp. 796–826

Marx, Karl (1971) *Capital Vol. III* (Moscow: Progress)

Marx, Karl (1975) *Contribution to the Critique of Hegel's Philosophy of Law*, pp. 4–129 in *Karl Marx Friedrich Engels Collected Works* Vol. 3 (Marx and Engels 1843–44) (London: Lawrence & Wishart)

Marx, Karl (1975a) *On the Jewish Question*, pp. 146–174 in *Karl Marx Friedrich Engels Collected Works* Vol. 3 (Marx and Engels 1843–44) (London: Lawrence & Wishart)

Mastyugina, T. and Stelmakh, V. (1994). 'Maliye narody severa i dalnevo vostoka. Osnovy pravovovo statusa v svete printsipov mezhdunarodnovo opyta' (Minor peoples of the north and far east. Foundations of their legal status in the light of international law and foreign experience) *Rossiiskii Byulleten' po Pravam Cheloveka (Russian Bulletin for Human Rights)* 4: 156–171

McBride, Jeremy (2003) 'Study on the Principles Governing the Application of the European Convention on Human Rights during Armed Conflict and Internal Disturbances and Tensions' *Council of Europe, Steering Committee for Human Rights (CDDH), Committee of Experts for the Development of Human Rights (DH-DEV)*, DH-DEV(2003)001

McEldowney, John (1985) 'Dicey in Historical Perspective – a Review Essay' in Patrick McAuslan and John McEldowney (eds) *Law, Legitimacy and the Constitution* (London: Sweet & Maxwell)

McGoldrick, Dominic (2004) *From '9-11' to the Iraq War 2003: International Law in an Age of Complexity* (Oxford: Hart Publishing)

McWhinney, Edward (1962) ' "Peaceful Co-existence" and Soviet–Western International Law' 56:4 *American Journal of International Law* pp. 951–970

Memorial (1997) *Pravo Narodov na Samoopredeleniye: Ideya i Voploshcheniye (The Rights of Peoples to Self-Determination: Idea and Realisation)* (Moscow: Svenya)

Meron, Theodor (1991) 'Prisoners of War: Civilians and Diplomats in the Gulf Crisis' in 'Agora: The Gulf Crisis in International and Foreign Relations Law' 85:1 *American Journal of International Law* pp. 104–109

Mertus, J. (1999) 'From Legal Transplants to Transformative Justice: Human Rights and the Promise of Transnational Civil Society' 14 *American University International Law Review* pp. 1335–1389

Miéville, China (2004) 'The Commodity-Form Theory of International Law: an Introduction' 17 *Leiden Journal of International Law* pp. 271–302

Miéville, China (2005) *Between Equal Rights: A Marxist Theory of International Law* (Leiden: Brill Academic Publishers)

Miéville, China (2005a) 'Anxiety and the Sidekick State: British International Law After Iraq' 46:7 *Harvard International Law Journal* pp. 441–458

Mikhaleva, N. A. (1996) 'Constitutional Reforms in the Republics of the Russian Federation' *Russian Politics and Law* pp. 67–79

Miller, D. (1997) *On Nationality* (Oxford: Clarendon Press)

Mole, Nuala (2001) 'Who Guards the Guards – The Rule of Law in Kosovo' Part 3 *European Human Rights Law Review* pp. 280–299

Mole, Nuala (2005) *'Issa v Turkey*: Delineating the Extra-Territorial Effect of the European Convention on Human Rights' Part 1 *European Human Rights Law Review* pp. 86–91

Moltmann, Jürgen (1993) *Theology of Hope: On the Ground and the Implications of a Christian Eschatology* (Minneapolis: Augsburg Fortress Publishers), first published in 1967

Morgan, Bronwen (2002) 'What is Right with Ideology?' 22:3 *Oxford Journal of Legal Studies* pp. 517–538

Morsink, Johannes (1999) *The Universal Declaration of Human Rights. Origins, Drafting and Intent* (Philadelphia: University of Pennsylvania Press)

Müller, Jan-Werner (2003) *A Dangerous Mind: Carl Schmitt in Post-War European Thought* (New Haven: Yale University Press)

Murphy, Sean D. (ed.) (2000) 'NATO Air Campaign Against Serbia and the Laws of War' in 'Contemporary Practice of the United States Relating to International

Law: International Criminal Law' 94 *American Journal of International Law* pp. 690–697

Murray, Rachel (1999) 'Serious or Massive Violations under the African Charter on Human and Peoples' Rights: A Comparison with the Inter-American and European Mechanisms' 17:2 *Netherlands Quarterly of Human Rights* pp. 109–133

Negri, Antonio (1991) *The Savage Anomaly: The Power of Spinoza's Metaphysics and Politics* (Minneapolis: University of Minnesota Press)

Newton, S. (2001) 'Transplantation and Transition: Legality and Legitimacy in the Kazakhstani Legislative Process' SOAS Working Paper, p. 3

Nino, Carlos (1993) *The Ethics of Human Rights* (Oxford: Clarendon Press)

Norrie, Alan (1993) (ed.) *Closure or Critique: New Directions in Legal Theory* (Edinburgh: Edinburgh University Press)

Norrie, Alan (1999) 'Justice and Relationality' 3:1 *Alethia* pp. 1–5

Norrie, Alan (2000) *Punishment, Responsibility and Justice: A Relational Critique* (Oxford: Oxford University Press)

Norrie, Alan (2005) *Law and the Beautiful Soul* (London: Glasshouse Press)

O'Connell, Mary Ellen (2002) 'Debating the Law of Sanctions' in 'Symposium: The Impact on International Law of a Decade of Measures against Iraq' 13:1 *European Journal of International Law* pp. 63–79

O'Neill, John (ed.) (1996) *Hegel's Dialectic of Desire and Recognition* (Albany: SUNY)

Oquendo, Angel R. (2002) 'Deliberative Democracy in Habermas and Nino' 22:2 *Oxford Journal of Legal Studies* pp. 189–226

Örücü, E. 'Law as Transposition' (2002) 51 *International and Comparative Law Quarterly* pp. 205–223

Osakwa, C. (1998) 'Propter Honoris Respectum: Anatomy of the 1994 Civil Codes of Russia and Kazakhstan: A Biopsy of the Economic Constitutions of the Post-Soviet Republics' 73 *Notre Dame Law Review* pp. 1413–1514

Ossipov, Aleksandr (1997) *Pravo Narodov na Samoopredeleniye: Ideya i Voploshcheniye (Right of Peoples to Self-Determination: Idea and Realisation)* (Moscow: Zvenya)

Otto, Dianne (1997) 'Rethinking the Universality of Human Rights Law' 29 *Columbia Human Rights Law Review* p. 1

Packer, John (1993) 'On the Definition of Minorities' in John Packer and Kristian Myntti (eds) *The Protection of Ethnic and Linguistic Minorities in Europe* (Helsinki: Abo Akademi University) p. 23

Packer, John (1996) 'On the Content of Minority Rights' in J. Raikka (ed.) *Do We Need Minority Rights?* (Leiden: Kluwer) p. 121

Pashukanis, Yevgeny (1924) *The General Theory of Law and Marxism* in Evgeny Pashukanis, *Selected Writings on Marxism and Law* (eds P. Beirne & R. Sharlet) (London & New York 1980) translated by Peter B. Maggs, pp. 40–131

Pashukanis, Yevgeny (1925) *Mezhdunarodnoe pravo, Entsiklopediia gosudarstva i prava* (International Law, Encyclopedia of state and law) (1925–1926) (Moscow: lzd. Kommunisticheskoi akademii) Vol. 2, pp. 858–874, from Evgeny Pashukanis, *Selected Writings on Marxism and Law* (eds P. Beirne & R. Sharlet) (London & New York 1980) pp. 168–183, 184–185, translated by Peter B. Maggs at http://www.marxists.org/archive/pashukanis/1925/xx/intlaw.htm

Pashukanis, Ye. B. (1927) 'O revolyutsionnykh momentakh v istorii gosudarstva i prav' (On revolutionary moments in the history of state and law) *Revolyutsiya i prava* (*Revolution and Law*) No. 1

Pashukanis, Yevgeny (1932) 'Pismo tov. Stalina i zadachi teoreticheskovo fronta gosudarstva i prava' (The letter of comrade Stalin and the tasks of the theoretical front of state and law) *Sovetskoe gosudarstvo (Soviet State)* No. 1 pp. 4–48

Pashukanis, Yevgeny (1935) *Ocherki po Mezhdunarodnomu Pravu* (*Essays in International Law*) (Moscow)

Pashukanis, Yevgeny (1980) *Pashukanis: Selected Writings on Marxism and Law* (eds P. Beirne & R. Sharlet) (London: Academic Press)

Pashukanis, Yevgeny (1983) *Law and Marxism: A General Theory. Towards a Critique of the Fundamental Concepts.* Edited and introduced by Chris Arthur (London: Pluto Press)

Paust, Jordan J. (1983) 'Conflicting Norms of Intervention: More Variables for the Equation' 13 *Georgia Journal of International and Comparative Law* p. 305

Paust, Jordan J. (1986) 'Responding Lawfully to International Terrorism: The Use of Force Abroad' 8 *Whittier Law Review* pp. 711–733

Peacerights (2004) 'Report of the Inquiry into the Alleged Commission of War Crimes by Coalition Forces in the Iraq War During 2003' 20 January 2004, at http://www.peacerights.org/documents/A%20IRAQ%20REPORT%20Final.doc (accessed 16 October 2007), copy also on file with the author

Perrin, Colin (2004) 'Breath From Nowhere: The Silent Foundation of Human Rights' 13/1 *Social and Legal Studies* pp. 133–151

Peter, Fabienne (2001) 'Health Equity and Social Justice' 18:2 *Journal of Applied Philosophy* pp. 159–170

Pierse, Catherin (1997) 'Violation of Cultural Rights of Kurds in Turkey' 15 *Netherlands Quarterly of Human Rights* p. 325

Plasseraud, Y. (2000) 'How to solve Cultural Identity Problems: Choose your own nation' *Le Monde Diplomatique* May 2000, p. 4 at www.globalpolicy.org/nations/citizen/region.htm

Prince, Charles (1942) 'The USSR and International Organisations' 36:3 *American Journal of International Law* pp. 425–445

Puchalska-Tych, Bogumila and Salter, Michael (1996) 'Comparing legal cultures of Eastern Europe: the need for a dialectical analysis' 16 *Legal Studies* p. 157

Quaye, Christopher (1991) *Liberation Struggles in International Law* (Philadelphia: Temple University Press)

Quenivet, Noelle (2005) 'The World after September 11: Has It Really Changed?' 16:3 *European Journal of International Law* pp. 561–577

Quigley, John (2002) 'The United Nations Security Council: Promethean Protector or Helpless Hostage?' 35 *Texas International Law Journal* pp. 129–172

Rancière, Jacques (2004) 'Who is the Subject of the Rights of Man?' 103:2–3 *South Atlantic Quarterly* pp. 297–310

Rasch, William (2005) *Sovereignty and its Discontents* (London: Birkbeck Law Press)

Rawls, John (1999) *The Law of Peoples* (Cambridge, Mass.: Harvard University Press)

Rayburn, Joel (2006) 'The Last Exit from Iraq' 85:2 *Foreign Affairs* pp. 29–40

Reddaway, Peter and Glinski, Dmitri (2001) *The Tragedy of Russia's Reforms: Market Bolshevism Against Democracy* (Washington: United States Institute of Peace Press)

Reidy, Aisling, Hampson, Françoise and Boyle, Kevin (1997) 'Gross Violations of

Human Rights: Invoking the European Convention on Human Rights in the Case of Turkey' 15:2 *Netherlands Quarterly of Human Rights* pp. 161–173

Reidy, Aisling (1998) 'The approach of the European Commission and Court of Human Rights to international humanitarian law' 324 *International Review of the Red Cross* pp. 513–529

Rich, Roland (1988) 'Right to Development: A Right of Peoples?' in James Crawford (ed.) *The Rights of Peoples* (Oxford: Clarendon Press)

Rieff, David (2002) 'On the wishful thinking of eminent persons: the Independent Commission's *Kosovo Report*' in 'A Symposium on Kosovo' 1:1 *Human Rights Journal* pp. 111–119

Risse, Thomas, Ropp, Stephen, and Sikkink, Kathryn (eds) (1999) *The Power of Human Rights: International Norms and Domestic Change* (Cambridge: Cambridge University Press)

Roberts, Anthea (2004) 'Righting Wrongs or Wronging Rights? The United States and Human Rights Post-September 11' 15:4 *European Journal of International Law* pp. 721–749

Robertson, Geoffrey (2001) *Crimes Against Humanity: The Struggle for Global Justice* (revised edition, London: Penguin)

Rodley, Nigel S. (1995) 'Conceptual Problems in the Protection of Minorities: International Legal Developments' 17 *Human Rights Quarterly* p. 48

Rodley, Nigel (2000) 'Breaking the Cycle of Impunity for Gross Violations of Human Rights: The Pinochet Case in Perspective' 69 *Nordic Journal of International Law* pp. 11–26

Ronzitti, Natalino (2000) 'Is the Non Liquet of the Final Report by the Committee Established to Review the NATO Bombing Against the FRY Acceptable?' 840 *International Review of the Red Cross* pp. 1020–1021

Rose, Gillian (1995) *Hegel: Contra Sociology* (London: Athlone)

Rosenberg, Justin (2002) *The Follies of Globalisation Theory* (London: Verso)

Rostow, Eugene V. (1991) 'Until What? Enforcement Action or Collective Self-Defense?' in 'Agora: The Gulf Crisis in International and Foreign Relations Law' 85 *American Journal of International Law* pp. 506–516

Rubin, Isaak (1928) *Essays on Marx's Theory of Value* (1972, trans from 3rd edn 1928) (Detroit: Black and Red)

Salter, Michael (1997) 'Habermas' New Contribution to Legal Scholarship' 24:2 *Journal of Law and Society* pp. 285–305

Sands, Philippe (2006) *Lawless World: Making and Breaking Global Rules* (London: Penguin Books)

Scarborough, Kyla D. (2002) 'Foundational Ethics: A Look at Alasdair MacIntyre's Ethical Views' PSU/NSF-REU Program, Summer 2002 at www.pittstate.edu/reuret/ResearchReports2002/18scarboroughEthicsIndented.pdf

Schmitt, Carl (1985) *Political Theology: Four Chapters on the Concept of Sovereignty* (Cambridge, Mass.: MIT Press)

Schmitt, Carl (1996) *The Concept of the Political* (Chicago: University of Chicago Press)

Schmitt, Carl (2003) *Nomos of the Earth in the International Law of the Jus Publicum Europaeum* (New York: Telos), originally published in 1950

Scholte, Aart Jan (2005, 2nd edn) *Globalization: a Critical Introduction* (London: Palgrave Macmillan)

Scobbie, Iain (2006) 'Some Common Heresies about International Law: Sundry Theoretical Perspectives' in Malcolm Evans (ed.) *International Law* (2nd edn, 2006 Oxford: Oxford University Press), pp. 83–112

Scott, Shirley B. (1994) 'International Law as Ideology: Theorizing the Relationship between International Law and International Politics' 5:3 *European Journal of International Law* pp. 313–325

Segesvary, Victor (1995) 'Group Rights: The Definition of Group Rights in the Contemporary Legal Debate Based on Socio-Cultural Analysis' 2/3 *International Journal of Group Rights* pp. 89–107

Shea, Jamie (2002) 'NATO – Upholding Ethics in International Security Policy' 15:1 *Cambridge Review of International Affairs* pp. 75–82

Shivji, Issa (1989) *The Concept of Human Rights in Africa* (Dakar: Codesria)

Shustov, V. B. (1996) Discrimination Against Indigenous People of the North, A Statement by Social Organisations and Movements of Indigenous People of the North, 4 March, http://www.globalpolicy.org/nations/sovereign/sover/emerg/2003/0806russia.htm (accessed 1 January 2006)

Simma, Bruno (1999) 'NATO, the UN and the Use of Force: Legal Aspects' 10:1 *European Journal of International Law* pp. 1–23

Simpson, Gerry (2000) 'Review Article: The Situation on the International Legal Theory Front: The Power of Rules and the Rule of Power' 11 *European Journal of International Law* pp. 439–464

Simpson, Gerry (2005) 'The war in Iraq and international law' 6 *Melbourne Journal of International Law* pp. 167–188

Skripilev E. A. (1997) 'Nashemy zhurnalu – 70 let' (Our journal is 70 years old) *Sovetskoye Gosudarstvo i Pravo* (Soviet State and Law) No. 2 p. 17

Smith, A. D. (1983) *Theories of Nationalism* (London: Duckworth)

Smith, A. D. (1986) *The Ethnic Origin of Nations* (Oxford: Oxford University Press)

Smith, A. D. (1998) *Nationalism and Modernism. A critical survey of recent theories of nations and nationalism* (London: Routledge)

Smith, A. D. (2001) 'Nations and History' in M. Guibernau and J. Hutchinson (eds) *Understanding Nationalism* (London: Polity) pp. 9–31

Smith, A. D. (2002) 'Dating the nation' in D. Conversi (ed.) *Ethnonationalism in the Contemporary World: Walker Connor and the study of nationalism'* (London: Routledge) pp. 53–71

Smith, Steven B. (1989) *Hegel's Critique of Liberalism. Rights in Context* (Chicago: Chicago University Press)

Smith, T. B. (1958) 'Strange Gods', University of Edinburgh, Inaugural lecture No. 4, p. 1 reprinted in T. B. Smith (1962) *Studies Critical and Comparative* (Edinburgh: Green), pp. 72ff

Speed, Richard B. (2005) 'Review of Christopher Andrew and Vasili Mitrokhin, *The World Was Going Our Way: The KGB and the Battle for the Third World* New York: Basic Books, 2005', *History News Network* at http://hnn.us/roundup/comments/19470.html (accessed 16 October 2007)

Stack, Robert (2000) 'Western Law in Japan: the *Antimonopoly Law* and other Legal Transplants' 27:3 *Manitoba Law Journal* pp. 399–413

Stalin, J. V. (1913) *Marxism and the National Question* nos 3–5 *Prosveshniye (Enlightenment)* March–May 1913, at www.marxists.org/reference/archive/stalin/works/1913/03.htm

Stapleton, Julia (1995) (ed.) *Group Rights: Perspectives Since 1900* (London: Thoemmes Press)

Stein, Jonathan (2001) 'The Community Legal Service needs a social justice mission' 6 July 2001 *New Law Journal*

Steiner, Henry and Alston, Philip (2000, 2nd edn) *International Human Rights in Context* (Oxford: Oxford University Press)

Stephenson, Susan 'Narrative, Identity and Modernity' ECPR Workshop, Mannheim, March 1999, at www.essex.ac.uk/ecpr/events/jointsessions/paperarchive/mannheim/w22/Stephenson.pdf

Stuchka P. I. (1988) *Selected Writings on Soviet Law and Marxism* (edited, annotated, translated and introduced by Robert Sharlet, Peter Maggs and Piers Beirne) (Armonk: M E Sharpe)

Sumner, L. W. (1987) *The Moral Foundation of Rights* (Oxford: Clarendon Press)

Sypnowich, Christine (1990) *The Concept of Socialist Law* (Oxford: Clarendon Press)

Tasioulas, John (2002) 'From Utopia to Kazanistan: John Rawls and the Law of Peoples' 22:2 *Oxford Journal of Legal Studies* pp. 367–396

Tasioulas, John (2002a) 'Human Rights, Universality and the Values of Personhood: Retracing Griffin's Steps' 10:1 *European Journal of Philosophy* pp. 79–100

Tasioulas, John (2003) 'The Moral Reality of Human Rights' UNESCO Seminar, Oxford, March 2003, at http://portal.unesco.org/shs/en/file_download.php/8d5b01d4c9074aea070631bff932dc52jonh_Tasioulas.pdf

Taylor, Charles (ed. Amy Gutmann) (1994) *Multiculturalism. Examining the Politics of Recognition* (Princeton: Princeton University Press)

Taylor, Charles (1994a) 'Justice After Virtue' in John Horton and Susan Mendus (eds) *After MacIntyre: Critical Perspectives on the Work of Alasdair MacIntyre* (Cambridge: Polity)

Teubner, G. (1993) *Law as an Autopoietic System* (London: Blackwell)

Teubner, G. (1998) 'Legal Irritants: Good Faith in British Law or How Unifying Law Ends Up in New Divergencies' 61 *Modern Law Review* p. 11

Thompson, Edward P. (1975) *Whigs and Hunters. The Origin of the Black Act* (London: Allen Lane)

Thompson, John (1990) *Ideology and Modern Culture: Critical Social Theory in the Era of Mass Communication* (Cambridge: Polity) p. 56

Tomasi, John (1991) 'Individual Rights and Community Virtues' (April 1991) 101:3 *Ethics* pp. 521–536

Tomuschat, Christian (1992) 'Quo Vadis Argentoratum? The Success Story of the European Convention on Human Rights – And a Few Dark Stains' 13:11–12 *Human Rights Law Journal* pp. 401–406

Tomuschat, Christian (2003) *Human Rights: Between Idealism and Realism* (Oxford: Oxford University Press)

Triska, Jan (1958) 'Treaties and Other Sources of Order in International Relations: The Soviet View' 52:4 *American Journal of International Law* pp. 699–726

Trotsky, Leon (1926) *Trotsky's Writings on Britain*, at http://www2.cddc.vt.edu/marxists/cd/cd1/Library/archive/trotsky/works/britain/ch06.htm

Trotsky, Leon (1930) *History of the Russian Revolution*, at www.marxists.org/archive/Trotsky/workd/1930-hrr/ch39.htm

Tunkin, G. I. (1962) *Voprosy Teorii Mezhdunarodnovo Prava (Questions of Theory of International Law)* (Moscow: Progress)

Tunkin G. I. (1967) *Ideologicheskaya Borba i Mezhdunarodnoye Pravo* (The Ideological Struggle and International Law) (Moscow: Progress) see book review in (1968) 62 *American Journal of International Law* p. 208

Tunkin, G. I. (1967a) 'Borba dvukh kontseptsii v mezhdunarodnom prave' (The struggle of two conceptions in international law' 11 *Sovetskoye Gosudarstvo i Pravo* (Soviet State and Law) pp. 140–149

Tunkin, G. I. (1970) *Teorii Mezhdunarodnovo Prava (The Theory of International Law)* (Moscow: Progress, 2nd revised edition)

Tunkin, G. I. (1970a) 'Leninskiye printsipi ravnopraviya i samoopredeleniya narodov i sovremennoye mezhdunarodnoye pravo' (Lenin's principles of equal rights and the self-determination of peoples in contemporary international law) No. 2 *Vestnik Moskovskovo Universiteta* (Bulletin of Moscow University) pp. 62–71

Tunkin, G. I. (1974) *Theory of International Law* (trans. W. E. Butler) (London: Allen & Unwin)

Tunkin, G. I. (1993) 'Is General International Law Customary Only?' 4:4 *European Journal of International Law* pp. 534–541

van Dyke, Vernon (1977) 'The Individual, the State and Ethnic Communities in Political Theory' 29 *World Politics* p. 343

van Dyke, Vernon (1995) 'Collective Entities and Moral Rights: Problems in Liberal-Democratic Thought' in Julia Stapleton (ed.) *Group Rights: Perspectives Since 1900* (London: Thoemmes Press) p. 180

Vasak, Karel (1977) 'A Thirty Year Struggle – the Sustained Efforts to give Force of Law to the Universal Declaration of Human Rights' *UNESCO Courier* November 1977

Vishnyakov, V. G. (1998) 'Konstitutsionnoye Regulirovaniye Federativnikh Otnoshenii' (The Constitutional Regulation of Federal Relations), *Gosudarstvo i Pravo* (State and Law) pp. 20–28

Vyshinsky A. Ya. (1948) 'Mezhdunarodnoye pravo i mezhdunarodnaya organisatsiya' (International Law and International Organisation) No.1 *Sovetskoye gosudarstvo i pravo* (Soviet State and Law) p. 22

Vyshinsky, A. Ya. (ed.) (1979) *The Law of the Soviet State* (trans. H. W. Baab) (Westport, CT: Greenwood Press, Publishers)

Waldron, Jeremy (1987) *Nonsense Upon Stilts: Bentham, Burke and Marx on the Rights of Man* (London: Routledge)

Waldron, Jeremy (1990) *The Right to Private Property* (Oxford: Clarendon Press)

Wallerstein, Immanuel (2004) *World-systems Analysis: An Introduction* (Durham, NC: Duke University Press)

Warbrick, Colin (2003) 'The Use of Force against Iraq' 52 *International and Comparative Law Quarterly* p. 811

Warrington, Ronnie (1981) 'Pashukanis and the Commodity Form Theory' 9 *International Journal of the Sociology of Law* 1–22, at p. 3, in C. Varga (ed.) *Marxian Legal Theory, International Library of Essays in Law and Legal Theory* (New York: New York University Press, 1993)

Watson, Alan (1976) 'Legal Transplants and Law Reform' 92 *Law Quarterly Review* pp. 79–84

Watson, Alan (1981) *The Making of the Civil Law* (Cambridge, Mass.: Harvard University Press)

Watson, Alan (1985) *The Evolution of Law* (Baltimore: Johns Hopkins University Press)

Watson, Alan (1993) *Legal Transplants: An Approach to Comparative Law* (Athens and London: University of Georgia Press, 2nd edn 1993 – 1st edn 1973)

Watson, Alan (1996) 'Aspects of the Reception of Law' 44:2 *American Journal of Comparative Law* pp. 335–351

Watson, Alan (2001) *Society and Legal Change* (2nd edn) (Philadelphia: Temple University Press)

Weber, E. (1979) *Peasants into Frenchmen: The Modernisation of Rural France, 1870–1914* (London: Chatto & Windus)

Wedel, Janine (2001) *Collision and Collusion: The Strange Case of Western Aid to Eastern Europe* (New York: Palgrave)

Wegener, Bernd (2000) 'Political Culture and Post-Communist Transition – A Social Justice Approach: Introduction' 13 *Social Justice Research* pp. 75–82

Weiss, Thomas (2002) 'Instrumental humanitarianism and the *Kosovo Report*' in 'A Symposium on Kosovo' 1:1 *Human Rights Journal* pp. 121–127

Weller, Mark (ed.) (1993) *Iraq and Kuwait: The Hostilities and their Aftermath* (Cambridge: Grotius Publications)

Weston, Burns H. (1991) 'Security Council Resolution 678 and Persian Gulf Decision Making: Precarious Legitimacy' in 'Agora: The Gulf Crisis in International and Foreign Relations Law' 85 *American Journal of International Law* pp. 516–535

Wheatley, Steven (2003) 'Deliberative Democracy and Minorities' 14:3 *European Journal of International Law* pp. 507–527

White, Nigel D. (2004) 'The Will and Authority of the Security Council after Iraq' 17 *Leiden Journal of International Law* pp. 645–672

Wiener, J. (2001) 'Responding to the Global Warming Problem. Something Borrowed for Something Blue: Legal Transplants and the Evolution of Global Environmental Law' 27 *Ecology Law Quarterly* pp. 1295–1371

Wilde, Ralph (2005) 'The "Legal Space" or "*Espace Juridique*" of the European Convention on Human Rights: Is It Relevant to Extraterritorial State Action' Part 2 *European Human Rights Law Review* pp. 115–124

Williams, Patricia J. (1992) *The Alchemy of Race and Rights* (Harvard: Harvard University Press)

Williams, Paul (2002) 'The Rise and Fall of the "Ethical Dimension": Presentation and Practice in New Labour's Foreign Policy' 15:1 *Cambridge Review of International Affairs* pp. 53–63

Wilson, Heather Anne (1988) *International Law and the Use of Force by National Liberation Movements* (Oxford: Clarendon Press)

Wissenburg, Marcel (2001) 'The "third way" and social justice' *Journal of Political Ideologies* pp. 231–235

Wolf, Martin (2005) *Why Globalization Works* (New Haven: Yale Nota Bene)

Zile, Zigurds (1992) *Ideas and Forces in Soviet Legal History: A Reader on the Soviet State and Law* (Oxford: Oxford University Press)

Žižek, Slavoj (1993) *Tarrying with the Negative: Kant, Hegel, and the Critique of Ideology* (Durham: Duke University Press) Chapter 6, 'Enjoy Your Nation as Yourself!'

Žižek, Slavoj (2001) *On Belief* (London: Routledge)

Žižek, Slavoj (2002) 'Are we in a war? Do we have an enemy?' 24:10 *London Review of Books*

Žižek, Slavoj (2004) *Revolution at the Gates: A Selection of Writings from February to October 1917 by V. I. Lenin* (London: Verso)

Žižek, Slavoj (2004a) 'From Politics to Biopolitics . . . and Back' 103:2/3 *South Atlantic Quarterly* pp. 501–521

Žižek, Slavoj (2005) 'Against Human Rights' 34 *New Left Review* July–August 2005

Žižek, Slavoj (2005a) *Iraq: The Borrowed Kettle* (London: Verso)

Žižek, Slavoj (2006) *The Parallax View* (Cambridge, MA: MIT Press)

Index

Please note that page references to footnotes are followed by the letter 'n'. References to publications beginning with 'A' or 'The' are sorted by the first significant word.